A LAWYER'S GUIDE TO DOING BUSINESS IN SOUTH AFRICA

Editors

Vaughn C. Williams
William M. Hannay
Michael R. Littenberg
Lauren G. Robinson

American Bar Association
Section of International Law and Practice

©American Bar Association, 1996
ISBN: 1-57073-364-3
Printed in the United States of America
All Rights Reserved

Nothing herein shall be construed as representing the opinion, views, or actions of the American Bar Association unless the same shall have been first approved by the House of Delegates or the Board of Governors.

Published under the direction of the Publications Committee of the Section of International Law and Practice.

Publications Committee Chair: John E. Noyes
Publications Director: Susan Frensilli Williams

TABLE OF CONTENTS

		Page
	PREFACE By Vaughn C. Williams	1
CHAPTER 1	**INTRODUCTION** By William M. Hannay and Lauren G. Robinson	3
CHAPTER 2	**ESTABLISHING A JOINT VENTURE IN SOUTH AFRICA** By Michael J.R. Evans	9
CHAPTER 3	**ESTABLISHING A DISTRIBUTION BUSINESS** By Lee Falkow and John Janks	17
CHAPTER 4	**SOUTH AFRICAN FINANCIAL STATEMENT REQUIREMENTS** By Deloitte & Touche, South Africa	39
CHAPTER 5	**SECURITIES LAWS AND PORTFOLIO INVESTMENT IN SOUTH AFRICA** By Peter S. G. Leon and Nicola F. Newton-King	47
CHAPTER 6	**TAXATION AND FOREIGN EXCHANGE** By Kevin W. Joselowitz and Michael M. Katz	71
CHAPTER 7	**TAX ASSESSMENTS, PAYMENTS AND APPEALS IN SOUTH AFRICA** By Deloitte & Touche, South Africa	85
CHAPTER 8	**TRADE REGULATION IN SOUTH AFRICA** By Leora Blumberg	89
CHAPTER 9	**COMPETITION LAW** By Pierre E. J. Brooks	101

CHAPTER 10	THE PROTECTION OF INTELLECTUAL PROPERTY By David F. Sheppard	109
CHAPTER 11	SOUTH AFRICAN EMPLOYMENT LAW By Puke Maserumule	119
CHAPTER 12	PRIVATIZATION IN SOUTH AFRICA By Tiego Moseneke	131
CHAPTER 13	DEVELOPMENTS IN CURRENT SOUTH AFRICAN ENVIRONMENTAL LAW By Robyn Stein	141
CHAPTER 14	RESOLVING COMMERCIAL DISPUTES IN SOUTH AFRICA By David W. Butler	153
CHAPTER 15	SOUTHERN AFRICAN REGIONAL LEGAL FRAMEWORK By Robin B. Camp	173
ABOUT THE AUTHORS		189
ABOUT THE EDITORS		195
APPENDIX A	RESOURCES ABOUT SOUTH AFRICAN LAW IN THE UNITED STATES	197
APPENDIX B	SELECTED BUSINESS, TRADE AND LEGAL ASSOCIATIONS AND GOVERNMENT AGENCIES	201
APPENDIX C	SOUTH AFRICA FACT SHEET	207

PREFACE

By Vaughn C. Williams

In November 1995, the American Bar Association's Section on International Law and Practice sponsored a delegation to South Africa, comprised of thirty American lawyers from diverse practices and other employments.

This delegation, headed by William M. Hannay, was conducted under the auspices of the Section's International Legal Exchange (ILEX) program. These ILEX delegations are intended to provide Section and Association members an in-depth, firsthand learning experience regarding the legal and judicial systems of the host country or region. These delegations are often arranged by ILEX in conjunction with the committee of the Section corresponding to the host country or region (in this case, the Section's African Law Committee).

For ten days, we met with South African lawyers, businessmen, and politicians in Johannesburg, Pretoria and Cape Town. These meetings were intended to provide us a better understanding of current developments in South African law, business and politics.

By their generous sharing of information with us about South Africa -- and their ever-present offers of tea and sandwiches -- the South Africans communicated their eagerness to be re-integrated into the international business and professional communities. Their presentations focused on:

- Their current efforts to move from business practices dictated by an economy isolated by international boycott to one with currency regulations, monetary policy and securities regulation, for example, responsive to the modern international world;
- Their efforts to create a constitutional body politic that would be stable and would reflect the best norms of international human rights;
- The areas offering greatest opportunities for foreign investment in South Africa;
- An explanation of South African business and professional practices;

During our visit to South Africa, we were able to meet at length with the following:

- Political and economic officials from the United States Embassy in Pretoria;
- Senior officials of the South African Reserve Bank;
- Senior officials of the South African Department of Trade and Industry;
- Senior officials of the South African Justice Department, including the Minister of Justice;
- Senior officials of the Johannesburg Stock Exchange;

- Senior officials of Anglo-American Mining Corporation, a South African conglomerate;
- Senior officials of Old Mutual International, a South African insurance conglomerate;
- Members of the South African Constitutional Court;
- Senior officials of Deloitte & Touche Tohmatsu International;
- Members of the Johannesburg Black Lawyers Association;
- Senior members of the Moseneke & Partners law firm in Johannesburg;
- Senior members of the Adams & Adams law firm in Pretoria;
- Members of the South African Supreme Court (Cape of Good Hope Provincial Division);
- The Deputy Speaker of the South African National Assembly;
- The Premier of the Western Cape Provincial Government;

Despite the rigorous schedule of our trip, we also reserved some time to see a little of South Africa, including a day-long tour of Johannesburg's Soweto Township and visits to the Stellenbosch wine country and the Cape of Good Hope. These diversions, and the South Africans they introduced us to, exposed us to the optimism held by most of those who have lived through a social revolution and political transition that they call the "Miracle." These trips also let us see some of the incredible physical beauty of South Africa.

This trip made clear that the South African business, government and professional communities are eager to invite their foreign counterparts to South Africa to work in business and professional partnerships. We thought, as one gesture of this potential partnership, that it would be appropriate for the International Law and Practice Section to provide American lawyers an introduction to certain areas of South African law and to South African lawyers. That is the reason for this Guide To Doing Business In South Africa.

New York, New York
June 1996

CHAPTER 1

INTRODUCTION

By William M. Hannay
and Lauren G. Robinson

With the dismantling of apartheid and the implementation of a fully democratic government has come a ground swell of interest in South Africa. A significant amount of that interest is in the country's economic potential. Until now, South Africa, particularly, and the southern Africa region, generally, have comprised a largely untapped region of the world economically. It is vital for attorneys to be knowledgeable about southern Africa to respond effectively to their clients' interest in this dynamic area.

I.   **The End of Apartheid**

The current enthusiasm for South Africa was sparked largely by a series of events that began in February 1990. The political, social, and economic changes that have swept South Africa since that time have been profound and pervasive. Then-President Frederik W. de Klerk opened Parliament on February 2, 1990 announcing that he would repeal discriminatory laws, lift the ban against political organizations including the African National Congress (ANC), the Pan Africanist Congress, and the South African Communist Party, and release several political prisoners. On February 11, 1990, Nelson Mandela, the world-renowned anti-apartheid leader, was released from prison after serving 27 years of a life sentence.

The release of Mr. Mandela and the eventual dismantling of White minority rule was the culmination of decades of political struggle in which thousands of lives were lost.   The damaging effects of economic sanctions imposed by the international community and the recognition by the apartheid government that neither the world nor the majority of South Africans would continue to tolerate its repressive regime also contributed to the downfall of apartheid.

In connection with the release of Mr. Mandela, the apartheid government began to lift the state of emergency imposed in various parts of the country in 1985. The apartheid government had declared a state of emergency under which it detained 30,000 people and trampled individual liberties in response to Black protest to government efforts to entrench apartheid further. The government lifted the state of emergency in all of the provinces except Natal by June 1990.

Mr. Mandela's release from prison was followed by the apartheid government's repeal of the statutes on which apartheid was built. In 1990, Parliament repealed the Separate Amenities Act, which had segregated public facilities such as toilets by race; the Group Areas Act, which had segregated residential areas by race; and the Population Registration Act, which had classified citizens by race. The four major racial classifications established under apartheid were Black (who were further classified into subgroups based on tribal affiliations), Coloured (descendants of the indigenous Khoikhoi and people of mixed ancestry of the Khoikhoi, Whites, and slaves from Madagascar), and Indian. In June 1991, Parliament repealed the 1913 and 1936 Land Acts which, by denying Black South Africans full property rights, divested them of their property and permitted the government to remove Black South Africans from their land. Those acts comprised the foundation upon which the legal and physical separation of the races was built.

On December 21, 1991, delegates from all of South Africa's leading political organizations except the Conservative Party and extreme right-wing groups attended the Convention for a Democratic South Africa (CODESA) to form a multi-racial transitional government and to draft an interim constitution.

In March 1992, Mr. de Klerk sought and won a vote of confidence on his political reforms in a Whites-only referendum. Shortly thereafter in June, 42 unarmed men, women and children were massacred in Boipatong, a township south of Johannesburg, allegedly by government security forces and members of the Inkatha Freedom Party. The latter was originally a Zulu cultural movement founded in 1928 which evolved into a political organization by the mid-1970's. The ANC responded by withdrawing from the CODESA negotiations and accelerating the pace of political change. The apartheid government responded by prosecuting security forces allegedly involved in violence in order to bring the ANC back to the negotiating table. On April 1, 1993, representatives from 26 political parties met to begin multi-party negotiations for a new multiracial government. On October 15, 1993, Mr. Mandela and Mr. de Klerk were awarded the Nobel Peace Prize.

In November 1993, the governing National Party and the ANC endorsed an interim constitution which abolished the ten "homelands" created under apartheid and reincorporated Transkei, Ciskei, Bophuthatswana, and Venda, which opted for "independence" under the Bantu Homelands Citizenship Act, into South Africa as of the date of its first democratic election. Under the interim constitution, a transitional government was formed to govern South Africa until the country held democratic elections.

In the country's first democratic election on April 27, 1994, the people of South Africa elected Mr. Nelson Mandela president by a clear majority. Pursuant to the interim constitution, a new "Government of National Unity" was formed to operate by consensus. The leading political parties -- the ANC, the National Party and the Inkatha Freedom Party -- shared cabinet posts in the new government in proportion to their electoral totals. Mr. de Klerk and Mr. Thabo Mbeki served as Deputy Presidents in the coalition government. The interim constitution divided the country into nine provinces, each of which had control over regional services.

The interim constitution continued as the country's governing document until the democratically-elected representatives drafted a permanent document. On May 8, 1996, South Africa's first democratically elected Parliament adopted the final Constitution. The new Constitution, whose provisions will be phased in over three years, establishes majority rule and a bill of rights guaranteeing individual liberties similar to the governing legal documents of the leading democracies of the world. South Africa's bill of rights prohibits discrimination based on "race, gender, sex, pregnancy, marital status, ethnic or social origin, colour, sexual orientation, age, disability, religion, conscience, belief, culture, language, and birth." The Constitutional Court, the highest court of South Africa, has final jurisdiction regarding the interpretation of the Constitution. As a result of these profound changes, the formerly ostracized and isolated South Africa has been reunited and reconciled with the international community.

The political and social evolution of South Africa continues. Following the ratification of the Constitution, the National Party, led by de Klerk, announced its withdrawal from the Government of National Unity on May 9, 1996. Mr. de Klerk expressed his belief that true multi-party democracy requires a strong opposition and stated that the National Party would fulfill that role. The country's next general election will be held in 1999.

II.   The Economic Outlook

The profound political changes in South Africa, combined with the country's many attributes that make it ripe for economic growth, have triggered growing levels of investment in the country by American and other foreign multinational corporations since South Africa's first national democratic elections in April 1994. South Africa is an attractive market because of its strong physical and economic infrastructure and its growing manufacturing sector. In 1993, its gross domestic product (GDP) reached $112 billion. Known for its abundant mineral wealth, mining remains central to the economy, accounting for 60% of exports and 10% of GDP. South Africa is among the world's leading suppliers of gold, chromium, manganese, and platinum. Its abundant natural resources also include coal and uranium oxide. Its stock market, the largest in Africa, is the tenth largest in the world and growing rapidly, attracting $1.2 billion in new foreign capital in the first nine months of 1995, up from just $57 million a year before.

South Africa is the economic leader of the African continent producing 50% of the electrical output of Africa, 45% of the continent's mining output, and 40% of the continent's GDP. It is also Africa's largest agricultural exporter. The country has the continent's best telephone system, the best network of paved roads and railway lines, the most developed port system, and the most sophisticated financial and banking system.

From an economic perspective, South Africa is at the core of the southern Africa region which in addition to South Africa includes Angola, Botswana, Lesotho, Malawi, Mauritius, Mozambique, Namibia, Swaziland, Tanzania, Zambia, and Zimbabwe. Seventy-five percent of the exports and 68% of the imports of southern Africa are transported through South Africa's seven ports. This region has recently formed an economic union -- the Southern Africa Development Community (SADC) -- which represents an untapped market of 150 million potential consumers. Its members have agreed to engage in initiatives such as building infrastructure, eliminating trade barriers, and sharing resources to attract international investment to the region. South Africa, with Swaziland, Lesotho, Botswana, and Namibia, also comprise another economic union -- the Southern African Customs Union (SACU).

Major American, European, and Asian corporations have begun to invest in South Africa since nationwide democratic elections were initially held in April 1994. The majority of the investments by American companies in South Africa have consisted of opening offices, purchasing equity in existing companies or repurchasing enterprises divested under sanctions. More than 200 American companies have directly invested in South Africa while some 500 additional companies have non-equity ties or licensing agreements that could lead to further investments. Companies investing in South Africa include corporations operating in the financial services, communications, information technology, food, and hotel industries.

U.S. companies dedicated to serving the African-American market have also demonstrated enthusiasm for South Africa. Luster Products, Inc., Soft Sheen Products, Inc. and Johnson Publishing Company, for example, have all initiated economic ventures into the South African market. Johnson Publishing Company, publisher of Ebony Magazine, has launched a South African edition of its magazine.

The encouraging levels of American corporate investment have been buttressed by the responsiveness of foreign companies. Approximately 1,800 multinational corporations currently do business in South Africa. Foreign companies directly invested some $1 billion in the country in the first seventeen months after Mandela was elected president. This exceeds the average yearly amount previously invested in the whole continent.

The current level of investment reflects the termination of the economic sanctions imposed by the world community in 1985. After years of threats, economic sanctions finally became a reality for South Africa in the mid-1980's. Led by Chase Manhattan Bank in mid-1985, many foreign banks called in their loans which caused a financial crisis in South Africa. Europe and the United States followed with punitive trade sanctions. These economic measures seriously weakened the once robust South African economy. The value of the rand sank steadily, external debts had to be rescheduled several times, hundreds of American and other international corporations disinvested, and foreign investment dried up. South Africa went from being an importer to an exporter of capital.

Sanctions resulted from the rising pressure for the world community to respond to the increasing atrocities of apartheid and efforts to entrench this repressive and failing political regime. Specifically, sanctions were a response to Black uprisings against then-President P.W. Botha's campaign to entrench apartheid and the apartheid regime's ruthless response to Black political opposition.

The United States and the world community began retreating from economic sanctions in 1991. Although the ANC supported the lifting of cultural, tourism and athletic sanctions in 1991, it remained steadfast against the lifting of economic sanctions until the transitional government was established in late 1993. The sea change in the ANC's position was marked by Mr. Mandela's visit to the United Nations in September 1993 seeking the end of economic sanctions and urging increased investment in the new South Africa.

The current and growing levels of investment in South Africa of American and other foreign multinational companies following the country's first democratic elections have begun to create job opportunities for South Africans and bolster the economy. Among the profound economic tasks of the new South Africa is providing employment. Unemployment among the entire population is roughly 40%. Among Blacks, who comprise 75% of the population, unemployment is 45%. The South African economy grew at a healthy rate of about 3.5% in 1995 and during 1996, it is expected to expand at a marginally greater rate. Sustained growth of between 6-7% is needed to begin to decrease current levels of unemployment. This is a daunting economic goal.

III.   The Future

Today, like its famous cape, South Africa is truly a land of good hope. Despite this hope, the country confronts significant challenges. To encourage investment, South Africa must quell burgeoning crime in its major cities and increased illegal immigration of Africans from other countries who recognize and seek to benefit from the economic promise of South Africa. The country must also address the potential for ethnic violence from Chief Buthelezi, leader of the Inkatha Freedom Party and the Zulus. Its greatest challenge, however, is reducing the poverty and extreme level of economic inequality throughout the population. Both conditions are remnants of apartheid and alleviating them is inextricably linked to reducing unemployment.

The long-term nature of the problems that South Africa faces must not be underestimated. They were not created overnight, nor will they be solved overnight. Both direct action -- such as initiatives under the Reconstruction and Development Program (RDP) to build housing and other infrastructure to meet the basic needs of the majority of South Africans -- and market discipline are necessary to address these problems. The success of these efforts, however, will most likely be experienced in the long term, rather than immediately.

South Africa is the beacon of hope and promise of Africa. Its evolution from the oppressive regime of apartheid to a democracy has inspired the world and the adherents of freedom and justice everywhere. It provides a model for other fledgling democracies in Africa. It is hope, combined with substantial economic investment and progressive policies, that will move the country forward.

For those U.S. and foreign companies that choose to make an investment in South Africa, this book is offered as a guide through the legal landscape.

Chicago, Illinois
June 1996

CHAPTER 2

ESTABLISHING A JOINT VENTURE IN SOUTH AFRICA

By Michael J.R. Evans

Joint ventures are increasingly being utilized as a mechanism for investment, both internationally and within South Africa. The increasingly important and popular role that "joint venturing" is playing in modern commercial life is reflected in the fact that, according to certain published sources, the formation of joint ventures between American companies and international co-venturers has increased at an annual rate of 27% since 1985.

In South Africa, too, and particularly since the end of the sanctions era, foreign investors are looking towards joint ventures as an appropriate mechanism for investing in South Africa. Over the past five years, the number of South African joint ventures has increased exponentially in a range of business sectors, but particularly in the fields of telecommunications, fishing, pharmaceutical, undersea mining, general manufacturing, energy, financial services and consumer products.

This chapter will identify some of the key issues of which a foreign investor wishing to establish a joint venture in South Africa should take note. Given the complexity of the South African situation, however, and some of the peculiarities of South Africa, it is vitally important that such investors utilize the assistance of local (South African) counsel when embarking on such ventures.

Although this chapter only deals with joint ventures embarked upon in South Africa, many of the same points can be made in regard to joint ventures embarked upon in Namibia. South Africa and Namibia share similar legal structures and systems of law.

I. Nature And Purpose Of Joint Ventures

In South Africa, a joint venture is understood to be a business activity carried on by two or more persons under common control and management. Perhaps the one thing which distinguishes it from other forms of business associations is that no one person has absolute control over the joint venture activities.

Generally, a joint venture will not be the first choice of entity of either party to the joint venture. It is normally a vehicle of necessity brought into being for one or more of the following commercial reasons:
- the unwillingness of either party to assume the entire risk of the venture;
- a marriage of expertise in a particular field where no party has the experience or the resources to undertake the venture by itself and both parties wish to participate in the profits of the venture;
- the different functions of the parties (for example, manufacturer and distributor or inventor and financier);
- the desire for a share in profits;
- the desire to retain some element of control over the venture; and
- as a vehicle for penetration into foreign markets.

The term "joint venture" covers a wide variety of co-operation arrangements, whether of a short- or long-term duration. These arrangements can take various forms from more narrowly defined licensing, marketing, distribution, sales or manufacturing agreements to more loosely defined partnership arrangements or strategic alliances. In South Africa, most joint ventures have been established either as a partnership (between a foreign and a local partner and in respect of the undertaking embarked upon by the joint venture), or by way of a joint venture company (with foreign and local shareholders), or, in a limited number of cases, as a combination of both.

II. Structuring The Joint Venture

Under South African law, a partnership is not a separate legal entity. Accordingly, the partners do not have the same protection afforded, for example, to shareholders in a company. The main disadvantage of a partnership is that the partners are jointly and severally liable for the obligations of the partnership. Generally, this liability extends beyond the capital provided by the partners and means that any third party may elect to proceed against one of the individual partners before proceeding against the partnership's assets. For this reason, joint venture parties are often hesitant to structure their relationship on a partnership basis.

Foreign entities accustomed to the notion of limited liability partnerships often attempt to limit liability when setting up the joint venture by defining it as not being a partnership. Such an endeavor would generally not be successful in South Africa, as South African law would tend to require an analysis of the substance of any agreement entered into by the parties. If, on analysis, the essential prerequisites of a partnership are present, the venture would be treated as a partnership.

There are certain advantages in structuring a joint venture as a partnership which may influence the decision of the particular parties. Most important of these are the tax implications. A partnership is not taxed as a separate entity, but the burden of taxation is passed on to the individual partners. Thus, the individual joint venture partner may be able to write off start-up losses against its other income and may be able to receive other tax benefits such as depreciation allowances (depending on the tax laws in the country in which the respective joint venturers are incorporated).

In many cases, however, the joint venture parties will elect to structure the venture as a limited liability company. South Africa has a well developed and sophisticated body of corporate law which governs the establishment and operations of companies in South Africa. Unlike many federal systems of government, South Africa has a single and uniform system of corporate law and a single Registrar of Companies who has jurisdiction over the whole country.

The main advantage of structuring a joint venture as a company is that liability is limited except in certain very extreme situations of trading recklessly or with the intent to defraud creditors. A further advantage of structuring a joint venture as a company is that the vehicle of a company is understood by local banks and other suppliers of credit. Moreover, the sale by one of the investors of its shares in the company would not necessitate the joint venture having to renegotiate contracts entered into, as would be the case by the parties to an unincorporated joint venture.

The requirements of particular business sectors will often dictate whether the joint venture is formed on a partnership or a corporate basis. For example, the South

African Merchant Shipping Act provides that no ship can be registered in South Africa unless the whole of the ship is owned by persons each of whom is a South African citizen or by corporate bodies established in South Africa. Thus, for example, in the case of a fishing joint venture that wishes to register a vessel in South Africa (among other things, to assist the joint venture in its application for fishing quotas), it will be necessary for the joint venture to be incorporated as a South African company.

III.   Establishing A Presence In South Africa

Before embarking on a joint venture, the foreign party will need to decide the form and nature of its presence in South Africa. In many cases, the foreign party will decide that it does not require an independent presence and its involvement in South Africa will merely be by way of the joint venture. However, there may be good reason for the foreign party to establish a more formal presence, which will usually take one of two forms: either (i) a subsidiary company can be incorporated in South Africa or (ii) a branch office can be opened in South Africa and registered as an external company under the provisions of the South African Companies Act.

The choice of the structure will have important tax and other implications. Under South Africa's source-based system of taxation, both the subsidiary company and the branch office will be taxed on all profits derived from South African sources. However, the rate of tax differs in each case. The locally incorporated subsidiary company will be taxed at a rate of 35% (the same rate which applies to all South African companies). In contrast the South African branches of foreign resident companies will be taxed at a rate of 40%.

In addition to the flat rate of tax, however, the subsidiary company will be required to pay a secondary tax on companies ("STC") at a rate of 12.5% of the net amount of all dividends declared (This rate was recently reduced from 25%, at least partially as a result of pressure from overseas investors. Much pressure is currently being placed on the South African government to abolish STC altogether). The branch office, on the other hand, will not be exposed to STC.

In effect, the imposition of STC on the subsidiary company will more or less bring its rate of tax up to the same level as that imposed on the branch office. It is also worth noting that the significance of the various rates of tax may be reduced if the foreign holding or parent company is able to take advantage of any double taxation agreement concluded between South Africa and the country of residence of such holding or parent company. At present, there is no tax treaty between the United States and South Africa.

The major disadvantage of going the branch office route is that the parent company is obliged to disclose detailed information to the South African authorities, including its financial statements and information concerning its directors. There is also a great deal of information which must be disclosed in the letterhead of a branch office. Furthermore, the legal liability of a branch office is not limited. Accordingly, if a creditor were to prove a claim against the branch it would be entitled to execute such claim against the parent company. These factors may influence the foreign investor to incorporate a subsidiary company rather than to establish a branch office.

IV. Formalities And Documentation

South African law distinguishes between private and public companies, the former having a maximum of 50 members. In each case, there are certain formalities which have to be complied with, although the process of registering a company is not particularly complicated or cumbersome. In essence, it involves the registration of the company's memorandum and articles of association. To avoid possible delays in company registrations, "shelf" companies are generally available for use by those investors who need a company incorporated quickly. At the same time, if the company has more than a single shareholder (as in the case of a joint venture company) it is advisable that a shareholders' agreement be concluded.

In the case of a joint venture partnership (assuming that the joint venture will not be conducted through a limited liability company), there are no formalities with which the parties have to comply. However, once again, it is advisable for an agreement to be concluded governing the relationship between the parties, among other things, to make it clear that the parties are partners only in respect of the activities of the joint venture. In South Africa, the relationship between partners is one of the utmost good faith which gives rise to a duty between partners not to compete with each other. The joint venture agreement must therefore clarify the differing duties which the partners owe to each other and the parameters of their relationship, such as the extent to which they can compete with each other and the extent to which they must account to each other.

V. Issues To Cover In A Joint Venture Agreement

Any joint venture agreement will necessarily have to deal with matters such as the particular contributions of the parties, the management of the joint venture and the respective interests of the parties with respect to profits and losses. However, there are particular matters to which attention should be given when establishing a cross-border joint venture, which are discussed below.

A. Financing Of The Joint Venture

This is often the issue which causes most difficulty in establishing the joint venture, particularly where the parties have unequal financial resources. For example, in the past few years, many joint ventures have been established in South Africa in which one of the parties (usually from the previously disadvantaged sector) has limited access to capital. In such situations, it is common practice to provide that, until the parties' respective capital accounts are equalized, the profits of the joint venture (or at least a major portion of the profits) will first be applied towards equalizing the capital accounts before being distributed in the form of dividends.

Another problem which sometimes arises concerns the need which the joint venture may have to raise additional financing. Particularly in situations where the joint venture cannot raise the necessary finances from outside sources (for example, through commercial borrowings), the joint venture will need to look to the parties to inject additional capital into the venture. The joint venture agreement will need to deal with the possibility that one party may be unable or unwilling to inject any further capital into the venture.

B.   Choice Of Law

If the joint venture's operations are going to be conducted in South Africa, it will usually be sensible for the chosen law to be South African law. In this regard, South Africa has a sophisticated legal system, with its corporate law being very closely modeled on the English system.

C.   Dispute Resolution

It is important that the parties decide at the commencement of the joint venture the basis on which disputes are to be resolved. While the parties can obviously elect to have recourse to the courts, it is common (although by no means uniform) in joint venture agreements for an arbitration clause to be included under which most or all disputes are referred to arbitration. In order to avoid time consuming and costly arbitration proceedings, the parties often elect a short-form arbitration procedure whereby disputes are referred to an arbitrator for resolution in a summary manner and without recourse to the usual rules of evidence.

There are, however, other methods of resolving disputes. These methods include, but are not limited to, providing that the chairperson of the joint venture company or of the management board of the joint venture will have a deciding vote or appointing an individual unconnected to the joint venture as an additional director or member of the management board who can exercise a deciding vote in particular deadlock situations. Deadlocks can also be resolved by terminating the joint venture.

D.   Termination

There are numerous situations which may give rise to one or both of the parties considering the termination of the joint venture: (i) the parties may reach an irresolvable deadlock; (ii) they may simply decide that they no longer wish to continue the relationship with each other; (iii) the joint venture itself may fail; (iv) the joint venture agreement may be breached; (v) one or both of the parties may be unable to provide the necessary finance; (vi) the purpose of the joint venture may come to an end; or (vii) one of the parties may be declared insolvent or undergo a change of control.

It is important that the agreement specify the bases upon which the joint venture can be terminated and the consequences of such termination. For example, should the parties be entitled to terminate the joint venture on notice and, if so, what notice is required? Should particular circumstances be identified which would entitle a party to terminate the joint venture and, if so, what circumstances?

Once a decision to terminate the joint venture has been reached, the parties will need to dispose of the assets and settle all liabilities. The joint venture agreement should provide for the mechanisms for such a winding-up, for example, by the sale of the entire issued share capital or the assets of the joint venture company to a third party, by the sale by one party of its shares or interest to the other, by the sale by one party of its shares or interest to a third party or by the liquidation of the joint venture.

It is also fairly common for the parties to include a buy/sell ("Russian roulette") clause in the joint venture agreement pursuant to which the one party can offer its shares in the joint venture to the other party at a specified price and the other party can elect whether to buy the first-mentioned party out or sell its own share in the joint venture to the first-mentioned party at the same price. This type of provision is particularly beneficial when the partners participate in the joint venture on a 50/50 basis. This provision can also be used as an alternative to arbitration. In other words, the agreement could give either party the right to invoke the "Russian roulette" clause in the event that the parties reach an irresolvable deadlock.

E. Intellectual Property

In cases where the joint venture parties own intellectual property rights, the use of which is required by the joint venture, appropriate agreements will have to be entered into to govern their use by the joint venture. This will particularly be the case in sectors such as manufacturing and consumer products where confidential information and knowledge will inevitably pass from one party to the other. This issue will also have to be considered when considering the consequences of termination.

VI. Political And Economic Considerations

No investor should consider investing in South Africa without taking account of the socio-political and economic climate. While there are numerous matters which should be investigated in the course of a due diligence exercise, particular consideration will need to be taken of the matters discussed below.

A. Tax

As already mentioned, South Africa has a source-based system of taxation which offers the investor the possibility of effective tax structuring. Thus, for example, a number of foreign investors have utilized South Africa as a base for investment into the rest of Africa. At the same time, South Africa has a burdensome tax rate of 35% plus STC of 12.5% of dividends declared in the case of companies, and a maximum of 45% in the case of individuals. In addition, there are a number of indirect taxes such as Value Added Tax (currently 14% on most goods and services, although input credits can be obtained).

B. Exchange Control

While the South African authorities have indicated an intention to abolish exchange control on a phased basis, the repatriation to and expatriation of funds from South Africa are still regulated. In general terms, a foreign investor is entitled to repatriate its profits and foreign investment via share capital without exchange control approval. On the other hand, exchange control approval is required prior to any foreign investment via loan capital. The exchange control authorities generally require that a 3:1 ratio be maintained between loan capital and share capital and the terms of any loan (including interest rate, repayment terms or period of repayment) must first be approved by the South African Reserve Bank. Furthermore, companies in which foreign entities have an ownership stake of 25% or more have certain limitations imposed on their borrowing ability. These requirements have implications for a joint venture company which has a significant foreign shareholding.

C. Competition Law

A joint venture between two or more companies which are, or could be, competitors raises inevitable competition law questions. Chief among these are the potential lessening of competition and the heightened risk of collusion between competitors. South African rules relating to restrictive practices and monopolies will need to be taken into account when structuring the joint venture.

D. Changing Political Climate

While South Africa is now structured on the basis of a relatively stable liberal democracy (with a Constitution and a Bill of Rights), the recent political turmoil means that investors should monitor the political climate carefully. This is particularly important in regard to the termination clauses in joint venture agreements. Whether expressed implicitly in the agreement (by reference to certain dates or targets) or explicitly through force majeure provisions, parties to a joint venture should consider the effects on the venture of significant changes of a political and economic nature as well as possible legal and regulatory changes which may be introduced.

E. Black Empowerment And Affirmative Action

Many new joint ventures in South Africa have been established between parties (often foreign) with access to capital, resources and expertise and South African parties from previously disadvantaged communities. These South African parties, while lacking capital and expertise, now, as a result of the changed political situation, have access to contracts, licenses and other opportunities. For example, in numerous sectors (such as fishing, building, printing, telecommunications and health care) government contracts, licenses and quotas are increasingly only being awarded to companies with significant black participation at both a shareholder and management level. This has influenced numerous companies either to restructure themselves or to embark on joint ventures with emerging black companies. Furthermore, a company's ability to obtain government contracts, licenses and the like is going to be influenced by the extent to which that company applies affirmative action policies aimed at redressing past racial and gender imbalances. Any foreign investor wishing to embark on a joint venture in South Africa is going to have to take account of this situation.

Cape Town, South Africa
June 1996

CHAPTER 3

ESTABLISHING A DISTRIBUTION BUSINESS

By Lee Falkow and John Janks

I.   Introduction

The establishment of a distribution business in the Republic of South Africa ("RSA") requires knowledge of the forms of business entities and their advantages and disadvantages, the tax implications and the exchange controls applicable to such entities and other relevant considerations in respect of such business entities. A brief guide as to the foreign exchange, tax and other implications of such business entities is provided, which is of a general nature and is only intended as a guide to establishing a distribution business in RSA. Specific details of the tax and foreign exchange implications are covered in another chapter of this guide.

II. Forms Of Business Entities

There are a variety of vehicles available to investors interested in setting up an active business in RSA. The main forms of business enterprise through which an investor can conduct business are the limited liability company, external company (branch operation), close corporation, partnership and sole proprietorship.

RSA has a well developed and formally regulated company regime. The Companies Act, 1973 regulates the formation, conduct of affairs and winding up of all companies. The Close Corporations Act, 1984 regulates the formation, conduct of affairs and winding up of close corporations (a simpler and less expensive corporate form which will be discussed in more detail). Partnerships are another form of business enterprise which are not formally regulated by statute. In addition, RSA has an extensive and economically powerful informal sector which is not regulated by legislation.

A.   Limited Liability Companies

The most common form of business entity in South Africa is the limited liability company. Two types of limited liability companies are available in RSA, public companies and private companies. Both are created in terms of and governed by the provisions of the Companies Act and the following characteristics and requirements apply to each:

- they are separate legal entities with separate legal personalities;
- the shareholders of such companies have limited liability in relation to the debts and obligations of the company;
- the shares in the companies do not need to be held by RSA residents;
- they are subject to a strict maintenance of capital rule which prevents shareholders from accessing the share capital of a company and provides that a company cannot buy its own shares and may not provide financial assistance for the acquisition of its shares. This has led to company funding by way of loans. Where the loans are made

by non-residents, exchange control regulations will be applicable. This will be more fully dealt with later on in this chapter.

Public companies are identified by the word "Limited" after the name of the company.

The formation of a public company requires a minimum of seven shareholders, none of whom are required to be local shareholders. There is no restriction upon the maximum number of members which it may have. There is no restriction on the transfer of shares in a public company.

A public company must file its annual financial statements and interim reports with the Registrar of Companies, where they are available for inspection by the general public during the Registrar's office hours.

Public companies may raise capital from the general public and are the only form of company which is capable of being listed on The Johannesburg Stock Exchange. A minimum of two directors is required and such directors need not hold qualification shares and need not be residents or nationals of RSA.

Private companies are identified by the words (Proprietary) Limited after the name of the company.

The articles of association of a private company (the constitution documents of the company) must restrict the right to transfer the shares of the company, limit the number of members of the private company to fifty (plus employees who hold shares) and prohibit any offer to the public for the subscription of any shares or debentures of the company.

A private company must have a minimum of one member which need not be a RSA resident and at least one director, who is not required to hold qualification shares.

A private company is formed without the necessity to mobilise or use public funds and as such, a private company does not have to comply with the strict requirements of publicity. Financial statements need not be lodged with the Registrar of Companies, nor need members be provided with half yearly interim reports and provisional annual financial statements.

B.   External Company (Branch Operation)

A foreign company not wishing to incorporate a subsidiary in RSA may instead set up a branch office. A company incorporated outside of RSA which establishes a place of business in RSA is required to register as an "external company" within 21 days of establishing such a place of business in RSA. The term "external company" denotes a company or other association accorded corporate status in another country.

Once registered, an external company is required to comply with the provisions of the Companies Act including the submission of statutory returns and the filing of annual financial statements relating to the RSA operations and the operations of the company in the country of incorporation. An exemption may be obtained from filing the annual financial statements of the parent company provided no prejudice will be suffered by any interested parties. In practice, this exemption is easily obtained.

An external company is not required to appoint a local board of directors, but is required to appoint a person resident in the RSA who is authorised to accept service of process and any notices served on the branch in the RSA.

C. Close Corporations

The Close Corporations Act, 1984 introduced a far simpler and less expensive form of corporate entity referred to as a "close corporation", which still provides for separate legal personality, perpetual succession and limited liability. The overriding intent of the legislation was to relieve closely held businesses of the complex requirements of the Companies Act while retaining their corporate status and a legal identity distinct from their members. The close corporation achieves corporate status by filing a founding statement with the Registrar of Close Corporations. A close corporation does not require either a memorandum or articles of association, but the members of the close corporation can elect to have an association agreement to regulate their relationship. A close corporation indicates its status by the letters "CC" after its name.

Close corporations do not have share capital. Members' interests in the close corporation are expressed as percentages of the total and are arrived at by agreement with the other members. The sale of a member's interest requires the consent of the other members, failing which the member can sell his or her interest back to the close corporation. Close corporations may give financial assistance for the acquisition of a member's interest and may themselves acquire members' interests from any member (this procedure is forbidden in relation to companies due to the maintenance of capital rule). If the close corporation does not remain both solvent and liquid immediately after giving that assistance or acquiring that interest, the members will be personally liable to creditors prejudiced as a result.

A close corporation may be formed by at least one but not more than 10 members. Membership is restricted to natural persons, including non-residents, and to trustees of testamentary trusts or a trustee, administrator, executor or curator for a member who is insolvent, deceased, mentally disordered or otherwise incapable of managing his or her affairs. A juristic person may not directly or indirectly hold an interest in a close corporation.

Each member of a close corporation stands in a fiduciary relationship to the close corporation and may become liable to the close corporation for losses suffered as a result of breach of that relationship. Close corporations are managed by their members. There is no separate board of directors or management body. Every member is entitled to participate in the management, unless the members agree to the contrary.

D. Partnerships

Business may be carried on in RSA by a partnership. The Companies Act limits the membership in a business partnership to 20 persons (who may be either natural or juristic persons). Apart from this restriction, a partnership is not subject to the requirements imposed on companies and close corporations by legislation.

No other statutory provisions govern partnerships. They are subject to the general principles of the law of contract and to various special principles of the law applicable particularly to partnerships. They are not separate legal entities, the partners, subject to certain specific exemptions, do not enjoy limited liability and no registration formalities exist in relation to partnerships.

A partnership may be constituted by contract or by implication through the conduct of the partners. For tax purposes the partnership must keep proper books and records and submit a copy of the partnership balance sheet and income statements in support of each individual partner's annual tax return to the Receiver of Revenue. This is not a statutory requirement of partnerships but is a requirement in terms of the Income Tax Act. There is no fixed format for the management and administration of the affairs of a partnership and there is no requirement to disclose the financial position to the public. The allocation of profits in the partnership is decided on by the partners.

E. Sole Proprietorships

There are no formalities required where a person commences business as a sole proprietorship. There are no audit or public disclosure requirements for a sole proprietor. The business is not a separate legal person and all transactions are concluded directly by the person concerned. The sole proprietorship does not enjoy limited liability and the sole proprietor's private estate is personally liable to make good any deficiency in the business.

Any income earned by the sole proprietorship is taxable in the sole proprietor's hands.

III. Formation Procedures
A. Limited Liability Companies

The following documents and information are required to be furnished to the Registrar of Companies in order to register a limited liability company:

- a memorandum and articles of association which are the constitution of the company. The memorandum specifies the name, object and the capital structure of the company and the articles contain regulations governing the management and directorship of the company and the rights of its shareholders;
- full names, business address, postal address and residential address of the subscribing shareholders;
- the name and consent to act of the auditors of the company;
- details of the registered office and postal address of the company;
- details of the financial year end of the company;
- names, addresses and other relevant details of the directors and officers of the company;
- a statement by the directors regarding the adequacy of the capital of the company. If the statement is to the effect that the capital is

nominal the directors must declare in what way the company is to be financed.

The annual financial statements must be drawn up in accordance with the provisions of the Companies Act, must be audited by an independent auditor (who must be a chartered accountant) and must be made available to the shareholders and directors of the company.

The approximate cost of registering a new company is currently R2 500.

B. External Company (Branch Operation)

The following documents and information are required to be lodged with the Registrar of Companies in order to register a branch of a foreign company in RSA as an external company:

- a notarially certified copy of the memorandum and articles of association (or their equivalent) of the "parent" company;
- the name and consent to act of the auditors in the RSA;
- details of the registered office and postal address of the company within the RSA;
- details of the financial year end;
- full names and addresses and associated details of the directors and officers (not only of the RSA branch but of the entire "parent" company);
- name and address of a person in the RSA authorised to accept service on behalf of the "parent" company.

Unless exemption is obtained from the Registrar of Companies, an external company is required to lodge a certified copy of its complete annual financial statements with the Registrar within six months of the end of its financial year. Such exemption is easily obtainable.

The approximate cost of establishing an external company is currently R2 100.

C. Close Corporations

A close corporation comes into existence through the registration of a duly completed founding statement by the Registrar of Close Corporations. The founding statement can be drawn up by any one or more persons who intend to form a close corporation and must be signed by, or on behalf of, all persons who will become members of the close corporation on registration.

The founding statement must contain the following particulars:

- the full name of the close corporation;
- the principal business to be carried on by the close corporation;
- the postal address and office address of the close corporation;
- the full names of each member and the identity number or date of birth of such member;
- the size of the interest of every member in the close corporation expressed as a percentage;

- the name and address of the accounting officer who must accept the appointment in writing;
- the date of the end of the corporation's financial year.

The approximate cost of registering a close corporation is currently R900.

IV. Advantages And Disadvantages Of Different Business Entities
A. Limited Liability Companies

The Exchange Control Department of the Reserve Bank of South Africa ("Excon") and other government departments prefer the setting up of a locally registered subsidiary, as this indicates a degree of permanence while an external company or branch operation may be regarded as a temporary entity only. This may place the external company or branch operation at a disadvantage in relation to a locally registered company if both are competing for a government or parastatal tender or an import permit in a specialised field if import permits are restricted at such time.

An RSA company need only disclose to the Registrar of Companies the details of its own directors and officers and need not disclose details in respect of its parent company.

Unless the RSA company is a public company within the meaning of the Companies Act, the company need not lodge its financial statements with the Registrar of Companies and need only present these to its shareholders and directors.

If the enterprise wishes to raise money locally, local lenders prefer, on the whole, to lend money to a locally registered entity rather than an external company. The exchange control restrictions applicable to local borrowings only entitle a foreign owned company to borrow locally in accordance with a specific formula. The formula together with the exchange control restrictions will be briefly dealt with in this chapter but more fully dealt with in another chapter of this Guide.

The disadvantage of registering an RSA company as a resident of RSA is that exchange control restrictions are far greater on RSA residents than those applicable to external companies.

B. External Company (Branch Operation)

As a non-resident of the RSA, the external company is not subject to the full impact of the Exchange Control Regulations. With the gradual lessening of exchange control restrictions, it is easier for an external company to repatriate its funds to the non-resident "parent" company. This topic is dealt with in more detail in another chapter of this Guide.

The disadvantages of registering an external company are:
- the details of the capital structure, directors and officers of the parent company must be lodged with the Registrar of Companies;
- unless a specific exemption is granted by the Registrar of Companies, certified copies of the complete annual financial statements must be lodged with the Registrar of Companies within six months from the end of its financial year;

- local lenders prefer, on the whole, to lend money to a locally registered company rather than an international entity as it will be easier to litigate against a locally registered company. Furthermore, local lenders may require expensive guarantees or other security from the international company. This will not differ in relation to a locally registered foreign owned subsidiary company in RSA;
- as the branch of the foreign company is not a separate legal person, all the assets of the foreign company will be at risk in an action for damages against the foreign company as a result of actions or omissions of the branch or its employees. In the case of a subsidiary company, the assets at risk are limited to such subsidiary company. Although the assets of a foreign company are at risk in an action for damages against the foreign company as a result of actions or omissions of the branch or its employees, in the event that a judgment is obtained in RSA for the attachment of such assets, such judgment will be required to be enforced in the relevant state of the "parent" company. This will prove expensive and difficult to enforce.

C. Close Corporations

The limited liability of the members of a close corporation is not as extensive as that provided by a limited liability company, but for normal trading purposes there is no significant difference. The limited liability of the members of a close corporation will be lost if the close corporation provides financial assistance subsequent to which the close corporation is no longer solvent or liquid, or, if a member of the close corporation is a "disqualified member" as determined by the Close Corporation Act.

Only natural persons or a trustee of a testamentary trust can be members of a close corporation.

A close corporation is, however, cheaper to form and administer than a limited liability company or branch and there are much fewer formalities. There is no prohibitions (provided the close corporation remains liquid and solvent) on the provision of financial assistance given to members for the acquisition of a members interest.

There are no tax benefits in forming a close corporation as a close corporation is regarded as a company for tax purposes and pays tax at the corporate rate of tax.

D. Partnerships And Sole Proprietorships

No limited liability arises in relation to partnerships or sole proprietorships. The partners and the sole proprietor are, subject to, a few specific and restricted exceptions, liable for all the debts of the entity. They are, however, very simple to form and administer.

V. Taxation

Taxation shall be more fully dealt with in a separate chapter of this Guide. The basic principles and sources of direct and indirect taxation revenue are briefly referred to in this chapter. More detailed information can be obtained from the chapter specifically dealing with this issue.

A. Income Tax

The principal source of direct taxation revenue in the RSA is income tax which is payable by both private individuals as well as companies. Income tax liability is determined and regulated by the Income Tax Act, 1962.

For any amount to be subject to South African Income Tax, such amount must have been received by or accrued to the taxpayer from a source within or deemed to be within South Africa. Liability for South African Income Tax is therefore not dependant on the place of that person's residence. A person will be liable for Income Tax on all the income derived from sources within, or deemed to be within the Republic no matter where such person resides.

The liability of a foreign company for RSA tax will be based on the principles of RSA tax law applicable to companies subject to the following important distinctions:
- a branch of a foreign company will not be subject to Secondary Tax on Companies ("STC") on profits remitted out of the RSA by it to its foreign company;
- there is no STC on dividends declared by foreign companies out of their RSA sourced income;
- on the income of the branch which has its place of effective management outside the RSA.

B. Value Added Tax

The principal source of indirect tax revenue in RSA is value added tax ("VAT"). The manner in which VAT is levied is closely modelled on the New Zealand Goods and Services Tax Act, 1985. The present standard rate of VAT in RSA is 14%.

Section 7(1)(a) of the VAT Act imposes invoice-based VAT liability in respect of the supply of goods and services by a vendor in the course of or furtherance of his enterprise. Section 7(1)(b) of the VAT Act imposes VAT liability on the value of the importation of goods into RSA by any person. Section 7(1)(c) levies VAT on the value of the supply of imported services by any one person.

Potential liability for VAT is a relevant tax issue for foreign investors, as VAT liability in terms of section 7(1) is incurred by any person who qualifies as a vendor.

C. Secondary Tax On Companies

Dividends received by an RSA company are exempt from income tax. Dividends declared by an RSA company to a resident shareholder are not subject to income tax.

During March 1993 a new corporate tax known as Secondary Tax on Companies was introduced in RSA. This is a tax payable by a company, which is presently at a flat rate of 12.5%, on the "net" amount of dividends declared by it. The net amount of the dividends declared is the amount by which the dividend declared by a company exceeds the sum of any dividends which have accrued to the company. Although STC is a tax imposed on the company declaring the dividend, and not on its shareholders, it increases the effective rate of company tax and accordingly impacts on the profits ultimately distributable to the company's shareholders.

D.   Other Relevant Sources Of Taxation Revenue

There are numerous other sources of taxation revenue in the form of transfer duty, marketable securities tax, stamp duty, regional services and local authorities levies and customs and excise duty. In establishing a distribution business in the RSA, it is more than likely that goods will be imported into the Republic. The importation of such goods are subject to the Customs and Excise Act, 1964 and to the import duties levied in terms of the Schedules to that Act will apply to the importation of such products. This again will be more fully dealt with in the chapter on Trade Law.

E.   Interest And Royalty Payments, Management And
     Administration Fees To RSA Non-Residents

Interest by a non-resident company received or accrued after April 1, 1996 will be exempt from normal tax on interest only if, in addition to the fact that it is managed and controlled outside RSA, it does not carry on business in RSA. If a "non-resident" company establishes a subsidiary in RSA, but does not itself carry on business in the RSA, it will be entitled to the tax exemption on interest. Any interest payable by a local branch or subsidiary will be deductible as an expense providing it is not a notional interest charge, which does not constitute interest actually incurred and it is incurred in the production of income.

Royalties paid by residents of RSA to non-resident companies are subject to a withholding tax of effectively 12%. Royalties are not subject to STC and are deductible for RSA income tax purposes, while dividends are paid from after tax profits. Therefore, it is generally more tax efficient to remit income in the form of royalties. However, the amount of the royalty which may be paid is limited by Excon, and the tax deductibility of excess charges may be queried by the Department of Finance.

In the ordinary course, a management fee charged by a non-resident holding company would qualify for a deduction for South African income tax purposes. Requests for payment of management and administration fees are considered by Excon on merit taking into account the reason for the fees, nature of the service and the basis of calculation. The fee cannot be excessive and must comply with all other requirements for deductibility of expenditure.

Where a distribution business is established in RSA, in the event that management fees are charged by a non-resident holding company, and are not merely an attempt to repatriate capital out of RSA in the guise of a management fee, such management fee may be approved by Excon and deducted by the local company for income tax purposes provided that it is not excessive.

It must be remembered that interest payments, royalty fees, licence fees and management, consultancy and administration fees require the prior approval of Excon. This will be dealt with more fully in the chapter on exchange control in this guide but a brief summary of such exchange control regulations is dealt with below.

VI. Exchange Control

Residents of the RSA are bound by several restrictions in respect of the remittance by them of funds abroad. These restrictions are contained in the Exchange Control Regulations published by the State President in terms of Section 9 of the Currency and Exchanges Act, and would apply to any entity established by non-residents in the RSA.

Generally, the Exchange Control Regulations provide that no person may, without Excon approval, make any payment to a person resident outside the RSA, or place any sum to the credit of such person.

Accordingly, the remittance of interest, royalties, licence and similar fees (including consultancy fees) requires the prior approval of Excon. In particular, the amount of such payments and the method of their calculation are critical. The following should be noted in this regard:

- royalty payments in respect of know-how are usually calculated as a percentage of the manufacturing cost or of the net ex-factory selling price of goods excluding any taxes such as VAT. A distinction is made between royalty agreements covering consumer goods and those for intermediate and capital goods. In the former case, a royalty of up to 4% of the ex-factory selling price is regarded as acceptable while in the latter, a payment of up to 6% may be in order. Any agreement involving the payment of royalties by a South African entity to a foreign concern must be submitted to the Department of Trade and Industry. The Department of Trade and Industry will then pass the request, with their recommendations on to Excon which will then make a final decision;
- all requests for payment of management, consultancy and administration fees are considered on merit taking into account the reasons therefor, the nature of the services provided and the basis of calculation (i.e., whether they are based on a percentage of turnover or actual time spent, the latter calculation being preferred since the fees paid must be based on the benefit received);
- payments of the above amounts to a holding company or another entity which directly or indirectly owns the RSA company or branch will be more difficult to justify since Excon prefers that profits be remitted out of the RSA by way of dividend or direct remittance of the profits to ensure that RSA tax is not avoided or materially reduced.

An external company or a company, of which 25% of the share capital is controlled by a non-resident of the RSA is restricted in respect of local borrowings from an RSA person by Excon regulations. Furthermore an RSA resident is restricted by Excon in respect of foreign loans to such RSA resident. Both such local borrowings and foreign loans require Excon approval.

As previously mentioned, this topic is more fully dealt with in a separate chapter in this Guide.

VII. Intellectual Property

Trade marks, copyright and patents and other intellectual property rights are statutorily protected in RSA. Thus, any distribution business established in RSA will be subject to and protected by such statutes.

The right to use a name in respect of a company is subject to common law limitations whereby a company is restrained from passing itself off as another by suggesting or creating the impression that its own undertaking is that of another. The Business Names Act, which is applicable to partnership names and trading names, effectively prohibits the carrying on of a business in a name calculated to deceive or mislead the public or cause annoyance or offense to any person. The Companies Act entitles a person to apply to the Registrar of Companies to register a defensive name in terms of which the exclusivity of certain words is protected. Furthermore, before incorporation of the company, the name of such company must be reserved.

VIII. The Main Distribution Channels in RSA

The main types of international arrangements for distributing products in South Africa are contained in this chapter, although such list is not exhaustive. The reference to "products" is intended to include services.

A. International Salesman

An international salesman is quite able to operate from an international base and, due to the ease of communication by modern methods is not required to reside in or trade while in RSA. Only in regard to relatively important and complex transactions do international salespersons have to spend extensive periods in RSA selling their products. During such periods in RSA, an international salesperson faces no legal requirements to register or report on his business activities.

There are fiscal implications in relation to such sales activities. Section 9(1)(a) and (d) of the Income Tax Act deems the proceeds of any sales agreement entered into in RSA or provision of services in RSA to be of RSA source, and hence, in the normal course of events, to be taxable in RSA.

The international salesman, if he is carrying on an enterprise in RSA which supplies goods or services to a total value which exceeds R150 000, will be regarded as a "vendor" for the purposes of the VAT Act and will be liable to charge and pay VAT.

An international salesman who supplies products to an RSA entity faces the difficulty that, if the sales price is to be paid to a non-resident outside RSA, the permission of Excon for such payment is required.

B. Agents

An agent in terms of RSA law is a person who performs a juristic act on behalf of another person (the principal), the agent himself not being bound by the rights and duties that stem from such act and bind the principal. The distribution of products in RSA can be undertaken by such class of agent. The law of agency in RSA is based on the common law. Statutory law is incidental to the contracts of agency, which may require the agent to comply with certain statutory formalities incidental to the relationship of agency.

It is necessary to distinguish an agent from a distributor, who buys and sells products for its own account and from persons who seek out potential buyers and sellers and facilitates transactions between them while themselves acting for their own account and having no power to conclude or execute these transactions.

There is a vast range of agency relationships in RSA and a large number of agents concerned only with the distribution of goods and services. Some of the principal classes of agents are:

- firstly, true agents;
- secondly, del credere agents who are true agents, but who, for an extra commission, guarantee to their principals the solvency of the person to whom they sell; and
- thirdly, factors who are also true agents but are employed to sell goods on behalf of their principals for remuneration by way of the goods and may buy and sell in their own name.

Agency agreements for the sale of products in South Africa may be written, oral, or even tacit. There is no legislation stipulating the form they should take. In practice, the agents will from time to time be called upon to prove their authority or status and for this purpose at least a written power of attorney, and a document fully setting out the agent's rights and obligations, are desirable.

Like the international salesman, the commission earned by the agent will be subject to income tax. Further, if the agent is a "vendor" for the purposes of the VAT Act, he will be liable to charge and pay VAT.

C. Distributors

Distributors, as previously mentioned, buy and sell products for their own account and not as agents of either the supplier or their own customers. They derive their remuneration from a mark-up margin they place on the products when selling them.

No formalities are required to conclude a distributorship agreement in RSA, and the agreement need not even be in writing. Although there are exceptions, distributorship agreements usually are written, and it normally is desirable to both parties that they be written.

Much confusion of terminology exists between the concepts of agency and distributorship. A written agreement clearly setting out the nature and terms of the relationship assists in removing such confusion. Distribution agreements have arisen as a result of practice and the RSA common law and statute has not developed in this regard.

Since distributors buy products from their foreign suppliers and proceed to resell them, they need not officially record or request approval from Excon for such appointment. The purchases of products made from time to time by the distributors will require them to make payments through their South African commercial banks to the suppliers. The banks being authorised dealers are able to authorise these payments under their delegated powers derived from the Reserve Bank.

D. Franchisees

Franchising is a method of licensing where the licensee or franchisee obtains the right to use and replicate the name, symbols, equipment, products and organizational procedures and selling techniques of the licensor or franchisor. Franchising has, since the April 1994 elections, developed extensively in RSA and is a rapidly growing method of distribution.

All license fees, royalties, management fees or the like, which are payable by the licensee or franchisee, will be subject to Excon approval.

E. Licensees

Manufacturing activities in RSA often take place under license in terms of technology transfer agreements with foreign suppliers in terms of which the licensee manufactures and sells the products for his own account and pays the licensor remuneration usually consisting, in part or exclusively, of royalties.

If the agreement provides for the payment of royalties or similar remuneration to a foreign licensor and such agreement is in respect of the manufacture of industrial products, the agreement must be in writing, and must be submitted together with other relevant documentation to the Department of Trade and Industry and thereafter to the South African Reserve Bank for Excon approval before payment can be made by the RSA licensee of the royalty to the foreign licensor.

F. Assemblers

A foreign supplier may appoint and be represented in RSA by an assembler of goods which are manufactured by the foreign supplier, and placed on the local market by such assembler through whatever distribution channels are available and appropriate.

G. External Company

A foreign supplier of products may establish an external company in RSA to distribute its own or other products. Such external company will not be a separate legal entity of the parent company. The characteristics and legal implications of such external company are discussed earlier in this chapter.

H. Subsidiaries

A foreign corporate supplier may distribute its products in RSA through a local subsidiary in the form of a limited liability company, which may be wholly or partly owned by the supplier. The arrangements for funding and other aspects of financial operations and the characteristics and legal implications of such limited liability RSA company are more fully discussed earlier in this chapter.

I. Joint Ventures

Joint ventures, whether as individuals, partnerships, close corporations or companies, jointly participate and engage in an activity in terms of which all parties can benefit from each others contacts and experience. A joint venture is usually a partnership although the parties can and often do incorporate the joint venture in the form of an ordinary company in terms of which the "partners" become shareholders. Such joint venture company is a separate legal entity and an RSA resident.

Joint ventures will be more fully discussed in a separate chapter of this Guide.

J. Direct Relationships

A proportion of the products entering RSA are acquired as a result of sales directly from a foreign seller to an RSA customer. The importation of such goods will be subject to the provisions of the Customs and Excise Act, 1964. The applicability of the Customs and Excise Act is not limited to the area of "direct relationships". The importation of goods into RSA or the exportation of such goods from RSA, whatever the relationship between the parties, will be subject to the provisions of the Customs and Excise Act. The details of such activities in relation to the importation or exportation of goods are more fully discussed in the chapter on Trade Law. Excon approvals for the remittance of funds to pay for the supply of such goods will be required.

K. Consignment Sales

In commercial practice goods are sometimes supplied by a wholesaler or a manufacturer to a retail trader "on consignment". This means that there is no contract of sale between them, but that the retailer is, in the course of his business, to dispose of the goods as the agent or the wholesaler or manufacturer, accounting to him for the proceeds and receiving a commission for such sale.

IX. Ancillary Considerations Applicable To Product Distribution In RSA
A. Parallel Imports

A comprehensive definition of parallel importation or "grey goods" describes a situation where "articles made by or with the authority of a copyright owner in one country are imported into another country in competition with the rights under copyright in a work granted to another person in the importing country". It is an entirely legitimate business provided the goods are genuine goods and the unlicensed importing entity does not infringe rules of copyright, trade marks and passing-off.

Parallel imports are an issue of concern to both parties to a product distribution agreement. For many years legal battles against grey marketeers have been waged to safeguard licensed importers' rights and protect the huge sums invested annually.

Up until recently RSA licencees and distributors have been powerless to prevent this trade practice. Court cases based on trade mark infringement, passing-off and unfair competition have been unsuccessful because the goods are genuine branded goods. The breakthrough came when the Appeal Court overturned a Durban Supreme Court decision and ruled that parallel importation in this particular case constituted an infringement of copyright.

The reason that such case succeeded is because the manufacturer had assigned the RSA copyright to the distributor. Most overseas manufacturers retain copyright to themselves for fear of giving a foreign distributor too much power. Accordingly, this cause of action depends wholly on the co-operation of the overseas principal.

Therefore, in order to take advantage of this landmark decision distributors must ensure that the item imported incorporates in its packaging or on the item itself elements of trade dress and get-up which fall within the meaning of artistic and/or literary works as defined by the Copyright Act and such copyright must be assigned by the manufacturer in the exporting country to its licenced distributor in South Africa.

The Business Practices Committee, in terms of the Harmful Business Practices Act, 1988 received various complaints from local distributors and agents in terms of the Harmful Business Practices Act to the effect that consumers were exploited by grey marketeers and that the trade in "grey goods" constituted a Harmful Business Practice. The Harmful Business Practices Act provides for investigations by the Committee. The Committee, in response to the complaints, merely proposed a consumer code to force dealers to indicate in their warranty whether their guarantees are backed by a manufacturer or licenced distributor. This proposal was contained in a report in the Government Gazette. The consumer code is merely a guideline as to what the Committee believes to be good sales practices which have no force of law. However, should a consumer complaint arise in relation to a contravention of such consumer code, it may lead to action in terms of the Harmful Business Practices Act. The Harmful Business Practices Act is dealt with in more detail below.

In general, parallel imports cannot be prevented where the parallel goods have been acquired lawfully and imported into RSA and the manufacturer or his licensee had not, when placing the goods on the market initially outside the RSA, stipulated to such parallel importer that they were not to be sold on the RSA market.

B.   Product Liability

Product liability is a relatively untested area of RSA law and one where conservative norms still prevail. There are two areas of common law applicable to product liability claims, namely delict (tort) and contract.

In South Africa, the requirements for a delict under the common law are an unlawful act or omission (in the sense of a breach of the complainant's rights), fault (whether deliberate intention or negligence) on the part of the perpetrator of the act or omission, damage to the complainant, and a causal connection between the unlawful act or omission and the damage. For the causal connection to exist, the damage must be reasonably foreseeable, and not too remote. In regard to product liability, the wrongful act is constituted by the production of a defective article that causes damage. In other words it is the manufacturer and not necessarily the seller who would attract delictual liability. However, sellers and distributors who are not manufactures may find themselves delictually liable by virtue of some other act or omission, namely, their failure to have inspected the goods prior to the sale in circumstances where the law imposes such an obligation.

There are few instances of manufacturers or distributors being sued for damages in South Africa on the grounds of delict arising from defects or alleged defects in their products.

Under the law of contract, only the purchaser will have a remedy (since only he has a contractual nexus with the seller), and usually a manufacturer whose products are sold by a distributor or retailer will have no contractual obligations towards the purchaser. In terms of RSA common law, parties can contractually exclude the manufacturer's warranty. This practice is commonly undertaken, and in addition, the manufacturer may require the distributor to limit the distributor's liability to the consumer. The manufacturer may provide limited warranties which, in effect, tend to limit rather than extend the manufacturer's liability. These warranties usually extend to the manufacturer undertaking to repair or replace defective goods at the election of the manufacturer. Further, provision is usually included in such contracts that the manufacturer is not liable for any damages which may be suffered as a result of any defect in a product. It is intended that legislation be drafted to provide consumers with better protection but, as yet, no specific statute has been introduced.

In the law of contract, suppliers of products are divided between those who have no specialist knowledge of the products they stock and who sell them indiscriminately, such as supermarket chains, and those who are specialists and expressly or by inference hold themselves out to be specialists in the products that they deal.

In the normal course of events, every product sold is, in law, automatically assumed to be fit for the purpose it was sold and to be of reasonable "merchantable" quality unless the seller has disclaimed liability for the state or condition of the product before conclusion of the contact and in a way that clearly amounts to a term of the contract. This can be undertaken by standard term contracts provided such terms are clearly brought to the attention of the purchaser. Such terms cannot simply be introduced in the invoice or delivery note.

If a guarantee attaches to goods sold, it may be the manufacturer or a distributor or a retailer who issues the guarantee and is liable under it to a customer. If the guarantee is given by or on behalf or the manufacturer, and the goods reach the customer through an agent or distributor or retailer in circumstances where it is known that the guarantee emanates from the manufacturer, the customer can assume that the trader from whom the goods have been bought has acted as an agent of the manufacturer in respect to the guarantee and its fulfilment, and will not be entitled to conclude that this agent is personally bound by the guarantee.

If the guarantee is disclosed to the customer but the identity of the grantor is not mentioned, the customer normally will be entitled to assume that the seller of the goods is issuing the guarantee and will be bound by it. If a guarantee is so limited as to be unconscionable, it will be invalid and normally the common-law warranties of fitness for purpose and merchantability will apply. It must be kept in mind that in RSA, it is difficult to persuade the courts that a clause in a contract or a contract itself is unconscionable. Although RSA courts are moving towards a more equity-based system, a court will not go so far as to hold a clause unconscionable if it merely results in hardship.

If no guarantee, whether express or implied, applies to the sale, the customer and those claiming through him will have no contractual basis for holding liable either the manufacturer or the seller from whom the customer bought the goods if the goods prove defective and cause the customer harm.

If there is an express or implied guarantee other than the warranties of fitness for purpose and of merchantability, it will be a question of interpretation of that guarantee to determine whether damage suffered by a complainant was of a nature the guarantee covered. If the damage went beyond that scope, the complainant will be without a remedy to that extent.

If the only guarantee was the warranties of fitness for purpose and of merchantability, the party bound by it (whether the manufacturer or a distributor or a retailer) will be bound for all reasonably foreseeable damage caused to the customer as a result of a defect in the product covered by the warranty. It is common in RSA law to restrict liability in contracts and to require a similar restriction to be contained in the onward sale contracts between the distributor and the purchaser. Such limitation can restrict the liability of the manufacturer for consequential damages. The party bound by the warranty will not have any contractual obligations to any third party who is damaged as a result of the defect, although there may be delictual liability.

C.   **Competition Law**

Competition Law in RSA is governed by the Maintenance and Promotion of Competition Act, 1979 (the "Competition Act"). This Act is presently in the process of being amended to ensure more stringent consequences for non compliance as well as to, inter alia, introduce stricter anti-trust legislation. Presently, the Competition Board is empowered to conduct investigations into "acquisitions or mergers", "monopoly situations" and "restrictive practices" as defined in the Competition Act. The Competition Board has no executive authority in that it merely makes recommendations to the

Minister of Trade and Industry who need not act on the Competition Board's advice, but, if he wishes to act, has a discretion as to the number of powers that he may exercise.

The policy objective underlying the Competition Act and its application by the Competition Board is the striving for effective competition in the economy of RSA. RSA competition law is relatively under-developed and the Competition Act has been criticized for failing to provide for real enforcement powers. The White Paper on the Reconstruction and Development Programme ("RDP") deals with, as one aspect of the reconstruction and development of RSA, the present government's policy on Competition Law. The objective of the new government's competition policy, as stated in the RDP white paper, is to remove or reduce the distorting effects of excessive economic concentration and the abuse of economic powers by enterprises in a dominant position.

In order to implement the new Government's competition policy, preparatory investigations were undertaken and a report was issued that new legislation was to be introduced. A Bill was introduced which received a negative reaction from industry. Thereafter, there was a change in the Minister of Trade and Industry and the new Minister has withdrawn the Bill and intends to begin the process of negotiating a new competition policy with business, labour and government.

D. Harmful Business Practices

A further important statute which governs trade and industry in the RSA is the Harmful Business Practices Act referred to above. This Act provides for the prohibition or control of certain business practices. The Harmful Business Practices Act establishes the Business Practices Committee. The functions of the Committee are to provide information on current policy in relation to harmful business practices, receive and dispose of representations in relation to matters provided for in the Harmful Business Practices Act, and make preliminary investigations into harmful business practices.

Any consumer who has a complaint that a harmful business practice is being performed may lodge such complaint with the Harmful Business Practices Committee who will undertake investigations into the practice. If the practice is found to be a harmful business practice the Harmful Business Practices Committee will issue a report which will be published in the Government Gazette. A harmful business practice is defined in the Harmful Business Practices Act as any business practice which, directly or indirectly, has or is likely to have the effect of harming the relations between business or consumers, unreasonably prejudicing any consumer, or deceiving any consumer.

Accordingly, business practices must be performed in such a manner so as not to contravene the Harmful Business Practices Act or the Regulations or notices promulgated in terms of the Harmful Business Practices Act. Any person failing to comply with the Harmful Business Practices Act or its regulations shall be guilty of an offence.

E. Law Of Sale Of Goods

Agreements for the sale of goods need not be in writing, unlike agreements for the sale of land and buildings. Distributorship agreements are usually concluded in writing between a foreign supplier and an RSA distributor and such agreements usually make provision for all conditions under which individual sales transactions between these parties will occur. These specific terms may be contained in the distributorship agreement itself or may require the distributor to apply the supplier's standard terms and conditions.

The parties are free to select the law of RSA, or that of the country of domicile of the foreign seller (or apparently any other legal system with which there is some formal or practical connection) as the governing law.

For the agreement to be one of sale, payment must be made wholly or partially in money. If no money is involved, the contract will be of a different nature, such as a barter or a donation, and not a sale.

Sales may be for cash, in which case payment must be made before or at the time of delivery of the goods, or on credit, in which case delivery (or at least dispatch) precedes payment or a portion of the payment. The commercial banks, which act as the authorised dealers for Excon may approve the remittance of cash payments for such goods.

Unless the parties agree otherwise, risk in the goods passes to the purchaser once the agreement of sale comes into force. Ownership (if the seller has it) passes on payment in the case of cash sales and on delivery in the case of credit sales. Despite the passing of risk, the seller is obliged to take care of the goods until delivery takes place, much as he would of his own goods. If he fails to observe this standard of care, the seller will be responsible for loss or deterioration of the goods.

If the goods sold to a purchaser who was unaware of defects prove to have been defective at the time of sale, even although the seller was unaware of the defect, the purchaser may cancel the sale and claim restitution of the price paid or retain the goods and claim the return of a portion of the purchase price. The defect must have been such as to interfere with the use intended for the goods. The remedy is also available if the seller was aware of the defect but failed to disclose it or if a material statement about the characteristics of the goods is made by the seller during the negotiations and proves to be false. The remedies are not available where the parties agreed that the purchaser would take the risk of defects at the time of the sale, or where the defects were patent or obvious. Liability for latent defects may be excluded. Contracts which contain such exclusion are referred to as "voetstoots sales" which protects the seller against any latent defects except where the seller knew and failed to disclose such defects to the purchaser.

Where there has been an express or implied warranty that the goods sold are fit for the purpose they were sold, an action based on breach of contract may be brought by a purchaser who shows that the goods failed to conform to the warranty. In appropriate circumstances, the purchaser may abide by the contract but claim a reduction in the price, or may cancel the contract and claim the return of the purchase price, returning the goods himself. If the purchaser has suffered loss as a result of the goods' failure to conform to the warranty, he may cancel the sale, tender the return of the goods sold, and claim compensation for the loss. Consequential loss may be claimed and recovered provided such loss was foreseeable and was in the contemplation of the parties at the time of the conclusion of the contract. Consequential loss or damages are, however, usually excluded by the agreement between the parties.

X.   Conclusion

Due to sanctions and balance of payments problems, RSA trade policy, until 1994, with international markets tended towards a resistance to trade liberalisation. Now that RSA is in a post apartheid era it is coming out of its political and economic isolation and is joining the international trading community. RSA has been under substantial pressure to open its markets to foreign manufacture and products.

RSA, with its relations with its Southern African neighbours is a key country for facilitating trade with and into Africa. It is a country with a new political legitimacy and a strong infrastructure, which, in terms of investment and trade, should be explored to the fullest.

Johannesburg, South Africa
June 1996

Bibliography:

Werksmans, Handbook On Doing Business In South Africa

Bamford, B.R., The law Of Partnership And Voluntary Association In South Africa, Cape Town, Juta (3rd edition 1982)

Boberg, P.Q.R., The Law of Delict, Cape Town, Juta (1984)

Christie, R.H., The Law of Contract In South Africa, Burban, Butterworths (1983)

Silke, J.M., The Law Of Agency In South Africa, Cape Town, Juta (3rd edition 1981)

Henochsberg, E.S., The Companies Act, edited by P.M. Meskin, Durban, Butterworths (4th edition 1985)

Kerr, A.J., The Law Of Agency In South Africa, Durban, Butterworths (2d edition 1979)

Coaker, J.F. and Zeffertt, D.T., Wille and Millin's Mercantile Law Of South Africa, Johannesburg, Hortors Stationary (18th edition 1983)

CHAPTER 4

SOUTH AFRICAN FINANCIAL STATEMENT REQUIREMENTS

By Deloitte & Touche, South Africa

I. Reporting Requirements
    A. Companies

The Companies Act governs the accounting principles and practices to be followed by all public and private companies in that it requires annual financial statements to conform to generally accepted accounting practice ("GAAP"). Guidance is provided in statements of GAAP approved by the Accounting Practice Board.

The fact that many large companies in South Africa have foreign shareholders has had an important effect on the evolution of GAAP. The influence of foreign accounting developments has been strong. South African statements of GAAP are similar to those in a number of other countries, particularly the United Kingdom. The published statements of the International Accounting Standards Committee, which seeks to achieve a degree of international conformity, have received a significant response in South Africa, as South African GAAP requires the professional accounting bodies to use their "best endeavors" to ensure compliance with international standards. In the absence of a South African statement on a particular accounting issue, an international statement serves as an authoritative guide.

Annual financial statements comprise a balance sheet, an income statement, a cash flow statement, relevant notes to the financial statements and a director's report. When a company has subsidiaries, group annual financial statements must also be prepared. In practice, this is usually done in the form of consolidated financial statements. When group financial statements do not take this form, various disclosure requirements laid down in Schedule 4 of the Companies Act must be met. The annual financial statements must be approved by the board of directors and signed on its behalf by representative directors.

The financial statements must fairly present the company's results in accordance with GAAP. Apart from this general rule, there is no statutory requirement as to the format or layout of any individual statement. A schedule to the Companies Act, however, lists the information that must be disclosed.

The statutory requirements are supplemented by disclosure requirements contained in accounting standards published by the accounting profession in consultation with commerce and industry, for example, on matters such as equity accounting for associated companies, deferred tax and earnings per share. Both the statutory disclosure requirements and the accounting standards produced by the accounting profession are substantially complied with in practice.

In accordance with GAAP, disclosure must be made of the accounting policies adopted in preparing financial statements. Schedule 4 of the Companies Act also requires the disclosure of various policies. Changes in accounting policies are accounted for by restating the comparable figures and, when applicable, the opening balance on retained income. The effect of any change and the reason for it must be disclosed.

Financial statements are generally prepared using the historical cost convention. There is no generally accepted method of accounting for the effects of inflation. Effects of inflation are partially dealt with via the revaluation of properties and other fixed assets. Companies are encouraged to provide supplementary inflation-adjusted information, and a limited number of listed companies are doing this. Some accounting guidelines and exposure drafts offer guidance in this area. In only a few isolated instances do companies combine a method of accounting for inflation into their primary accounts.

Annual financial statements are expressed in either English or Afrikaans and must be drawn up in South African rands.

B. Close Corporations

The reporting requirements for close corporations are governed by the Close Corporations Act. The members are required to prepare annual financial statements consisting of at least a balance sheet and an income statement. All members must approve these statements. The rules concerning the financial statements of companies apply broadly to close corporations, but fewer statutory disclosures are required. In general, more flexibility is allowed in drawing up a close corporation's statements than those of a company.

Although there is no explicit statutory requirement for the preparation of consolidated financial statements, the fair presentation principle would necessitate consolidation if the figures for subsidiaries were material.

C. Partnerships

A partnership is not a separate legal entity and there is no statutory requirement for it to produce financial statements. A partnership must, however, supply financial statements with the tax return for the partnership. These accounts are generally prepared in accordance with GAAP.

II. Accounting Principles And Standards

Financial statements of companies and close corporations are not required to conform to valuation principles set out in tax or commercial legislation, but they must "fairly present" the financial position and results based on the circumstances. Separate financial statements are not prepared for tax purposes. Adjustments required by tax law to the statements prepared for the proprietors are made as part of a tax computation schedule.

In general, assets are not understated or liabilities overstated as a recognized policy of extreme conservatism and financial statements must be drawn up on a consistent basis year after year. As a result, the creation or operation of secret reserves is not encountered to any material extent in South Africa. Banks and insurers were exceptions to these rules. However, banks and insurers are now required to comply with GAAP and, as a result, the creation or operation of secret reserves is no longer acceptable in South Africa.

III. Accounting Practices

The accounting practices described below are generally adopted by companies and close corporations.

A. Revaluation Of Assets

There are no legal requirements regarding the revaluation of assets. Revaluations are permitted, but appropriate disclosure must be made. Directors are specifically required to disclose their valuation of investment property and the basis on which it has been determined. Director's valuations of unlisted investments, although not the basis of valuation, must also be disclosed. The market value of listed investments must be shown. Intangible assets, such as trademarks and brands, are generally not revalued due to the absence of a generally accepted method of calculation.

B. Depreciation

Depreciation rates used in preparing annual financial statements are based on economic principles rather than tax principles and have regard to estimated useful life. Depreciation is calculated on the cost or, if applicable, the revalued amount of the asset. Various depreciation methods are used, but the straight-line and declining-balance methods are the most prevalent.

C. Goodwill

There is no generally accepted method of accounting for goodwill. A range of treatments exists at present. Goodwill arising on consolidation is generally carried unamortized to the balance sheet. Currently, the most common method of dealing with purchased goodwill is to write it off on acquisition.

D. Dividends

Proposed dividend distributions are accounted for by a charge to the income statement and the inclusion of a corresponding current liability in the balance sheet.

E. Merger Accounting

All mergers are accounted for as purchases of one company by another.

F. Leased Assets

Assets acquired under finance leases are capitalized in the hands of the lessee and a corresponding liability is raised equal to the cash cost of the asset. Finance charges are written off as the liability is repaid over the term of the lease. The asset acquired is subject to the same depreciation rules as other assets.

Assets acquired under operating leases are not capitalized and the lease payments are written off as incurred. Disclosure is made of operating lease commitments.

G. Research And Development Expenditure

South Africa has no GAAP for research and development expenditure. The practice currently followed by most companies is to charge all research and development expenditure to the income statement as incurred. Few companies disclose the amounts they spend on research and development.

H. Capitalization Of Interest

Interest can be capitalized as part of the cost of assets if all the following apply:
- expenditures on the assets are being incurred;
- activities that are necessary to prepare the asset for its sale or intended use are in progress; or
- borrowing costs are being incurred.

I. Inventory Valuation

Inventory can be valued by any method considered appropriate to the type of inventory and the characteristics of the industry concerned. Portions of production overhead that are considered to be costs incurred in bringing inventory to its present location and condition are included in the cost of manufactured finished goods and work in progress.

Inventory is valued at the lower of cost or net realizable value. "Net realizable value" is the estimated selling price in the ordinary course of business, less costs of completion and costs necessarily incurred in order to make the sale. Inventory should be written down to net realizable value item by item or by groups of similar items. The method used should be consistently applied.

J. Deferred Tax Accounting

Deferred tax is provided for on the liability basis, preferably using the comprehensive method. However, the partial method is an allowed alternative. Under the comprehensive method, full provision is made for any timing differences. Under the partial method, provision is made only to the extent that timing differences are expected to reverse in the foreseeable future. The extent to which full provision has not been made on all timing differences is disclosed as a contingent liability.

K. Currency Translations

Transactions in foreign currency that are not specifically covered by a forward exchange contract are recorded by applying the spot rate at the transaction date. At the reporting date, any uncovered monetary item denominated in foreign currency is stated at the current equivalent by applying the spot rate at that date. Resulting exchange gains or losses are recognized as income at that date.

When forward exchange contracts are entered into specifically for a particular transaction and are entered into prior to or immediately after the transaction date, the transaction is translated and recorded at the forward exchange contract rate. Gains or losses on speculative forward exchange contracts are recognized as income for the period in which the exchange rate movement occurred.

L. Equity Capital

"Equity capital" is normally defined as those instruments of capital that carry the right to share in the profits of the company and are not limited by a specific coupon or interest rate. General voting powers are normally attached to such instruments. Convertible bonds are in most instances disclosed as equity. There is, however, no specific legal requirement preventing the disclosure of convertible bonds as debt. The terms of the conversion have a significant influence on the classification.

M. Unusual Items

If items of income and expense are of such size, nature or incidence that disclosure is relevant, they should be separately disclosed and included in profit before tax. Items that are clearly distinct from the ordinary activities of the enterprise — and do not occur frequently or regularly — are extraordinary and should be separately disclosed on the face of the income statement.

Prior-year adjustments are material adjustments to net income for prior years. They arise either from changes in accounting policies or from the correction of fundamental errors. Prior-year adjustments should be accounted for by restating the comparative amounts and the opening balance of retained income. The effect of any change should be disclosed by showing the amounts involved, either through the restatement of the comparative amounts or in a note to the financial statements. When a prior-year adjustment results from a change in accounting policy, the reason for the change should be disclosed.

N. Consolidation Practices

A company is a "subsidiary" of another company if that other company is a member and if the majority of voting rights are controlled by the other company. Subsidiaries are fully consolidated into group accounts. Investments in joint ventures are proportionately consolidated. "Joint ventures" are investments in entities in which joint control is exercised. Entities that are neither subsidiaries nor joint ventures and over which significant influence can be exercised are termed "associates." Interests in associated entities are equity accounted. All other investments are accounted for on the cost basis.

Goodwill or negative goodwill is calculated on the acquisition of a subsidiary.

IV. Audit Requirements And Standards

There are various groups of professional accountants in South Africa, each with specializations, as shown in the table below. Foreign investors wanting to set up business in South Africa are advised to consult with the South African Foreign Trade Organization ("SAFTO"). SAFTO, which is a private company, is a national export organization whose activities cover export marketing, export administration, foreign market intelligence, publications and liaison between the authorities and the private sector in South Africa and abroad. In addition, foreign investors are advised to consult with a firm of chartered accountants registered with the South African Institute of Chartered Accountants ("SAICA"). The SAICA is a member of the International Federation of Accountants.

Professional Accounting Groups in South Africa and Their Specializations

Group	Specialization
South African Institute of Chartered Accountants	Wide range of business expertise, including audit, accounting, tax and secretarial services.
Institute of Commercial and Financial Accountants	Accounting services.
Chartered Institute of Management Accountants	Cost and management accounting services.
Institute of Chartered Secretaries	Secretarial services.
Chartered Association of Certified Accountants	Accounting services.
Association for the Advancement of Black Accountants of Southern Africa	Black accounting development.

A. Companies

All companies, whether private or public, must appoint independent, professionally qualified auditors. The auditor's main function is to report to shareholders on the fair presentation or otherwise of the annual financial statements.

Auditors' rights and duties are governed by the Companies Act and the Public Accountants and Auditors Act 1951. Audit firms may provide tax, consulting and other services to their audit clients, provided that professional independence is maintained.

Audit firms may be appointed as auditors. They are normally appointed by the shareholders at the annual general meeting. Should there be a casual vacancy during a financial year, the directors are empowered to appoint auditors for that financial year. Any audit firm accepting an appointment as an auditor is legally bound to confirm directly with the previous auditor that there is no professional reason not to accept the appointment.

B. Close Corporations

A close corporation is not required to appoint an auditor but must appoint an accounting officer. The accounting officer must have prescribed minimum qualifications, but these are of a lower order than those required for company auditors.

Accounting officers do not necessarily have to be independent, nor do they have to report on whether the financial statements "fairly present" the results and financial situation. Their most important task is to see that the statements agree with a summary of the accounting records and to report on this fact. They do not perform an audit.

Accounting officers must report any contraventions of the Close Corporations Act. The accounting officer also must report to the registrar of close corporations if the close corporation ceases to carry on business or if its annual financial statements show that its liabilities exceed its assets.

C. Other Entities

A partnership's accounts need not be audited, except in special cases such as the trust funds of a partnership of attorneys. The annual financial statements of a South African branch of a foreign company must include a report by a South African auditor.

Johannesburg, South Africa
June 1996

CHAPTER 5

SECURITIES LAWS AND PORTFOLIO INVESTMENT IN SOUTH AFRICA

By Peter S. G. Leon and
Nicola F. Newton-King

Corporate and securities operations in South Africa are primarily regulated by statute. This chapter first briefly discusses the investment vehicles available to investors in South Africa and the requirements for obtaining a listing on the Johannesburg Stock Exchange (the "JSE"). It then deals with the requirements for membership of the JSE and of South Africa's only licensed futures market, the South African Futures Exchange ("SAFEX"). Finally, the chapter discusses portfolio management and unit trust operations in South Africa.

I.   Investment Vehicles

The decision as to which investment vehicle is the most appropriate for an investor's requirements will depend on numerous factors, including the need for limited liability and tax transparency.

A.   Limited Liability Companies In General

A limited liability company will generally be the most suitable investment vehicle as its allows great flexibility and can also be used in joint ventures. There are two types of limited liability companies in South Africa: public companies and private companies. Both are created pursuant to and are governed by the provisions of the Companies Act, 1973 (the "Companies Act").

A limited liability company has limited liability and a separate legal personality from its shareholders. Furthermore, a limited liability company must appoint an auditor, is subject to company tax levied at a flat rate of 35% and a secondary tax on companies ("STC") levied on the company in an amount of 12.5% of the difference between dividends declared and dividends received or accrued by the company. The rate of STC was reduced from 25% to 12.5% in South Africa's 1996 budget.

The requirements of the founding shareholders will determine whether a limited liability company is formed as public or private company. The differences between such private and public companies are discussed below.

B.   Characteristics Of A Public Company

A public company must have a minimum of seven shareholders, but there is no upper limit on the number of shareholders in a public company. A public company must file its annual financial statements and interim reports with the Registrar of Companies, where they are available for inspection by the general public.

Public companies must have a minimum of two directors, although such directors need not hold qualification shares and need not be residents or nationals of South Africa. Similarly, there are no provisions in the Companies Act requiring a minimum number of South African shareholders in a public company.

The quorum at general meetings of the shareholders of public companies is three members who have voting rights.

Only public companies may offer shares to and raise capital from the general public and are capable of being listed on the JSE.

C. Characteristics Of A Private Company

A private company must have at least one and may have no more than fifty shareholders. The articles of association of a private company must restrict the right to transfer the shares of the company, limit the number of members to fifty and prohibit any offer to the public for the subscription of any shares or debentures of the company.

In contrast to a public company, copies of the audited financial statements of a private company need not be lodged with the Registrar of Companies, nor need members be provided with semi-annual interim reports or provisional annual financial statements. The provision of such reports and statements to shareholders of a private company may, however, be required pursuant to the articles of association of the company or a shareholders' agreement entered into between the shareholders of the company.

A private company must have at least one director, although the director is not required by statute to hold qualification shares. As with a public company, the director does not need to be resident in or a national of South Africa.

The quorum at meetings of shareholders where there is more than one shareholder of a private company is two members who have voting rights. Voting rights in a private company may be unequal and must be determined by the company's articles.

D. Section 53(b) Company

Pursuant to section 53(b) of the Companies Act, a private company may provide in its memorandum of association that the directors of the company are jointly and severally liable for all debts and liabilities of the company incurred during their term of office. Section 53(b) companies are identified by the word "Incorporated" or "Inc." after the name of the company.

Professionals who are statutorily prevented from forming private companies may incorporate a section 53(b) company to regulate their affairs. Stockbroking members of the JSE have, in the past, conducted business through section 53(b) companies, although following the deregulation of the JSE discussed below, most such companies have been converted to companies with limited liability.

E. Branches

A foreign company which does not wish to incorporate a subsidiary in South Africa may instead set up a branch office. Such a branch office does not have a separate legal identity apart from its parent company.

A branch is required to be registered as an external company within twenty-one days after the establishment of a place of business in South Africa. An external company must furnish the Registrar of Companies with a certified copy of the memorandum and articles of association of the company (if it is not in one of the official languages of South Africa, a certified translation thereof must be furnished). A "memorandum" is defined in section 1 of the Companies Act as "the charter, statutes, memorandum of association and articles; or other instrument constituting or defining the constitution of the company." An external company must also furnish the Registrar with: (i) a notice specifying the registered office and postal address of the company; (ii) the name, address and consent to act of the auditor of the branch in South Africa; (iii) the financial year-end of the company; (iv) certain information concerning the local manager and secretary; (v) a list of the directors of the company; and (vi) a notice in the prescribed form giving the name and address of a person resident in South Africa who is authorized to accept service of process and any notices served on the branch company in South Africa.

When the memorandum of an external company is registered, the company becomes a body corporate in South Africa and is subject to certain provisions in the Companies Act which deal, among other things, with the effect of registration as an external company and the power of such company to own immovable property in South Africa.

An external company must comply with the Companies Act by appointing a South African auditor and by submitting statutory returns and filing annual financial statements within six months of the end of the financial year of the head office. Exemption from the filing of financial statements may be applied for from the Registrar. There is no need for an external company to appoint a local board of directors.

Branches are taxable entities and their taxable income will be taxed at the rate applicable to corporate entities in South Africa, which currently is 40%. Branch profits can be remitted to the head office free of withholding taxes. STC on branches was abolished in the 1996 Budget.

Branches are useful investment vehicles and can, for instance, be used to conduct banking and portfolio management operations. However, the JSE and SAFEX will not allow a branch of a foreign company to become a member of the JSE. Thus, before a foreign investor decides on the investment vehicle through which to conduct business operations, the particular requirements of the industry in which the investment is to be made should be carefully investigated.

F.   Partnerships

Because of their flexibility, partnerships are useful for tax planning purposes and are frequently used to create joint ventures between two or more corporate entities or natural persons. It is possible for a partnership to become a member of the JSE.

Partnerships are not regulated by statute and may be constituted by contract or be implied from the conduct of the parties. Every partner in a general partnership is liable jointly and severally for all the debts and obligations of the partnership, while, in a limited partnership, the liability of the partners is limited to their respective partnership contributions. Limited partners may not participate in the management of the partnership or hold themselves out to the public as partners.

A partnership is not a legal person distinct from the persons comprising the partnership (including for tax purposes). The partnership must keep proper books and records and submit to the Receiver of Revenue a copy of the partnership balance sheet and income statements in support of each individual partner's annual tax return.

The Companies Act prohibits an unincorporated company, association or partnership from including more than twenty people, except for certain professional partnerships (such as lawyers and accountants).

G. Close Corporations And Joint Ventures

There are a number of other investment vehicles available in South Africa, including close corporations (a simpler, less expensive form of corporate body than the limited liability company) and joint ventures. These are, however, not widely used in the securities industry and are, therefore, only briefly outlined here.

While a close corporation (which is established pursuant to the Close Corporations Act, 1984) provides for separate legal personality, perpetual succession and some form of limited liability, it is unlikely to be of interest to the majority of foreign investors as close corporations are often considered not to be of the same financial standing as companies. The key characteristics of a close corporation are that only individuals (not companies or trusts) may be members of a close corporation and the number of members must be at least one but is limited to ten. Members of a close corporation may not sell their interests in the close corporation without the consent of the other members. Close corporations are taxed in the same manner as companies.

Joint ventures may be conducted through any of the vehicles discussed above and can be constituted between any two such vehicles. International joint ventures represent a significant proportion of international operations in South Africa. The economic sectors of activities in which joint ventures are most common are research and development, national resource exploration and exploitation, engineering and construction, production/manufacturing, trade and services.

Typically, a joint venture is formed as a company whose share capital is held by the joint venturers, as an unincorporated association which has the legal status of a partnership or as an unincorporated association which does not have the legal status of a partnership (such as by means of a contract between the parties). The choice of joint venture vehicle will depend upon a variety of different factors, including legal implications, commercial objectives, tax aspects, market usage and professional or political pressure. Some of the factors discussed above in relation to the different corporate structures are relevant.

II. Obtaining A Listing On The JSE
A. General

South Africa has one licensed stock exchange, the JSE, which operates pursuant to the Stock Exchanges Control Act, 1985 ("SECA"). The structure and regulation of the JSE are discussed in a subsequent section of this chapter. This section of the chapter addresses only the manner in which a listing is obtained on the JSE.

Pursuant to the SECA, the Committee of the JSE may grant listings of securities issued by companies and other institutions and may prescribe the minimum requirements with which any issuer of securities must comply before a listing of its securities will be granted and with which the issuer must comply while its securities are listed. These requirements are known as "the listing requirements" and are set out in a volume published by the JSE. The listings requirements were substantially reviewed during 1995 to take account of international developments and to address the needs of the Government's Reconstruction and Development Program. The new listings requirements for all issuers other than mining companies came into effect on July 1, 1995. The new listings requirements relating to mining companies were reviewed in conjunction with the South African Chamber of Mines and came into force on October 1, 1995.

B. The Different Sectors Of The JSE

The JSE lists securities in three main markets. High risk securities are listed under the venture capital market (the "VCM"), while the development capital market (the "DCM") caters to small, high growth companies. Beginning in August 1994, companies have been able to obtain a listing on the financial-redevelopment sector of the main board if their principal objective is to invest in undertakings or entrepreneurial businesses which the JSE Committee considers to be of a socio-economic development nature.

The main board has more substantial requirements than the three sectors mentioned above. The requirements for each sector are set out below and relate to minimum subscribed capital, issued shares, minimum pre-tax profits, acceptable trading record and minimum number and prescribed public spread of shareholders.

C. Requirements For A Main Board Listing

An applicant seeking a listing on the main board must:
- have subscribed capital (including reserves, but excluding minority interests, revaluations of assets that are not supported by a valuation by an independent professional expert acceptable to the JSE Committee prepared within the last six months and intangible assets) of at least R2,000,000;
- have not less than 1,000,000 issued equity shares;
- have a satisfactory profit history for the preceding three financial years, the latter of which reported an audited pre-tax profit of at least R1,000,000;
- ensure that at least 10% of each class of equity shares is held by the public;
- ensure that there are at least 300 public shareholders in respect of the listed equity shares, 25 public shareholders in respect of the listed preference shares and 10 public shareholders in respect of the listed debentures issued by the issuer; and

- issue all securities to be initially listed on the main board at a price of at least R1

D. Requirements For A Listing On The DCM

While the general listings requirements apply to companies whose securities are or are sought to be listed on the DCM, the listings requirements contain a number of permissible deviations and guidelines relevant to listings on the DCM. An applicant seeking a listing on the DCM must:

- have subscribed capital (including reserves, but excluding minority interests, revaluations of assets that are not supported by a valuation by an independent professional expert acceptable to the JSE Committee prepared within the last six months and intangible assets) of at least R1,000,000;
- have not less than 1,000,000 issued equity shares;
- have a satisfactory profit history for the preceding two financial years, the latter of which reported an audited pre-tax profit of at least R500,000;
- ensure that at least 10% of each class of equity shares is held by the public;
- ensure that there are at least 75 public shareholders in respect of the listed equity shares, 25 public shareholders in respect of the listed preference shares and 10 public shareholders in respect of the listed debentures issued by the issuer; and
- issue all securities to be initially listed on the DCM at a price of at least 50 cents.

Companies without a track record in the business in which they wish to be listed, without adequate management or without a qualified auditor's report for either of the two financial years prior to the application for listing are considered to be unsuitable for listing on the DCM.

E. Requirements For A Listing On The VCM

While the general listings requirements apply to companies whose securities are or are sought to be listed on the VCM, the requirements contain a number of permissible deviations from compliance with such requirements. An issuer seeking a listing on the VCM must, prior to the submission of its application for listing, submit to the JSE a memorandum summarizing its nature, method of doing business, business plans and prospects.

In addition, an applicant seeking a listing on the VCM must:

- have subscribed capital (including reserves, but excluding minority interests, revaluations of assets that are not supported by a valuation by an independent professional expert acceptable to the JSE Committee prepared within the last six months and intangible assets) of at least R500,000;

- have not less than 1,000,000 issued equity shares;
- ensure that at least 5% of each class of equity shares is held by the public;
- ensure that there are at least 75 public shareholders in respect of the listed equity shares, 25 public shareholders in respect of the listed preference shares and 10 public shareholders in respect of the listed debentures issued by the issuer;
- issue all securities to be listed on the VCM at a price of at least 50 cents;
- have a majority of directors and managers who have successful records of achievement in their respective roles; and
- contain a prominent warning, in bold, in the form of a notice, at the beginning of the applicant's prospectus or pre-listing statement, of the speculative nature of investment in such issuer.

It should be noted that it is not necessary for a company seeking a VCM listing to have a profit history. However, the issuer should, in its analysis of its future earnings, indicate credible returns on capital which, on a time-weighted basis, are above average.

F. Requirements For A Listing On The Financial-Redevelopment Sector Of The Main Board

In evaluating the listing of securities on the financial-redevelopment sector of the main board, the JSE Committee closely examines the principal objective of the redevelopment entity, which must be the provision of assistance to persons, communities or undertakings which in the opinion of the JSE Committee would make a positive contribution to the socio-economic development of South Africa. Companies may be listed on this sector of the main board notwithstanding that the normal main board requirements regarding details of assets, liabilities and profit history are not given or that the redevelopment entity consists wholly or substantially of cash or liquid assets.

The JSE should be approached at an early stage so that the company seeking the listing can obtain an indication of which listings requirements will be waived and what additional requirements will be imposed.

G. Procedure For Listing

All applications for listing must be submitted to the JSE Committee for approval by a sponsoring broker. Applications for listing must also be accompanied by prescribed documentation, including a formal application and a pre-listing statement (alternatively, a prospectus or an offer for sale may be submitted). The JSE charges a fee for the review of listings applications and other documents that issuers of listed securities are required to submit to the JSE.

Before an issue of securities may be listed, the articles of association of the issuer and its subsidiaries must be approved by the JSE. The JSE requires that the articles meet requirements covering such diverse topics as unissued shares, transfer of shares, signature of certificates, calls on shares of external companies and share warrants. In addition, the JSE Committee may require a company whose securities are listed on the DCM or VCM to appoint advisers such as accountants, lawyers and merchant bankers in addition to the company's sponsoring broker.

For listings in connection with a public offering, the listings requirements require 30% of the shares to be placed with the sponsoring broker, which must, in turn, offer 30% of the shares to the broking community.

H.   Features Of The New Listings Requirements

As previously discussed, the JSE recently revised its listing requirements. The major amendments to the old listing requirements are the following:

- The JSE Committee may now approve the listing of "high" or "low voting equity instruments," provided that the issue of such securities is approved by the majority of shareholders of the issuer other than the controlling shareholders.
- Shareholder spread requirements for each sector have been introduced. New applicants will be required to have, or obtain, the required spread upon listing, whereas existing listed companies will have until January 1, 2000 to obtain the required spread. These requirements were introduced to address the historical illiquidity in the JSE. In a 1995 survey of world stock markets, the JSE was rated 35th in terms of liquidity, despite being the 11th biggest market in the world by market capitalization.
- The listing of first-tier pyramids in respect of companies whose securities are listed on the main board is permitted provided such companies have been listed for at least two years and provided further that minority shareholders in the subsidiary are offered access to the pyramid.
- The previous listings requirements required publication of press announcements and circulars in the previous two official languages (English and Afrikaans). As there are now eleven official languages, the requirement to publish in all official languages is clearly impractical and the proposed listings requirements now specify that documents should be published at least in English and one other official language.
- New provisions have been included to give the JSE Committee greater power to censure companies which do not comply with the listing requirements. In certain cases, the listing of securities may be suspended or terminated after the issuer has been given adequate opportunity to make representations regarding such proposed suspension or termination.
- Companies whose securities are listed on the main board are now required to indicate in their annual financial statements the extent of their compliance with the King Code of Corporate Practices and Conduct set out in the King Report released during November 1994. Such statement need not be audited. The King Code is largely based

on the similar code produced by the Cadbury Committee in the United Kingdom.

I. **Responsibilities Of The Sponsoring Broker**

As indicated above, all documents submitted to the JSE for approval and all applications for listing must be submitted through the issuer's sponsoring broker. The sponsoring broker must ensure, having made due and careful inquiry, that, on the production of a pre-listing statement, all listing requirements have been met and that there are no other matters that should be disclosed (either in the pre-listing statement or to the JSE Committee) or that should be taken into account in considering the suitability for listing of the securities. The sponsoring broker must also guide and advise the issuer on the application of the listings requirements and brief the directors of new applicants and new directors of listed companies concerning their duties and obligations with regard to the listings requirements. Furthermore, the sponsoring broker is required to ensure, having made due and careful inquiry, that a new applicant has satisfactory reporting procedures from which the directors can make proper judgments as to the financial position and prospects of the new applicant and its group. The sponsoring broker also is required to ensure that any statements regarding working capital and profit forecasts to be published in pre-listing statements have been made after due and careful inquiry by the issuer.

J. **Continuing Disclosure Obligations Of Issuers**

Any Company whose securities are listed on the JSE is required to announce any information necessary to enable holders of its listed securities and the public to appraise the position of the listed company and avoid the creation of a false market in its listed securities. Companies are also required to disclose any major new developments in their sphere of activity which are not public knowledge and which may, by virtue of the effect of those developments on their assets and liabilities or financial position or in the general course of its business, lead to substantial movements in the price of their listed securities. Companies will thus be required to announce not only details of transactions and possible takeovers but other matters that could affect their share price, for example, major contracts obtained or new mineral resources discovered. Information which has not been published when required by the listings requirements may not be given to a third party except in limited circumstances relating primarily to information furnished to professional advisers and statutory bodies. Where the necessary confidentiality cannot be maintained, the company is required to publish, by way of a cautionary announcement, information which could lead to material movements in the price of its securities.

An annual report is required to be sent to shareholders at least twenty-one days before the shareholders' annual general meeting and interim reports must be issued half yearly. The disclosure requirements for such reports are governed by the Companies Act and are supplemented by the JSE requirements. In addition, the JSE requires various kinds of public disclosure to be made in relation to transactions carried out by listed companies, including, in particular, acquisitions, disposals and reverse takeovers. The degree of disclosure required varies from circulars supported by approving shareholders' resolutions, to stand alone circulars, press announcements and the inclusion of reports in the company's public annual financial statements. The required disclosure depends on whether the relevant transaction falls into one of four different categories specified in the listings requirements. These categories are based on the amount of the consideration for the transaction relative to the market value of all the company's shares and the number of shares to be issued relative to the number of issued shares.

The previous listing requirements were incongruous in stating that investors should receive substantial quantities of information when given the opportunity to invest in new applicants, but received very little when asked to participate in major issues by existing listed companies. Accordingly, the new listing requirements stipulate that pre-listing statements should be produced by existing listed companies seeking a listing for a significant amount of new shares (taken to be 30% of the existing share capital) as well as by new applicants.

K. Review Of Listings, Suspension And Delisting Of Securities

Pursuant to the SECA, the JSE Committee is required to review the listing of a company's securities once a year. The JSE charges a fee for such review.

The JSE Committee is also empowered to suspend the listing of securities or to delist such securities if the Committee is of the opinion that it is desirable to do so or if the listed company has failed to comply with the listings requirements. Such suspension or delisting may only be effected once the listed company has had the opportunity of making representations to the Committee in support of the continued inclusion of the securities in the relevant list.

While a decision by the Committee to suspend or terminate the listing of a security will be reviewable (in the appropriate circumstances) in a court of law as a matter of South African common law, the SECA provides that only a decision to terminate the listing of a security will be appealable to the Stock Exchanges Appeal Board.

III. Securities Trading And Portfolio Management
A. Introduction

While the JSE is, at present, the only licensed stock exchange in South Africa, only one licensed futures market, SAFEX, exists alongside it. Although the JSE has, until very recently, listed bonds, the Bond Exchange was licensed on May 15, 1996 and all listed bonds will, in the future, be traded on the Bond Exchange. Both the JSE and SAFEX are regulated by the Financial Services Board (the "FSB"). The Bond Exchange also will be regulated by the FSB. The FSB also regulates the insurance industry and the portfolio management and unit trust industries, the latter two of which are discussed below.

B. Role And Structure Of The FSB

The FSB was created by the Financial Services Board Act, 1990 (the "FSB Act") following the report of the Van der Horst Committee of Inquiry which reported to the Minister of Finance in September 1989. The Committee recommended that a statutory board be created to exercise supervision over financial institutions, independently of the public service, but responsible to the Minister of Finance.

The functions of the FSB are essentially to supervise the activities of financial institutions, including licensed exchanges, and financial services and to advise the Minister of Finance on matters concerning financial institutions and financial services. The FSB itself consists of members appointed by the President and is, in turn, supported by professional and administrative staff, including a chief executive, who are employed outside the financial discipline of the Public Service Commission with a view to attracting private sector employees.

In addition to administering financial services legislation, the FSB has also acquired significant powers with respect to policy-making, which had been the exclusive province of the Minister of Finance under the former Financial Institutions Office, the precursor of the FSB. The interposition of the FSB between the Minister and the financial services industry in relation to policy issues has caused uncertainty about the role and function of the various participants involved in regulation and has led to serious problems in practice. An attempt to ameliorate this situation was made in 1993 by the creation of the Policy Board for Financial Services and Regulation (the "Policy Board"), which comprises representatives from industry and the FSB and advises the Minister on policy matters.

The FSB has wide ranging powers both in terms of the FSB Act and in terms of the relevant enabling legislation governing stock exchanges, financial markets and the financial services industry generally. On the other hand, while the FSB is the statutory regulator of the financial services industry, the industry is characterized by self-regulating organizations which control and regulate the day-to-day activities of persons active in the financial services industry. For example, the committees of the licensed exchanges, and not the FSB, are the bodies primarily responsible for the regulation of the business of their members and for the listing of securities and instruments on such exchanges.

IV. Membership Of And Trading On The JSE
A. Introduction

Pursuant to section 12 of the SECA, a stock exchange is required to promulgate rules governing the business of such stock exchange. Section 12 requires that such rules deal with certain basic issues, among other things, relating to the admission to the membership of the stock exchange, the management of the stock exchange by a committee, the delivery of securities pursuant to a transaction, the settlement of transactions and the provision of adequate capital or guarantees by members for all their activities. Section 12 of the SECA also requires that a stock exchange enact rules providing that (i) every transaction note to the buyer or seller of listed securities discloses the date and time at which the transaction was effected and whether such transaction was effected by the stockbroker concerned in the capacity of principal or agent and (ii) that members may negotiate fees for their services.

B. Deregulation Of The JSE

The SECA was substantially amended in 1995 through the promulgation of the Stock Exchanges Control Amendment Act, 1995 (the "Amendment Act"), which facilitated the deregulation of the JSE. Following the promulgation of the Amendment Act, the JSE's new rules became effective on November 8, 1995.

Prior to November 1995, the SECA provided that membership on the JSE was limited to natural persons over the age of 21 who were South African citizens and to partnerships or companies comprised of and solely owned by South African citizens. Furthermore, stockbrokers were not allowed to act as principals in any transactions with clients and were not permitted to negotiate fees or commissions in respect of transactions, except to the extent that the nominal value of a transaction exceeded R3,000,000.

These provisions effectively limited the membership of the JSE to South African citizens and prevented companies in which foreigners had an interest from becoming members of the JSE. The JSE increasingly came under both local and international pressure to deregulate and, in 1995, the promulgation of the Amendment Act, together with the promulgation of the JSE's rules on November 8, 1995, facilitated such deregulation.

The JSE's rules now recognize corporate membership and do not require such companies to be wholly-owned by South African citizens. Dual trading capacity has been introduced together with negotiated commissions. These rules are discussed in more detail below.

C. Membership Of The JSE

The JSE's new rules distinguish between stockbrokers on the one hand, and members of the JSE on the other. Stockbrokers are natural persons who are members of the South African Institute of Stockbrokers and who are sole proprietors, partners, directors or employees of a member of the JSE. It follows that only stockbrokers who practice as sole proprietors will also be members of the JSE.

Under the new JSE rules, the following categories of persons may become members of the exchange: (1) natural person sole proprietors; (2) partnerships consisting of natural persons; (3) private companies whose shareholders have unlimited liability together with the company; (4) public or private companies with limited liability, all of whose shareholders are stockbrokers; and (5) public or private companies with limited liability and non-stockbroker ownership. Although natural persons who are stockbrokers, and officers and employees of members are not required to be South African citizens, in certain circumstances, corporate members are required to have a minimum number of executive directors who are resident in South Africa. Furthermore, all JSE members that are corporate entities are required to be incorporated and registered as domestic companies under South African law. Branches of foreign companies may not become members of the JSE. There are, however, no restrictions on foreign ownership of a JSE member.

D.   JSE Membership Rights

Each member of the JSE is required to hold a certain number of rights in the JSE. Rights are, in essence, entitlements to become a member of the JSE. Rights can be purchased from existing right holders or, if sufficient rights are not available for purchase in this manner, from the JSE.

Under the new rules, each category of member is required to hold at least the following number of rights: (i) natural person sole proprietors — 3 rights; (ii) partnerships comprised of natural persons — 3 rights per stockbroker who is a partner; (iii) private companies whose shareholders have unlimited liability together with the company — 3 rights per director; (iv) companies with limited liability owned entirely by stockbrokers — 3 rights per stockbroker owner; and (v) companies with limited liability with non-stockbroker ownership — 60 rights. Partnerships, corporate members with unlimited liability and corporate members owned entirely by stockbrokers are not required to hold in excess of 60 rights, but in the event that more than 60 rights are held, these will not carry any voting rights at meetings of members of the JSE.

No member may hold more than 30 rights beyond that number required to be held by the member. Individual stockbrokers are not required to hold any rights unless they practice in sole proprietorship, but they may hold up to 10 rights each.

E.   Capital Requirements Of Members

No person may be admitted to JSE membership or continue as a JSE member unless the person holds net assets in South Africa which comply with the minimum capital requirements set out in the JSE's new rules. Under these rules, a member's minimum liquid capital must at all times be sufficient to meet both the member's base requirement and the member's risk requirement. A member's base requirement is equal to the greater of: (i) a member's operating expenditures over the preceding 13-week period, as calculated in accordance with the applicable directives of the JSE; and (ii) either (a) R200,000, if the member does not have discretionary authority over client accounts or client funds or securities, or (b) R400,000, in all other cases. A member's risk requirement is the sum of the member's position risk requirement, counterparty risk requirement, foreign exchange requirement and large exposure requirement, each of which is determined by reference to the applicable directives of the JSE.

If a member fails to comply with the minimum capital requirements set out in the JSE's rules and directives and the member does not immediately thereafter comply with such requirements, the JSE Committee may, in its discretion: (i) prohibit the member from trading; (ii) restrict the trading activities of the member; (iii) give the member such instructions as the JSE Committee deems necessary in the interests of the member's clients, other members of the JSE or a JSE settlement system; or (iv) levy a fine on the member equal to the lesser of 5% of the shortfall in the member's adjusted liquid capital or R25,000 for each day that the shortfall occurs.

F. Resident Director Requirements

Under the JSE's new rules, JSE members with limited liability and non-stockbroker ownership (category (v) members) are required to have at least one stockbroker as an executive director. Such stockbroker is required to be permanently resident in South Africa. From January 1, 1997, such corporate members will be required to have two stockbrokers who are permanently resident in South Africa as executive directors and from January, 1998, this requirement will be increased to three executive directors. If a JSE member company with limited liability that is owned entirely by stockbrokers (a category (iv) member) appoints a person other than a stockbroker as a director, such member must also comply with the resident director requirements described above.

G. Compliance Officer Requirements

From April 1, 1996, all members of the JSE were required to appoint a compliance officer. It is the responsibility of a member's compliance officer to ensure the member's compliance with the provisions of the SECA, the rules of the JSE and the directives and decisions of the JSE Committee. In order to act as a compliance officer a person must be a stockbroker and must, among other things, have passed the JSE's compliance officer examination on or before October 31, 1996.

H. Dual Trading Capacity And Negotiated Commissions

One of the features of the JSE prior to its deregulation in November 1995 was the fact that brokers were permitted to act only as agents in transactions with clients in equity securities, except in certain limited circumstances, such as to correct a trading error. Brokers were, however, permitted to act in a principal capacity with any counterparty in a transaction in bonds provided that they had made prior disclosure of their intention to act in such capacity. Failing such disclosure, brokers were permitted only to act as agents in transactions in bonds.

Another feature of trading under the old JSE rules was the fact that brokers were required to charge clients commission on any deal in equity securities executed for the clients according to a fixed tariff determined by the JSE Committee and set out in the JSE rules. This tariff worked on a sliding scale for all equity transactions up to a nominal value of R3, 000, 000, after which commission was fully negotiable. Commission for agency transactions in bonds was, however, fully negotiable.

The requirements that brokers act only as agents and that they charge fixed commissions for transactions in equity securities were deleted from the SECA by the Amendment Act. Members of the JSE are now allowed to act either as agents or as principals and to negotiate commission in respect of all transactions in respect of securities traded on the JET system. Since June 6, 1996, all equity securities have been traded over the JET system.

I. Stamp Duty And Marketable Securities Tax

Marketable securities tax ("MST") is payable pursuant to the Marketable Securities Tax Act, 1948 (the "MST Act") in respect of the purchase of all marketable securities (such as shares listed on the JSE) by a stockbroker on behalf of any person at the rate of .5% of the consideration for which such securities are purchased. This rate was reduced from 1% in the 1996 Budget. The purchase of marketable securities issued by certain issuers specified in the MST Act (which includes certain parastatals), is exempt from MST. Similarly, the purchase of any interest-bearing debentures (such as bonds) listed on the JSE is also exempt from MST.

If shares or bonds are not purchased through a stockbroker, MST is not payable, although stamp duty levied pursuant to the Stamp Duties Act, 1968 (the "Stamp Duties Act") may be payable. Stamp duty is levied on the registration of transfer of a marketable security at .5% of the higher of the consideration paid or the fair market value of the marketable security. As with MST, the rate of stamp duty was reduced from 1% to .5% in the 1996 Budget. The registration of transfer of certain bonds issued by local authorities and other issuers set out in the Stamp Duties Act is exempt from stamp duty as in the regulations of bonds listed on the JSE. In certain circumstances, it is possible for a foreign purchaser to obtain exemption from stamp duty under what is known as the "arbitrage exemption," although this exemption is currently under review by the revenue authorities.

J. The JSE Guarantee Fund

In circumstances in which a member of the JSE has been declared to be a defaulter by the JSE Committee — essentially where the member is no longer able to meet its commitments to its clients — the JSE Guarantee Fund is liable to clients and fellow members in the circumstances outlined in the rules of the JSE Guarantee Fund. However, where a client incurs losses arising out of transactions in securities with a JSE member, the JSE Guarantee Fund is only liable for losses incurred by such client or foreign dealers up to a maximum aggregate of R5,000,000. For transactions in bonds, the JSE Guarantee Fund must reimburse clients, in aggregate, up to a maximum additional amount of R5,000,000.

V. Membership Of And Trading On SAFEX
A. Introduction

SAFEX is South Africa's only futures exchange and is licensed under the FMCA. As with SECA, the FMCA empowers the executive committee of a licensed financial exchange (such as SAFEX) to list financial instruments and to promulgate rules governing the business of such a financial exchange. Such rules govern issues such as the admission to membership of a financial exchange, the management of the financial exchange and the manner in which trading on such exchange occurs.

B. Membership Of SAFEX

There are two classes of members of SAFEX: clearing members and non-clearing members. Members of SAFEX are also divided into broking members and non-broking members.

Any natural person, body corporate or partnership may apply for the membership of SAFEX provided that such person is resident in South Africa. A "resident" is defined in the rules of SAFEX to mean a natural person who is resident in the Republic of South Africa, Lesotho, Namibia or Swaziland or who is a legal entity registered in any such area. A foreign controlled subsidiary may, therefore, become a member of SAFEX, provided that the subsidiary is incorporated in South Africa pursuant to the Companies Act. A member who is a natural person must be at least twenty-one years of age and of full legal capacity and must be a citizen or permanent resident of South Africa.

C. Capital Requirements Of Members

A non-clearing non-broking member that does not have clients in any other financial market is required to have the initial capital required by his clearing member. A non-clearing member may only enter into a clearing agreement with one clearing member at a time.

A non-clearing broking member who does not receive or hold a resident client's margins or who does not receive any other assets of his client with respect to such client's buying and selling of financial instruments is required to have initial capital of at least R200,000. A non-clearing broking member who receives or holds a resident client's margins or receives any other assets of his client with respect to the client buying and selling of financial instruments is required to have initial capital of at least R400,000.

A clearing member must have funds of R200,000,000 or such other sum as the Executive Committee of SAFEX may determine, provided that the executive officer of the Executive Committee may, in his discretion, impose additional suretyship, guarantees or other requirements on a clearing member in certain circumstances. A clearing member is also required to maintain and keep in force a suretyship for the due performance of all or any of its obligations to the clearing house, of not less than R10,000,000, in favor of the SAFEX clearing house. The suretyship must be by a financial or other institution acceptable to the Executive Committee of SAFEX. The clearing member, however, remains jointly liable with the surety.

Pursuant to SAFEX rules, a broking member may be a clearing member or a non-clearing member but may not be a natural person. A non-broking member is not allowed to trade with clients or to enter into client agreements with any client.

D. Stamp Duty And Marketable Securities Tax

There is no stamp duty or MST payable in respect of transactions on financial instruments listed on licensed financial markets such as SAFEX.

E. Trading On SAFEX

Members of SAFEX are not allowed to trade with or on behalf of a client until the client has been registered with the SAFEX Clearing Company (Pty) Ltd, which acts as the clearing house for transactions in financial instruments listed on SAFEX. A member of SAFEX can act either as principal or agent in any transaction with a client, although the member must inform the client of the capacity in which he will act before he contracts with the client.

VI. Portfolio Management And Unit Trust Activities
A. Introduction

In South Africa, a distinction is drawn between the management and administration of investment portfolios owned by one person and the management of portfolios of investments in which members of the public are invited to purchase interests or units. The former is known as portfolio management and the latter as the management of unit trusts. While portfolio management and unit trust activities are regulated under different statutes, they both fall under the ultimate supervision of the FSB.

B. Portfolio Management
1. Regulatory Environment

The conduct of portfolio or asset management business is regulated by section 4 of the SECA and by section 5 of the FMCA. Section 4 of the SECA deals with portfolio management of listed securities as defined in SECA (essentially equity securities) and of investments of which listed securities form a part. Section 5 of the FMCA deals with portfolio management of financial instruments (essentially futures listed on the SAFEX) and of investments of which financial instruments form a part.

Both section 4 of the SECA and section 5 of the FMCA were amended in 1995, but section 4 of the SECA has not yet been promulgated and is, therefore, not yet in force or effect. It is expected that Section 4 will be promulgated in October 1996. Once section 4 has been promulgated, its main effect will be to require persons who manage listed or unlisted securities also to be registered as portfolio managers pursuant to the SECA. In addition, certain categories of persons who are, at present, under section 4 of the SECA automatically exempted from applying for authorization will be required to apply for authorization to conduct portfolio management business.

In addition to the SECA and the FMCA, the Financial Institutions (Investment of Funds) Act, 1984 is relevant to the activities and duties of portfolio managers and, in particular, their fiduciary duties. This Act is discussed later in this chapter.

2. Eligibility Requirements

At present, pursuant to the SECA, no person who wishes as a regular feature of his business to administer or hold in safe custody on behalf of any other person any investments in listed securities or any investments of which listed securities form a part may do so unless:

- Such person is an institution such as a bank or a stockbroker, which is interpreted by the FSB to be member of the JSE. A number of institutions are presently exempt under this section of the SECA. However, when the amended section 4 comes into effect, the automatic exemption granted to all such institutions other than members of the JSE will expire.
- Such person has been approved by the Registrar of Stock Exchanges.
- Such person is a member of a category of persons approved by the Registrar. However, no such category has yet been approved.

In each case, the portfolio manager must comply with the conditions determined by the Minister of Finance in the Government Gazette. These conditions are somewhat antiquated and currently are being reviewed by the FSB. It is, however, unlikely that new conditions will be published before October 1996.

As a result of the amendments to section 5 of the FMCA during 1995, persons who wish to hold in safe custody listed financial instruments or investments of which listed financial instruments form a part are no longer required to be registered as portfolio managers under that Act. On the other hand, all persons who wish to manage such financial instruments are required to be registered.

Any person who wishes to conduct portfolio management business through an entity, other than a member of the JSE or SAFEX, will need to apply for approval from the FSB to conduct such activities through such new corporate entity. This entity may be incorporated as a private or public company or may be a branch of a foreign company.

3. Investment In The Money Market

If a portfolio manager wishes to invest client funds in the money market or pool client funds in order to obtain a better rate of interest, such activities are regulated by the Banks Act, 1990 (the "Banks Act") and not by the SECA or the FMCA. Pursuant to the Banks Act, a portfolio manager may only invest client funds in the money market (i) if it registered as a bank or (ii) if it has a written contract with the client authorizing the portfolio manager to so invest the funds. The Banks Act stipulates the content of this contract, which can be incorporated with the mandate contemplated in the conditions to the SECA and the FMCA discussed later in this chapter.

A portfolio manager may, in addition, only pool client funds if it has been approved and designated to do so by the Registrar of Banks by notice in the Government Gazette and complies with the conditions that the Registrar may stipulate in such notice. At present, other than banks, only members of the JSE have been given permission to pool client funds. Thus, if a portfolio manager is not a member of the JSE, such portfolio manager will not be able to pool client funds without the approval of the Registrar of Banks.

4. Procedure For Application

The approval or rejection of an application for approval as a portfolio manager under either the SECA or the FMCA takes approximately one week after the application has been formally submitted. Such application must be accompanied by a cheque for R3,500,00, which is the FSB's fee for reviewing the application. This is a one-time fee payable only on application.

Once approval as a portfolio manager is granted, the FSB imposes an annual levy on approved portfolio managers. This levy is R700 plus a multiple of the total portfolio of securities or financial instruments under management. This levy is currently imposed only in respect of listed securities and listed financial instruments under management and is not calculated on any money market instruments or cash which a portfolio manager may hold.

5. Requirements To Be Fulfilled Before Application Will Be Approved

There are a number of requirements to be fulfilled before any application will be approved, the most significant being those pertaining to capital adequacy, educational requirements and mandates.

Capital Adequacy. Although neither the SECA nor the FMCA sets out any minimum capital requirements for portfolio managers, the FSB's practice is not to approve an application unless the applicant is capitalized in the amount of at least R20,000 paid up equity share capital (as opposed to loan capital) for the first shareholder, an additional amount of at least R20,000 paid up equity share capital for the second shareholder and another R10,000 paid up equity share capital for each shareholder thereafter. The FSB is not prepared to accept fidelity or other insurance or guarantees in lieu of equity capitalization, although this is presently under review.

It is likely that the FSB would require a South African branch of a foreign company that applies for approval to have adequate capital in South Africa and for its obligations to be guaranteed by the parent company.

Educational Requirements. These requirements apply to the persons actually administering the investment portfolios rather than to the shareholders of the approved portfolio manager. The FSB currently requires a person administering equity portfolios to have completed certain examinations set by the JSE and to have specified minimum experience as an portfolio manager of equity securities. Failing that, the person is required to have at least five years experience as a portfolio manager of equity securities. Similar requirements are imposed in respect of persons wishing approval to manage portfolios of financial instruments.

If the portfolio management operations are conducted in more than one premises or in different towns, a suitably experienced person must be present in each such office to supervise the business. Persons who have international experience but no South African experience in portfolio management will not be accepted as suitable administrators by the FSB.

Portfolio managers are not required to appoint compliance officers.

Mandates. The FSB will review the content of the mandates which the portfolio manager intends to enter into with its clients. The content of the mandates is largely determined by the conditions published under the SECA and the FMCA, respectively, which are discussed below.

6. Conditions Under The SECA And The FMCA

The conditions essentially regulate the relationship between a portfolio manager and its client. These conditions which are somewhat antiquated and are now under review, require, among other things:

- A client and portfolio manager to enter into a written agreement (mandate) which records the arrangement made by the client with the portfolio manager for the administration and holding in safe custody of the investments concerned.
- The mandate to stipulate the name in which the portfolio manager may hold investments on behalf of the client.
- The portfolio manager to deposit all monies received in connection with the administration or holding in safe custody of investments to which the agreement relates, either with JSE Trustees (Pty) Limited, where the portfolio manager is a stockbroker or member of the JSE, or in a designated trust account or in a client's account with a bank.
- The portfolio manager to mark any document of title relating to investments held on behalf of a client in a manner which will render it possible at all times to establish readily the identity of the owner of such investments. Alternatively, the portfolio manager is required to maintain a register to identify the ownership of the investments.
- The portfolio manager to keep proper accounting books and records and to submit the books to an annual audit in which the portfolio manager's auditor is required to certify that the portfolio manager has complied with the conditions set out in the notice. In addition, where a portfolio manager holds investments in safe custody on behalf of clients, it is required to satisfy the Registrar that adequate measures are in operation to ensure the continued safety of the investments and that, relative to the value of the investments of which it has safe custody, it holds sufficient insurance or other cover to make good any losses resulting from the negligence, dishonesty or fraud of such manager or any person in its employ.

C. Unit Trust Activities
1. Regulatory Environment

Section 37(1) of the Unit Trusts Control Act, 1981 (the "Unit Trusts Act") provides that, apart from an approved participation bond scheme, "no person shall do any act or enter into any agreement or transaction for the purpose of establishing, carrying on or managing any scheme, other than a unit trust scheme in terms of this Act, in pursuance of which members of the public are or will be invited or permitted for valuable consideration to acquire an interest or undivided share in an asset or one or more groups of assets and to participate proportionately in the income or profits derived therefrom."

A "unit trust scheme" is defined in section 1 of the Unit Trusts Act as "any scheme or arrangement in the nature of a trust in pursuance of which members of the public are invited or permitted, as beneficiaries under the trust, to acquire an interest or undivided share (whether called a unit or by any other name) in one or more unit portfolios and to participate proportionately in the income or profits derived therefrom."

A "unit portfolio" is, in turn, defined as a group of securities in which members of the public are invited or permitted to acquire units. "Securities" are broadly defined to include shares, stock, loan stock and debentures. It is notable that the definition is not limited to securities listed on a stock exchange licensed in South Africa or elsewhere.

2. Registration As A Management Company

Only a company which has been registered as a management company under section 4 of the Unit Trusts Act may manage or carry on any "unit trust scheme in securities" or issue unit certificates in respect of a unit trust scheme. Such a management company is required to be registered as a public company under the Companies Act and to have a paid-up share capital and non-distributable reserves which amount to not less than R2,000,000 which are actually employed or immediately available for employment in its unit trust business. Application for registration as a management company must be made to the FSB.

3. Elements Of A Unit Trust Portfolio

The Unit Trusts Act prescribes the content of a unit trust portfolio. One of the prescribed elements of a unit trust portfolio is "stock exchange securities." These are defined as those securities "which are listed and authorized to be dealt in on a recognized stock exchange, and the prices of which are quoted in a list issued for publication by such stock exchange." A "recognized stock exchange" includes, pursuant to section 1 of the Unit Trusts Act, "a stock exchange outside the Republic recognized by the Registrar for the purpose of this Act." A number of stock exchanges have recently been recognized for the purposes of the Unit Trusts Act. These include the stock exchanges of New York, London, Stockholm, Rome, Tokyo and Zurich.

D. The Financial Institutions (Investment Of Funds) Act, 1984

Pursuant to the Financial Institutions (Investment of Funds) Act, 1984 (the "Investment of Funds Act"), any financial institution which holds, controls or administers any asset (the "trust property") in its capacity as administrator, trustee or curator by virtue of a will, deed of settlement or order of court, or as an agent for any other principal, must comply with the provisions of the Investment of Funds Act. The ambit of the Investment of Funds Act extends beyond traditional trust companies or financial institutions and includes any company incorporated under the Companies Act, provided that such company invests, controls or administers trust property as defined. Accordingly, the management company of a unit trust, a portfolio manager and a member of the JSE or SAFEX which holds client funds in safe deposit will be required to comply with the provisions of the Investment of Funds Act.

The Investment of Funds Act prescribes the duties of a financial institution and its employees in relation to any trust property controlled by it. The provisions of the Act essentially codify the duties imposed on trustees under the common law. A director, official, employee or agent of a financial institution or nominee company controlled by a financial institution that invests, keeps in safe custody or otherwise controls any funds of the institution or any trust property held by or on behalf of the institution or any beneficiary or principal is thus required, in the management of the trust property, to observe the utmost good faith and exercise the usual care and diligence required of a trustee. Such a person may not administer the funds or trust property in a manner calculated to benefit him or herself or any other person at the expense of the institution, trust, beneficiary or principal concerned.

A financial institution is prohibited from investing trust property otherwise than in accordance with the agreement in terms of which the trust property is being administered. Where the agreement is silent in this regard, section 4(2) of the Investment of Funds Act provides that trust property may only be invested (i) in the name of the client, (ii) in the name of the financial institution in its capacity as trustee or agent of the client or (iii) in the name of a nominee company controlled by the financial institution.

Funds invested in the name of such a nominee company must be clearly identified, in the books of the financial institution, as property which belongs to specified principals. Pursuant to section 4(2)(b) of the Investment of Funds Act, such nominee company must be controlled by the financial institution and may incur no liabilities other than on behalf of the principals for whose benefit it holds assets. In addition, the nominee company may not incur liabilities which exceed the value of the assets belonging to the principals.

Trust property which is expressly registered in the name of the financial institution in its capacity as administrator, trustee, curator or agent, does not under any circumstances form part of the assets of the financial institution.

VII. The Securities Regulation Panel

The Securities Regulation Panel (the "SRP") was established pursuant to the Companies Act in 1991 and its functions are to regulate "affected transactions" (as defined below) and to supervise certain dealings in securities. The Securities Regulation Code on Take-Overs and Mergers (the "Code"), promulgated by the SRP pursuant to section 440 of the Companies Act, came into effect on February 1, 1991. The Code is based largely on the City Code on Take-overs and Mergers issued by the London Panel on Take-overs and Mergers and its underlying principle is to ensure fair and equal treatment of all holders of relevant securities in relation to affected transactions. The Code applies to "affected transactions" in which the offeree company is (i) a public company (whether listed or not), (ii) a statutory corporation resident in South Africa or (iii) a private company whose shareholders' interests (valued at the offer price) together with the loan capital exceed R5,000,000 and which has more than ten shareholders.

An "affected transaction" is one which: (i) taking into account any securities held before such transaction, has or will have the effect of (a) vesting control of any company in any person, or persons acting in concert, in whom control did not vest prior to such transaction or (b) any person or persons acting in concert, acquiring all the securities, or all the securities of a particular class of any company; or (ii) involves the acquisition by any person, or persons acting in concert, in whom control of any company vests of further securities of that company in excess of the limits prescribed in the rules. "Control" is defined as being 35% or more of the voting rights of a company.

It should be noted that the Code applies only in respect of transactions involving the acquisition of shares. Where assets are purchased from a company as a going concern, all that is needed is the approval by a simple majority of shareholders in general meeting. Although the Code applies to both listed and unlisted companies, in practice, the acquisitions most affected are those involving companies with numerous minority shareholders who do not participate directly in takeover negotiations.

The Code acknowledges that it is impractical to devise rules in sufficient detail to cover all possible circumstances. The spirit of the Code is, therefore, embodied in specified "General Principles" and the SRP seeks to interpret, enforce or relax the rules in accordance with these Principles. The Principles include the following:

- All holders of the same class of securities of an offeree company must be treated similarly by an offeror.
- During the course of an offer, neither the offeror nor the offeree company, nor any of their respective advisers, may furnish information to some holders which is not made available to all holders of such securities, except with the consent of the SRP.
- Holders of relevant securities must be given sufficient information and advice to enable them to reach a properly informed decision and must have sufficient time to do so. No relevant information may be withheld from them.
- All parties to an offer must take all reasonable steps to prevent the creation of a false market in the securities of an offeror or the offeree company. Parties involved in offers must take care that statements are

- not made which may mislead holders of relevant securities or the market.
- Rights of control are to be exercised in good faith and the oppression of a minority is unacceptable.
- After a bona fide offer has been communicated to the board of the offeree company, or after it has reason to believe that an offer might be imminent, it may not take any action in relation to the affairs of the company, without the approval of the holders of the relevant securities in general meeting, which could effectively result in any offer being frustrated or in the holders of relevant securities being denied an opportunity to decide whether to accept the offer on its merits.
- An affected transaction normally gives rise to an obligation to make a general offer to all other holders of the relevant securities. Where an acquisition is contemplated, the offeror must ensure that he is able to implement such an offer.
- The underlying principle is that persons holding an equity interest in an offeree company through shares or other securities in that company (whether or not such shares carry voting rights) are entitled to dispose of their interest on terms comparable to the parties of an affected transaction.

The Code contains extensive rules governing the conduct of take-overs and mergers. Some of the more important of such rules are as follows:

- A mandatory offer must be made to all other shareholders for the same or comparable consideration as those afforded to the parties to the affected transaction when any person (or persons acting in concert) becomes the holder of 35% or more of the voting rights of a company or a shareholder owning between 30% and 50% increases that shareholding by more than 5% in one year.
- The publication of cautionary announcements (in certain circumstances, where an offer is being negotiated) and of an announcement of a firm intention to make an offer (in certain other circumstances) is required.
- The offer must be put in writing to the board of the offeree company and must remain open for a least 21 days after the posting of the offeror document. The ultimate offeror must be disclosed to the board and the board must obtain competent independent advice on the offer, which advice is to be made known to the holders of the relevant securities.

Johannesburg, South Africa
June 1996

CHAPTER 6

TAXATION AND FOREIGN EXCHANGE

By Kevin W. Joselowitz
and Michael M. Katz

I. **Taxation**
   A. **Introduction**

South Africa taxes on a territorial, as opposed to a residence or worldwide, basis. Thus, both South African and foreign taxpayers are subject to tax on taxable income derived from a source within South Africa or deemed to have been earned within South Africa. Conversely, South African resident companies and individuals are exempt from tax on foreign source income. Certain foreign source income may, however, be deemed to have a South African source, the most important being dividends and income from contracts of sale of goods entered into in South Africa. At present, however, dividends received by South African residents are exempt from tax.

The Income Tax Act No. 58 of 1962, as amended (the "Income Tax Act"), governs companies, individuals and trusts, although there are certain provisions which are not common to all. This chapter will focus on the tax implications of foreign companies doing business in South Africa, whether through the vehicle of a subsidiary of the foreign company or a branch of the foreign company.

The corporate tax system applies, among other things, to all corporations and companies incorporated in South Africa and to similar bodies incorporated outside of South Africa that carry on business or have an office or place of business in South Africa and derive income from any source within or deemed to be within South Africa. Accordingly, the provisions of the Income Tax Act are applicable to external companies (being companies incorporated outside South Africa) in respect of their South African income.

In many cases, the domestic tax consequences are overridden by provisions in double tax agreements. At present, there is no double tax treaty in existence between South Africa and the United States. The tax situation in South Africa should, of course, be considered in conjunction with the method of taxation in the country in which the parent company carries on business.

   B. **The South African Tax System**

The system is in essence a unitary system, providing for the aggregation of all income received or accrued and the deduction therefrom of all losses and expenses incurred in the production of such income to arrive at a "taxable income" which is subject to tax in a single assessment.

C. Groups of Companies

There is no group taxation in South Africa. Each company in the group is taxed as a separate entity. Losses sustained by one company in the group cannot be set-off against profits earned by another. Group tax returns are not acceptable and group tax relief allowances are not available. It is, therefore, important to ensure that an expense incurred by a company in a group is recorded as an expense by the company to which the income earned would be attributable, in order for the expense to be allowed as a deduction. It is also important to ensure, where practicable, that an interest expense is borne by a company within the group having taxable income, since there will be no cash-flow advantage from the deduction if it is borne by a company with an assessed loss. Assessed losses of individual companies may not be surrendered in favor of other companies in the group with taxable incomes, nor may tax benefits be transferred or shared between companies. There are anti-avoidance provisions to prevent efforts to achieve group taxation, including endeavors to transfer assets within a group so as to achieve a stepped-up basis for depreciating the assets acquired.

D. Obligation to Register As A Taxpayer

If a foreign corporation has income from a South African source or which is deemed to be from a South African source, it will be obliged to register as a taxpayer and submit tax returns. The returns should disclose all taxable income (i.e., gross income less allowable deductions) derived from sources within South Africa. In other words, accounts should be prepared disclosing profits and losses related to the South African business, without reference to non-South African operations. The income disclosed will then be assessed according to the normal rules governing income tax pursuant to the Income Tax Act.

The corporate tax system requires the filing of annual returns in which all the information necessary to compute the company's tax liability must be furnished. The return for any company that carries on business or has an office in South Africa must be filed by the public officer appointed by the company to represent it in all dealings with the revenue authorities. The person appointed as public officer must be resident in South Africa and his appointment must be reported to and approved by the revenue authorities.

E. Rate of Taxation

Companies are at present taxed at a flat rate of 35% of taxable income. The Income Tax Act imposes a secondary tax on companies ("STC") in respect of dividends declared by a company on or after March 17, 1993. STC is at present determined at the rate of 12.5% of the net amount of any dividend declared by a company. STC is payable by the company declaring the dividend and not by its shareholders. No STC is payable in respect of the distribution by an external company of branch profits in respect of assessment years ending on or after April 1, 1996. However, a branch profit tax has been introduced at a rate of 40%. From a tax point of view, a foreign company that operates as a branch in South Africa is better off than a foreign company operating as a subsidiary, the latter of which pays corporate tax at a rate of 35% and STC at a rate of 12% on dividends declared; the benefit being a rate of 40% for a branch as compared to an effective rate of 42.2% for a subsidiary.

The effective rate of tax for a domestic company or local subsidiary of a foreign company varies depending upon what percentage of tax profit is distributed as a dividend. The following are some examples:

Percentage of Taxed Profit Distributed	Effective Tax Rate Percentage
0	35.00
50	38.81
75	40.42
100	42.22

Dividends which a domestic company distributes to foreign corporations and individuals are exempt from normal and withholding tax.

Interest payable by a South African subsidiary to an overseas parent company or other lender would be deductible for tax purposes. The interest received by the non-resident recipient is not taxable in South Africa, nor is it subject to any withholding tax. This is subject to the thin capitalization and transfer rules discussed later in this chapter.

F. Calculating Taxable Income

The profit reflected in the financial statements, in practice, forms the basis of calculating taxable income. Profits are reduced by (i) non-South African source income, (ii) receipt or accruals of a capital nature, (iii) exempt income (including dividend income) and certain tax-exempt state subsidies, (iv) certain special tax allowances as well as allowances in respect of doubtful debts, (v) future expenditure on contracts and (vi) amounts owing for goods or fixed property sold on a reserved ownership basis. The profits are then increased by (i) capital expenditures, (ii) provisions for anticipated liabilities or losses and general reserves and (iii) non-trading expenditures to the extent not incurred for the purpose of trade (e.g., charitable donations). As a general rule, interest payable (including finance charges on the acquisition of capital assets) is deductible according to the same rules applicable to all expenditures on an accrual basis. Although there are timing differences in the calculation of taxable income when compared with accounting income, more recent amendments to the Income Tax Act are designed to reduce these timing differences. Thus, for tax purposes, interest accrues, and is incurred, on a day-to-day yield-to-maturity basis.

G. Depreciation

A depreciation, or wear-and-tear, allowance is granted in respect of machinery, implements, utensils and articles used for the purpose of trade. Generally, depreciation is calculated on the cost of the asset excluding finance charges. No allowance is available in respect of goodwill.

Depreciation rates are based on the anticipated useful lives of the assets concerned. The reducing balance basis (the straight line basis) may be used. Depreciation may, however, not be claimed on office and shop buildings but may be claimed on certain building appurtenances. The cost of devising or acquiring patents, copyrights, designs, trade marks, etc. may be amortized in equal installments over their useful lives, with a maximum period of 25 years. Depreciation on plant used in a process of manufacture is calculated on a 20% straight line basis. More favorable rates apply to the mining and agricultural industries.

On the sale of an asset, any excess received over tax value (but not any excess over the original cost) will be taxed as a recoupment of depreciation. Any shortfall will normally be allowed as a deduction by way of a scrapping allowance. Any excess will normally be a non-taxable capital gain, except in the mining and agricultural industries.

H. Trade Losses

Where allowable deductions exceed income in any year, an assessed loss arises. Assessed loss is available to be set off against other trading income as well as non-trading income, the latter of which, for example, includes interest.

Where a company does not trade in any year of assessment, it loses its entitlement to carry forward the assessed loss to the subsequent year. The term "trade," however, is widely defined and includes the leasing of property.

As long as the company trades in each year, the assessed loss can be carried forward indefinitely. Anti-tax avoidance legislation exists which is designed to prevent trafficking in companies with assessed losses and to prevent the diversion of income to assessed loss companies.

I. Withholding Tax on Royalties, Know-How, etc.

Withholding tax is applicable to royalty payments made to non-resident individuals or companies not carrying on business in South Africa. Royalties paid to non-residents are subject to a withholding tax at a rate of 12%. There is no longer any withholding tax on dividends or interest on loans remitted to a non-resident.

There are a number of double taxation agreements in existence between South Africa and various countries which provide relief in respect of royalties and know-how withholding tax. At present there is no double taxation agreement with the United States.

J. Management Fees

Management fees payable by a subsidiary to its external parent company are deductible if the criterion normally applicable for the deduction of expenditures is satisfied – that the fees are incurred in the production of income – and are taxable at normal rates in the hands of the recipient. It should be noted that the exchange control authorities are not usually inclined to grant consent for the expatriation of management fees.

K. Capital Gains

At present, there is no capital gains tax in South Africa. Capital gains are not taxed and capital losses are not tax deductible in South Africa. The proceeds of the disposal of the share capital of a subsidiary which was held as an investment (i.e., a capital asset) would be treated as a receipt of a capital nature, which is not subject to tax. In the event that the shares were held as trading stock or were acquired for the sole or main purpose of realizing a profit on their subsequent disposal, different considerations would apply. In the case of shares in listed companies, the taxpayer can elect to have gains realized on a disposal which takes place more than five years after acquisition recognized as a capital asset even if on the application of normal principles it would otherwise have been revenue.

L. Transfer Pricing

Section 31 of the Income Tax Act provides, in the context of an international transaction, that the Commissioner for Inland Revenue (the "Commissioner") may, for purposes of determining tax liability, adjust the consideration in respect of a transaction to reflect the arms'-length price of goods or services supplied by, or acquired from, "a connected person" (which includes in relation to company A, the holding company of A, a subsidiary company of A, a co-subsidiary of A or any other company, if at least 20% of the equity share capital of such company is held by A and no shareholder holds the majority voting rights of such company). Such an adjustment may be made at the discretion of the Commissioner where:
- any goods or services, including intangibles, are supplied or acquired pursuant to an agreement between a company managed and controlled in South Africa and a company managed and controlled outside of South Africa (referred to in the Income Tax Act as an "international agreement");
- the acquiror is a connected person in relation to the supplier; and
- the goods or services are supplied at a price which is higher or lower than an arms'-length price.

Any amount disallowed in this manner will be treated as a dividend and thus will be subject to STC.

M. Thin Capitalization

Section 31 of the Income Tax Act further provides that interest, finance charges or any other consideration payable to a connected person shall be disallowed to the extent that it relates to financial assistance which is, in the opinion of the Commissioner for Inland Revenue, excessive in relation to the fixed capital of the recipient. Fixed capital means share capital, share premium, accumulated profits (whether of a capital nature or not) or any other permanent owner's capital. This provision applies where a company that is managed and controlled outside of South Africa ("the investor") grants financial assistance (including a loan, advance or debt or the provision of any security or guarantee) directly or indirectly to a company managed and controlled in South Africa ("the recipient") which is a connected person in relation to the investor, or not a connected person but one in respect of which the investor is entitled to participate in not less than 25% of the dividends, profits or capital or is directly or indirectly entitled to exercise not less than 25% of the votes.

While the Commissioner will, in due course, issue a practice note setting out how he proposes to deal with section 31, it is expected that the Commissioner will prescribe "safe-haven" debt/equity funding ratios which, if the financial assistance falls within, will not be considered by the Commissioner as being excessive. If the financial assistance results in the recipient's debt/equity ratio exceeding the "safe-haven" limits, then, unless such financial assistance can be shown not to be excessive under the applicable circumstances, the recipient would face the risk of the interest payable in respect of the excessive financial assistance being disallowed. Any amount which is disallowed under section 31 will be deemed to be a dividend for the purpose of STC.

The effect of the foregoing is that, where a foreigner makes a loan to a connected person in South Africa and exceeds the debt/equity ratio, interest payable on the excess debt will be disallowed as a deduction and subject to STC as a dividend. Even where the debt/equity ratio is correct, the rate of interest must be correct as any excess will be disallowed as a deduction and subject to STC. The correct rate of interest is, if the loan is denominated in a foreign currency, LIBOR plus 2%, and if denominated in Rand, the prime overdraft rate plus 2%.

N. South African Branch Of A Foreign Company

A branch of a South African company is not taxed separately from the company of which it is a branch. However, the branch of a foreign company is taxed as if it were a separate taxable entity from the foreign company. This is achieved in practice by the maintenance of separate accounts for the operations of the branch, which will be regarded as encompassing all activities relating to the business of the branch carried on in South Africa. The branch must be registered as a taxpayer describing itself as a branch. In South Africa's 1996/1997 budget, branch profits tax at the rate of 40% of taxable income was introduced and will apply from the commencement of years of assessment ending on or after April 1, 1996.

O. Anti-Avoidance Provisions

The revenue authorities are entitled to disregard transactions which are not entered into on a normal or arms'-length basis, which result in avoidance, postponement or reduction in tax, where the sole, or one of the main aims of the transaction was the avoidance, postponement or reduction of tax.

P. Individuals

Individuals pay income tax on exactly the same basis as companies, although the rates of tax differ and there are certain rebates and deductions available to individuals which are not available to companies. Moreover, individuals are taxed at progressive rates.

In the case of employees, the employer withholds tax from remuneration (known as "PAYE"). Self-employed persons and others are exempt from PAYE pay provisional tax.

In the case of certain employees, where the remuneration does not exceed a certain maximum per annum, the PAYE payment is known as the Standard Income Tax on Employees ("SITE"). This SITE is a final, non-refundable tax, so that if an employee does not have significant other income he will be relieved from submitting a tax return.

Q. Trusts

A trust is taxed on the same basis as an unmarried person, although none of the rebates and deductions are available. However, where the trust distributes its income to the beneficiaries, the beneficiaries are taxable instead.

R. Partnerships

A partnership is not taxed as a separate entity. The taxable income of the partnership is ascertained and then allocated amongst the partners in their profit-sharing ratio. Thereafter, the partners will be subject to either individual or corporate income tax on this income. In the case of a limited partnership, however, the law effectively prohibits a limited partner from claiming a loss for tax purposes in excess of the amount for which he is liable to creditors, whether by way of his contribution to the partnership, by way of accumulated income or in any other manner.

S. Other South African Taxes
1. Value-Added Tax

Value-Added Tax ("VAT") is charged at the rate of 14% on the supply of goods and services by South African business entities, including South African branches of foreign entities. Certain supplies of goods and services are exempt (certain financial services, residential accommodation and public transport) from VAT while others are zero-rated (mainly exports).

2. Land and Buildings

Transfers of immovable property are subject to transfer duty on the greater of the purchase price or fair market value. Different rates are applicable to properties acquired by natural persons and companies. The present rate for a corporate purchaser is 10%. No duty is payable where a sale is subject to VAT or is zero-rated. Under a recent practice note, both input and output VAT on property transactions will be levied on the payment or receipt of cash. Annual rates (property taxes) are payable to local authorities by the owner based on a local authority valuation.

3. Stamp Duties

Marketable securities tax and stamp duty are payable on the registration of transfer of share certificates at the rate of 0.5% of the value or purchase consideration and 0.25% of the original issue price, respectively.

4. Social Security Taxes

There are no social security taxes as such. Both employers and employees are obliged to contribute to the State Unemployment Insurance Fund if the employee's annual remuneration does not exceed R69,420.

5. Regional Service Council Levies

Two levies, namely, a levy on sales and a levy on payroll, are payable to various Regional Services Councils operating in various parts of the country. The levies are tax deductible. The levies vary between regions but approximate 0.14% and 0.35%. In addition, VAT is payable on these levies.

6. Customs and Excise Taxes

Customs duty is payable on certain imports, while excise duty is payable on certain products.

7. Donations Tax

Donations tax is levied on donations made by a person ordinarily resident in South Africa and by South African domestic companies. The rate of the tax is 25% on donations made on or after March 14, 1996.

8. Tax Incentives

Under the June 7, 1996 Macro-Economic Proposals of the South African Government, certain tax incentives will be available.

II. Exchange Control Considerations
A. Introduction

Pursuant to the Exchange Control Regulations, Orders and Rules, 1961 (the "Regulations"), exchange control measures were originally introduced to stem the outflow of capital from South Africa and to ensure a measure of stability in the currency market. The general principle in terms of the Regulations is that no South African company or resident may acquire foreign assets or incur foreign liabilities without exchange control approval.

Exchange control applies, in the main, to South African residents and, although there are generally no restrictions on the inward or outward transfer of funds of which non-residents are the sole beneficial owners, there are certain constraints and conditions applicable to them. Branches and subsidiaries are normally both treated as resident in the country in which they are situated or incorporated and transactions between a branch or subsidiary in South Africa and a head office or a holding company outside South Africa are regarded as being between a resident and a non-resident. In most circumstances, transactions connected with the investment by non-residents in projects in South Africa will require the approval of the exchange control authorities under the regulations dealing with the issue of shares and the borrowing of money.

The South African Reserve Bank ("SARB") delegates considerable authority to the commercial banks to deal with exchange control matters. Applications to the SARB involving issues outside the authority of commercial banks must be made through the applicant's normal bankers.

The government has on numerous occasions stated its intention to continue the gradual process of abolishing exchange control.

B. Limitation on Local Borrowings By South African Companies With Foreign Ownership

Where 25% or more of a South African company's income is received by a non-resident, or 25% or more of the voting or non-voting securities are held or controlled, directly or indirectly, by non-residents, the company's local borrowings are restricted. The restriction commences immediately when foreign ownership or control reaches 25% and the restriction increases as the foreign ownership increases to 100%.

Local borrowing by non-resident controlled companies is restricted to ensure adequate capitalization from abroad and to prevent excessive leverage. Companies owned wholly by non-residents may borrow up to 50% of their total shareholders' funds/investments, as described below. The total is sometimes referred to as the company's "borrowing base." Financial assistance or local borrowing includes any form of borrowing other than normal trade credit, including off-balance sheet financing.

To encourage local participation in enterprises, the basic 50% is increased depending on the percentage of local shareholding. The equivalent of the percentage of the shareholders' funds that may be borrowed locally is calculated in terms of the following formula:

$$50\% + \left(\frac{\%\ \text{local shareholding}}{\%\ \text{foreign shareholding}} \times 50 \right)$$

Thus, a 25% local equity interest will increase maximum local borrowing to 66.67% of the borrowing base, while a 50% local equity interest yields a 100% figure. The following table further illustrates the formula:

Percentage of Foreign Shareholding or of Company's Income Received by Non-Residents	Local Borrowing as a Percentage of the Borrowing Base
less than 25	No restriction
25	200
40	125
50	100
75	66-2/3
100	50

Under the recently announced Macro-Economic Proposals of the South African Government, the above limits on local borrowings are to be doubled. At the time of going to press on this chapter, the official Government Notice confirming the doubling of the local borrowing limits had not been published.

Shareholders' funds/investment consists of the following:
- paid-up share capital;
- share premium;
- distributable reserves;
- retained earnings;
- shareholders' loans and preference share capital;
- hard core trade credit; and
- deferred tax balances.

Excluded from shareholders' funds/investment are reserves resulting from the revaluation of assets. Shareholder's loans are included in shareholders' funds investment to the extent that these are provided in the same proportion as the capital is owned as between residents and non-residents. Where the non-resident shareholders' loans are in excess proportion, the excess will rank for inclusion as shareholders' funds. Where, however, the resident shareholders' loans are in excess proportion, the excess will not rank as shareholders' funds but, instead, as local borrowing.

Preference shares are normally treated the same way as shareholders' loans for purposes of determining local borrowing. They are considered as local borrowing if held by South African residents but not if held by the overseas shareholders.

Applications may be made for permission to borrow in excess of the above borrowing base limitations. These applications will be considered on merit in exceptional cases, but only for short periods, such as three years. Applications for excess local facilities will not be allowed where the resources so provided are to be applied in accelerating payments abroad, such as for the (i) repayment of shareholders' loans, (ii) settlement of shareholders' trade credit and (iii) payment of dividends. The SARB must be advised once per year of local borrowing in excess of R10,000. This is done through the authorized dealer. New local borrowing must be disclosed immediately and, thereafter, be advised once per annum.

The acceptance of loans from non-resident shareholders is subject to prior SARB approval.

C. Dividends

Dividends may be remitted from all net retained earnings derived from normal trading, provided that such earnings arose subsequent to January 1, 1984. However, where local borrowing is in existence, SARB approval is required to remit dividends to non-resident shareholders. Approval of payments is granted where it can be shown that the remittance will not result in the company becoming overborrowed locally in terms of the formula set out above.

D. Interest

The remittal of interest to non-resident parent or associated companies will normally be allowed upon production of evidence of the indebtedness, provided that the rate is reasonable as compared with current interest rates and past practice.

E. Branch Profits

There are no restrictions on the transfer of taxed profits of local branches of a foreign parent, provided such profits arose after January 1, 1984 and provided that such transfers are financed from available cash funds without the need to resort to excessive local borrowing.

F. Royalties, License Fees, Patents, etc.

Agreements for South African companies to pay royalties, license fees and patent fees are subject to prior approval from the exchange control authorities and, where local manufacture of goods is concerned, also from the Department of Trade and Industry. In general, sympathetic consideration is given to applications in those cases where the acquisition of such rights would be in the interest of the further development of the local industry.

G. Management and Technical Assistance Fees

Payments to non-residents of management and technical assistance fees require the prior approval of the exchange control authorities who will have to be satisfied as to the basis on which the payments are calculated and whether such payments are merited. The exchange control authorities are not usually inclined to grant consent for the expatriation of management fees payable by a subsidiary company to its foreign parent company, as exchange control prefers foreign investors withdrawing their profits from South Africa in the form of dividends.

Directors' fees of up to R8000 per annum may be remitted to a non-resident director upon production to an authorized foreign exchange dealer in South Africa of a resolution by the company confirming the fees payable.

H. Imports and Exports

Foreign currency is made freely available for permissible imports, which are those imports for which import permits have been issued (a limited range of products) or are not required (the majority of goods). Payment is permitted only against proof of importation or shipment to South Africa. Import permits serve for customs purposes and for the granting of foreign exchange facilities by the SARB.

The proceeds from exports, both visible and invisible, must be remitted to South Africa within six months of the date of export. However, authorized dealers may allow extended credit terms of up to twelve months if conditions in a particular market warrant such terms. Exporters of capital goods, on application to the SARB, may be allowed to extend credit terms in excess of twelve months. South African exporters who export on credit are required, within seven days of the date of shipment of the goods, to take out a forward exchange contract for the sale of the foreign currency proceeds. The receivable must thereafter be continuously covered until the proceeds are transferred to South Africa.

Under the South African Government's recently announced Macro-Economic Proposals, export and import proceeds occurring within 30 days of each other may be offset against each other.

I. Contract Workers and Immigrants
1. Contract Workers

A contract worker, in the exchange control context, is a person who is normally resident outside South Africa but is on secondment to a local firm or has been recruited under a definite pre-existing contract. He or she may have temporary or permanent residence. Most have the latter. However, the intention is to return to the home country at the end of the period of secondment/contract.

Contract workers who are employed as mentioned above, may transfer a portion of their earnings abroad, provided they comply with the following three requirements:

- they declare on arrival in South Africa (or subsequently) to an authorized dealer, for onward transmission to the exchange control authorities, whether or not they possess foreign assets and, if so, undertake in writing that they will not place such assets at the disposal of any third party normally resident in South Africa;
- the amount to be remitted must be reasonable in relation to earnings; and
- the initial request to the bank to transfer funds must be accompanied by a letter from the applicant's employer stating that the applicant is employed on contract/secondment and providing details of his earnings.

Generally, the norm applied by the SARB is that contract workers should, while they are in South Africa, be treated more or less like residents in order to avoid unnecessary administrative procedures which would have resulted from treating them as non-residents. That implies, for example, that they can keep bank accounts or obtain funds from financial institutions for the purchase of a house in the same way as a resident.

On completion of tours of duty, or upon the expiration or prior termination of their original contracts, contract workers may transfer, through normal banking channels, savings accumulated from their earnings in South Africa when returning permanently to their home countries. The amount transferred must be reasonable in relation to earnings.

2. Immigrants

Immigrants in the exchange control context, are defined as nationals of another country who come to South Africa with the intention of residing in South Africa permanently. In other words, the foreign national formally immigrates and takes up permanent residence.

Immigrants are required to declare on arrival in detail to an authorized dealer any foreign assets and income thereon and give a written undertaking that they will not place such assets at the disposal of any third party resident in South Africa. On taking up permanent residence in South Africa, immigrants become subject to the exchange control regulations. Any income on foreign assets must be transferred to South Africa within seven days of receipt.

To encourage immigration, the authorities permit immigrants to retain their assets abroad. On the fifth anniversary of an immigrant's arrival in South Africa, he or she will be required to once again declare foreign assets. Assurance is given that (prospective) immigrants who decide to relinquish South African residence within five years of arrival may re-transfer freely to the monetary area from which they came all funds introduced to South Africa, provided the transfer is not funded by local borrowing facilities.

Immigrants may be permitted to transfer premiums due on foreign currency life assurance policies or make pension fund payments, provided that (i) the commitment was entered into prior to the applicant's immigration, (ii) documentary evidence is produced and (iii) no cash resources from which the payment can be made are available abroad. Loans taken out by immigrants in their previous country of domicile for the specific purposes of financing their migration to South Africa may be repatriated from South Africa, provided that (i) the amount involved does not exceed R1,000, (ii) no cash resources from which the payment can be made are available abroad and (iii) the loan was obtained for the specific purpose of financing their immigration to South Africa. Similarly, tax commitments can be settled from South Africa against documentary evidence, provided no foreign cash resources are available.

After five years in South Africa, immigrants are, for exchange control purposes, regarded as permanent residents of the country. On subsequent immigration, they will be accorded a normal settling-in allowance and other facilities available to immigrants under exchange control.

Johannesburg, South Africa
June 1996

Bibliography:

De Koker, Income Tax In South Africa, Durban, Butterworths (1989)

Silke, Silke On South African Income Tax, Durban, Butterworths (11th edition 1995)

Danzinger, International Income Tax: The South African Perspective, Durban, Butterworths (1991)

Moss-Morris, Exchange Control Service, Durban, Butterworths (1990)

Exchange Control Encyclopedia, Northlands, International Law & Tax Institute (2nd edition 1995)

South African Reserve Bank Exchange Control Manual, Pretoria, South African Reserve Bank (2nd edition 1996)

CHAPTER 7

TAX ASSESSMENTS, PAYMENTS AND APPEALS IN SOUTH AFRICA

By Deloitte & Touche, South Africa

I. **Tax Year**
   A. **Companies**

A company's tax year coincides with its financial year for accounting purposes. Under the Income Tax Act 1962, as amended, a company is generally required to close its financial year on the last day of February. Any company that wants to end its financial year on any other date or change the closing date of its financial year must obtain the Commissioner's permission. Permission is invariably given, unless there has been a change in the tax rate, in which case permission is normally refused, at least in relation to years affected by the change.

   B. **Individuals**

The tax year for individuals ends on February 28th. However, certain taxpayers may make a prior election for their year to end on June 30th.

II. **Returns And Assessments**
   A. **Companies**

A company whose financial year ends between January 1st and the end of February must normally file its tax return by the middle of the following May, although an extension may be granted. A company whose financial year ends in March or later must agree with the Commissioner on a filing date. The Commissioner for Inland Revenue (the "Commissioner") will usually agree to a date within the six months following the end of the company's financial year without question. Penalties are levied if returns are not filed on time.

The return must include or be accompanied by the following:
- a balance sheet, an income statement and any special reports by the auditor relating to the financial statements;
- a computation of taxable income;
- schedules of tax depreciation claimed; and
- particulars of:
- nontaxable amounts credited and disallowable expenses charged in the income statement, as well as special allowances not claimed in the income statement;
- loans and advances not in the ordinary course of business or at rates of interest below normal commercial rates;
- increases or decreases in provisions and reserves;
- capital profits on the sale of properties and other assets;
- interest, royalty and know-how payments to non-residents;
- traveling expenses for journeys outside South Africa;

- in the case of a private company, remuneration payable to directors and their relatives; and
- details of shareholdings in foreign tax-haven companies.

Each company must appoint a resident public officer to assume responsibility for the accuracy of the tax return and to accept service of any notice or demand. All persons employed in carrying out the provisions of the Income Tax Act take oaths of secrecy. Any breach of confidentiality constitutes a criminal offense.

Companies must calculate their own taxable income on their returns. Tax returns are checked by Inland Revenue assessors, who prepare an official assessment showing (i) taxable income, (ii) provisional tax payments, including the third payment described under "Payment of Tax" below (if any), (iii) the final balance of company income tax due by the company and (iv) the due date of payment.

B. Individuals

Individuals must file returns of income within sixty days of a date published by the Commissioner. Husbands and wives file separate returns. This date is normally in mid-March, but taxpayers who are unable to file their returns by mid-May may apply for an extension. Usually an extension of a number of months is granted. Tax return forms are mailed to all registered taxpayers. Individuals who are not registered and taxpayers who do not receive forms but are required to file returns must obtain forms from the tax authorities. Particulars of all (i) income, property or share transactions, (ii) deductions claimed and (iii) donations made in excess of R5,000 or received in excess of R3,000 must be included in an individual's return.

An individual whose employment income does not exceed R50,000 and who is not in receipt of any other income does not generally need to file a return. Standard income tax on employees ("SITE") deductions are regarded as fully accounting for the tax liability.

Unlike companies, individuals are not obliged to make any calculations for assessment purposes. However, they may do so if they wish. Tax information brochures enable them to do this. Assessment procedures are basically the same as for companies. An additional item shown on the official assessment for an individual is the figure for the SITE and pay-as-you-earn ("PAYE") deductions.

III. Tax Audits

There is no formal system of government tax audits in South Africa. Audits take place from time to time on an ad hoc basis.

IV. Payment Of Tax
A. Companies

A company is required to make two provisional payments during each financial year on account of income tax finally assessable on the year's results. These two payments are usually based on the actual taxable income for the latest financial year for which the company has been assessed. In the case of the second payment, however, the company may choose to base the payment on an estimated figure of taxable income lower than its taxable income as last assessed, as long as the company is certain that the two provisional payments will, in the aggregate, be within 10% of the final assessed tax liability for the current year. If the provisional payments turn out not to be within this limit, the taxpayer must pay penalties. The first provisional payment is made at the end of the first six months of the company's current financial year, and the second at the year-end. Each payment is equal to roughly half of the total tax ultimately payable for the year, provided that taxable income does not fluctuate significantly compared with the previous year.

A company with taxable income of more than R20,000 in a financial year must ensure that the balance of any tax due on that year's income after deducting the two provisional payments is paid within six months following its year-end. If a company fails to make this third payment within this time limit and its tax liability as finally determined by the tax authorities proves to be more than the sum of the two provisional payments, interest is charged on the amount of the shortfall. The interest is charged at a prescribed rate, which is changed from time to time, from the end of the six-month period until the date of the official assessment. The Commissioner has discretion to reduce the amount of interest payable if the company had reasonable grounds for arriving at a figure of taxable income lower than that finally assessed.

When provisional payments, together with any third payment, fall short of the tax finally assessed, the balance is payable on the due date indicated by the assessment. Overpayments are generally refunded with interest calculated from six months after the end of the tax year.

B.   Individuals

Individuals receiving substantial income not subject to SITE and PAYE deductions are required to make two provisional tax payments per year. Furthermore, when such a taxpayer has taxable income of more than R50,000, he or she must make a third payment by August 31st in order to discharge fully the tax liability for the year. These rules are similar to those for companies.

Any balance of income tax due — after taking into account SITE and PAYE deductions, the semiannual provisional payments and the third payment described above — is payable on the due date indicated by the official assessment. Overpayments of PAYE (but not SITE) and provisional tax are refunded. Interest at 15% is charged on overdue tax.

An individual leaving the country permanently or indefinitely is usually required to file an interim return of income and pay any taxes due before departing. A visitor from abroad is not required to obtain a tax clearance before leaving the country. However, if the visitor has received any taxable income from South African sources during his or her stay, the tax authorities have the right to demand a return of income, issue an assessment and require payment of any tax due before the visitor's departure.

V. Disputes And Appeals

A taxpayer may dispute the correctness of an assessment, including some discretionary decisions of the Commissioner, by filing a written objection within thirty days following the date of the assessment notice. This objection must specify in detail the grounds for the objection. If the objection is disallowed, the taxpayer may appeal to the Special Court for Hearing Income Tax Appeals (the "Special Court"). If the taxpayer or the tax authorities is not satisfied with the decision of the Special Court, either party may appeal to the Supreme Court.

A specially constituted board is available to deal in the first instance with small appeals — namely, those involving tax of less than R20,000 and those to which the Commissioner gives consent. Persons aggrieved by a decision of the board may appeal to the Special Court.

A. Penalties

The Commissioner may by way of penalty impose additional tax of up to twice the normal tax payable if the taxpayer:
- does not render a return for any particular year of assessment;
- omits from a return any amount that should have been included; or
- makes an incorrect statement in a return that results, or would result, if accepted, in a lesser amount of tax being assessed than would otherwise be the case.

The penalty is in addition to the tax ordinarily chargeable on the income of the taxpayer and may be imposed not only for tax evasion but also for errors or omissions caused by carelessness or negligence on the part of the taxpayer. When the taxpayer has not deliberately evaded tax, however, the penalty is likely to be substantially reduced if not completely waived.

When a taxpayer has been assessed a tax and fails to pay any amount due under the assessment within the time allowed for payment, interest is payable on the amount outstanding at a prescribed rate, currently 15% per annum. Penalties and interest payable on the late payment of income tax are not deductible for income tax purposes.

In addition to the penalties and interest described above, fines and imprisonment can be imposed on taxpayers for a number of offenses.

Johannesburg, South Africa
June 1996

CHAPTER 8

TRADE REGULATION IN SOUTH AFRICA

By Leora Blumberg

I.   Background

South Africa was one of the founding members of the General Agreement on Tariffs and Trade (the GATT) and has always participated in the various rounds of negotiations. South Africa was not, however, a disciplined member of the GATT and tended to be protectionist in nature, pursuing a policy of import replacement, because of international sanctions against South Africa and because of its balance-of-payments problems. However, after decades of political and economic isolation, South Africa has undergone a major political transition. South Africa has once again become part of the international trading community and has had to re-address its international economic relations.

In the Uruguay Round, South Africa came under pressure from its major trading partners to fall in line with the GATT philosophy, and to make a substantial move to open its markets or face retaliation. Although the Uruguay Round was signed by the previous Government, its principles have been embraced by the ANC-led[1] Government of National Unity, elected in April 1994, which has confirmed South Africa's commitment to the GATT and to liberalization.

On 2 December 1994, South Africa deposited with the Secretariat of the GATT, a signed instrument of accession to the Agreement establishing the World Trade Organization (the WTO). It thereby became a member of the WTO and a party to all the multilateral agreements concluded in the Uruguay Round of trade negotiations, including the Agreement on the Implementation of Article VI of the GATT (the AD Agreement) and the Subsidies and Countervailing Measures Agreement (the SCM Agreement).

On 6 April 1995, Parliament approved the accession, subsequent to recommendations from both houses of Parliament, in accordance with the new Constitution of South Africa[2]. Parliament has not, however, declared that the Uruguay Round Agreements form part of the domestic law of South Africa, and therefore the Agreements cannot be invoked by citizens against the Government. This was probably a deliberate omission, and it is unlikely at this stage that Parliament will, in fact, take this step in the future.

II.   Industrial Products

In accordance with its Uruguay Round obligations, South Africa has bound (that is, set maximum limits upon) virtually all of the tariffs on industrial products. These tariffs include those that replaced the remaining quantitative restrictions and the

---

1   African National Congress.

2   Act No. 200 of 1993.

so-called formula duties[3]. By virtue of being bound, the tariffs cannot be increased above their bound levels except in accordance with special procedures allowed by the GATT. The tariffs on industrial products are generally bound at the following rates: 0% to 10% for primary and semi-primary products, and capital products, 10% to 15% for components and 15% to 30% for consumer products.

In the Uruguay Round, South Africa typically bound its maximum tariffs, which then became the point of departure for the staged reductions. In many cases, however, the effective tariff was lower than the maximum tariff, and South Africa chose to begin its reductions from the lower level, although it was not required to do so by its international obligations.

The tariffs on industrial products will generally be reduced in five equal annual stages. The first stage took effect on 27 January 1995, and the fifth stage is scheduled to take effect on 1 January 1999. The final bound rates represent an average reduction of 27% on industrial products.

III. Sensitive Industries

Some industries, including the automobile and textile and clothing industries, were protected by very high tariffs under the previous protectionist regime. As a result, their reduction will generally be more than the average of 27% for industrial products, but the phasing-down will take longer than the standard five years.

For the automobile industry, South Africa's GATT obligations were to reduce tariffs over eight years (with a four-year standstill) from 100% to 50% on motor vehicles, from 49% to 30% on components for original equipment, and from 50% to 30% on replacement parts. South Africa accelerated its schedule and reduced the tariff on built up motor vehicles to 70% last year. This was further reduced to 65% on 1 September 1995 and will be phased down to 40% by 1 January 2002. In the case of components imported as original equipment, duties will be reduced to 30% by 1 January 2002.

For the textile and clothing industries, South Africa's GATT obligations were to reduce tariffs over twelve years (with a four-year standstill) from 100% to 45% on clothing, from 50% to 25% on fabrics, from 35% to 17.5% on yarn, from 15% to 10% on fibers, and from 60% to 30% on household textiles. The Government's proposals are that the reductions will be greater and take place over a shorter term than is required by GATT, that is, the following duties are to be achieved in seven years: 40% on

---

3   A formula duty consists of a certain sum in Rand per unit of quantity (referred to as the reference price) less a percentage ad valorem on the export price. In most cases the effect of such a formula is that, where the export price of any consignment is less than the reference price, the duty will be equal to the normal ad valorem duty on that export price, plus the full amount of the difference between the reference price and the export price. Therefore in effect, the lower the price, the higher the duty.

clothing, 30% on household textiles, 22% on fabrics, 15% on yarn, and 7.5% on polyester fibre. A number of reductions were initiated on 1 September 1995.

IV. Agricultural Products

South Africa is committed to fulfilling its obligations under the Agreement on Agriculture.

First, South Africa eliminated most export subsidies on agricultural products, effective 1 January 1995. It did so in spite of the fact that its formal obligation was only to reduce export subsidies over time. South Africa intends to phase out the remaining export subsidy by 1997.

Second, South Africa will reduce its domestic price-support programs by 20% over six years, that is, by 3.3% per year, using a base rate of the average of the years 1986 to 1988. For the year 1995 South Africa was well within its commitment levels (although this was in part due to the high world prices in respect of a number of products)

Third, South Africa will eliminate all quantitative restrictions on agricultural products and convert these measures to customs duties. The policy has been that the customs duty should result in domestic production and consumption being more or less the same as was the case under import control. This process started in 1994 and is almost completed with the exception of a few products. South Africa has also begun to reduce its tariffs on agricultural products (once converted from quantitative restrictions) by 36%, on average, over six years.

Fourth, South Africa is obliged to provide minimum market access opportunities in respect of certain products. This obligation means that in respect of certain products a certain volume of imports should be allowed at a level of duty which is not higher than 20 per cent of the level to which the duty should be reduced, that is, the binding. In practice this obligation will be met by the creation of rebate provisions for each of the products concerned. These rebate provisions will be subject to permits issued by the Director-General of Agriculture.

V. Import Controls

In the early 1980's, more than three quarters of imports into South Africa were subject to import controls, consisting of import licenses and quantitative restrictions. Since that time, South Africa has been progressively phasing-out these controls and replacing them with tariffs. Those products that are currently involved in this process include textiles, clothing, rope and cable, certain metal products, arms and ammunition, and certain chemicals.

Under the authority of the Safeguards Agreement, which South Africa signed as one of the Uruguay Round agreements, South Africa is maintaining for four years controls over imports of petroleum and oil products, polymers, tires, and other rubber products. In general, the Safeguards Agreement allows a country to maintain controls over an article that is being imported in such increased quantities as to cause or threaten serious injury to a domestic industry.

Import controls will not be abolished over a few specified products, such as those that harm the environment.

VI. Import Surcharges

In 1985, South Africa introduced import surcharges. They originally covered numerous agricultural and industrial products and ranged from 5% to 40%. In 1994, the import surcharges applicable to capital and intermediate products (that is, those subject to a rate of 5%) were lifted. The remaining surcharges, ranging from 10% to 40%, covered electrical products, such as television sets and video cassette recorders, and appliances, like refrigerators, toasters and stereos. On 1 October 1995 these remaining import surcharges were abolished.

Certain preferential trade agreements with some Eastern and Central European countries, which allowed for the reduction or elimination of import surcharges, have therefore become redundant.

VII. Anti-Dumping and Countervailing Actions

Anti-dumping and countervailing legislation existed in the Customs and Excise Act[4] (the Customs Act) for decades, but there were very few anti-dumping investigations before 1992, mainly because local producers were able to use other more effective mechanisms to achieve the same (or better) results, such as formula duties[5], import controls, and applications for ad hoc increases in duties. However, these protectionist mechanisms were placed under the GATT spotlight, and have generally been dismantled. Increasing importance is now being placed on anti-dumping and countervailing measures, perceived to be the only remedies available to local producers facing the threat of low-priced imports, in an environment of reducing tariffs.

New anti-dumping and countervailing legislation was introduced in South Africa in May 1992, in the form of amendments to the Board of Trade and Industry Act, now renamed the Board on Tariffs and Trade Act[6] (the Board Act), and the Customs Act. The 1992 amending acts substantially narrowed the objects of the renamed "Board on Tariffs and Trade" (the Board) with more of an emphasis on investigations in connection with dumping, subsidies and a new concept of "disruptive competition".

The Board is a statutory body established in terms of the Board Act with Board members appointed by the State President by reason of their knowledge of and expertise in commerce, industry and the economy. The Board is the primary body concerned with anti-dumping and countervailing investigations and reports to and makes recommendations to the Minister of Trade and Industry (the Trade Minister).

---

4   Act No.91 of 1964.

5   See Note 3 above.

6   Act No. 107 of 1986.

The Board Act[7] provides that the Board may of its own accord investigate dumping in or to the Republic and, if authorized thereto by an agreement, in or to the common customs area of the Southern African Customs Union[8] (SACU). It is also provided that the Board may by order of the Trade Minister investigate any other matter which affects or may affect the trade and industry of the Republic and, if authorized thereto by an agreement, the common customs area of the SACU.

The basic procedure in terms of the Board Act and the Customs Act is that the Board conducts the anti-dumping or countervailing investigation and makes a recommendation to the Trade Minister who may accept or reject the recommendation.

If the recommendation is accepted by the Trade Minister, he will "request" the Minister of Finance to impose an anti-dumping duty and to amend the tariff schedules accordingly[9]. The reason for the involvement of the Department of Finance is that it is the only government department authorized to collect duties. The 1992 legislation, however, purported to limit the discretion of the Minister of Finance, with his only real function being the imposition and collection of duties, and with real control being given to the Board under the auspices of the Trade Minister.

The South African legislation, as introduced in 1992, was very rudimentary, and made no reference to a number of important international concepts, such as injury, dumping margin and causation. There was also no reference in either the Board Act or the Customs Act to the procedure of anti-dumping and countervailing actions. Although the Board Act provides for the promulgation of regulations, no regulations have yet been promulgated. At the time that the legislation was enacted in 1992, however, a document was published by the Board entitled, "Guide to the Policy and Procedure with Regard to Action against Unfair International Trade Practises: Dumping, Subsidies and other forms of Disruptive Competition" (the Guide). The 18 page Guide, which does not have any formal legislative force or effect, makes reference to South Africa's obligations to GATT, addresses some of the issues omitted in the legislation and sets out the procedure of an anti-dumping action in layman's terms.

---

7   Section 4 of Act No. 107 of 1986.

8   The Southern African Customs Union Agreement was concluded between the Governments of South Africa, the Republic of Botswana, the Kingdom of Lesotho and the Kingdom of Swaziland, on 11 December 1969, providing for the continuance of the custom union arrangements which had been in operation between the four countries since 1910. Namibia became a member of SACU after its independence in 1990. The SACU Agreement provides for South African law and customs regulation to be the central point around which the SACU operates and that members of the SACU implement the South African tariff as a common external tariff. It is specifically provided that the Governments apply laws (and any amendments thereto) relating to customs in force in South Africa from time to time (which would include anti-dumping and countervailing duties).

9   Section 4(2) of Act No. 107 of 1986.

When the legislation was introduced in 1992, various concerns were expressed by local industry and business organizations. It was recognized that the legislation was contrary to the GATT, and that it gave the Board an extremely wide discretion. The previous Government recognized its shortcomings in experience and resources in the implementation of anti-dumping and countervailing legislation and appeared to be giving itself some freedom to maneuver in its implementation of the legislation during the learning phase while committing itself to bring its legislation in line with GATT principles in the future.

Since the new legislation was introduced, local producers have vigorously used the legislation, with approximately 35 anti-dumping investigations being formally instituted since 1992. Presently there is no right of appeal from the Board's decisions. The only remedy for an aggrieved party is a review by the Supreme Court, based on the limited common law grounds of review (which do not extend to the merits of the case), such as, procedural unfairness, error of fact, misinterpretation of the law or unreasonableness. In the first Supreme Court review of an anti-dumping action, the State Attorney raised a technical preliminary point, the effect of which, if successful would have meant that a decision of the Board cannot be reviewed, even if based on dishonesty or fraud. This argument was, however, dismissed by the judge, reconfirming the principle of judicial review in respect of anti-dumping investigations.[10] There is, as yet, no actual case law on the anti-dumping legislation. However, as mentioned above, the first Supreme Court review of an anti-dumping investigation has now been instituted, which will result in the first judicial pronouncements on the subject.

Criticism has been levied against the Board in its implementation of the legislation, by all parties: local producers and unions, on the one hand, who believe that the anti-dumping legislation and procedure is not effective and that the Board is not sufficiently responsive to their particular problems, and, on the other hand, foreign exporters and importers who believe that the legislation is a new form of protectionism. In addition, there has been concern by South Africa's international trading partners as to its compliance with the requirements of the GATT, and now the WTO. Over the past four years the Board has, however, gained some experience and has developed its expertise in anti-dumping procedures. There is no doubt, however, that the South African legislation and procedure needs to be substantially overhauled in order to comply with the GATT and the WTO Agreements.

At the end of 1994 the Trade and Industry Working Group of the National Economic Forum[11] published a report on Anti-dumping and Countervailing Measures, and

---

10 Brenco Incorporated and Others v Chairman of the Board on Tariffs and Trade (unreported).

11 The National Economic Forum was launched in October 1992 with organized business, organized labor and the governing authority as principal participants. The NEF was established to provide a mechanism through which major economic stakeholders could address the economic challenges facing the coun-
(continued...)

has made certain policy proposals (the NEF Report). The purpose of the NEF Report was to review anti-dumping and countervailing measures in the SACU with particular reference to administrative procedures, organizational structure and legislation, and to make recommendations to the Cabinet. It was recognized in the NEF Report that anti-dumping and countervailing legislation and procedures must conform to the provisions of the GATT and the WTO Agreement and that the legislation would need to be substantially amended. The NEF Report recommended that a new statutory body (other than the Board) be formed, an "Anti-dumping Authority", which would be responsible for conducting anti-dumping investigations and should be seen as completely neutral and objective. The NEF Report was handed to the Trade Minister in early 1995.

On 31 August 1995, the Board on Tariffs and Trade Amendment Act[12] (the Amendment Act) was passed. The Amendment Act simply amended the definitions of dumping in the Board Act to comply more with the definitions in the GATT and the AD Agreement. The Amendment Act, however, did not deal with the restructuring of the legislation or the institutions, and was generally considered to be an interim measure, pending a complete restructuring.

At the end of 1995 the Trade Minister announced the appointment of an international trade lawyer, active in the area in South Africa, to the position of Deputy Chairperson of the Board, to lead the restructuring of the anti-dumping/countervailing system in accordance with the requirements of the WTO. The new Deputy Chairperson was appointed by the State President in accordance with the Board Act and took up office in January 1996.

The restructuring process has also now been formalized by an "Order" by the Trade Minister in terms of the Board Act[13], for the Board to urgently investigate the restructuring of the anti-dumping/countervailing system with a view to ensuring compliance with the requirements of the WTO and to take forward the proposals of the NEF Report. Notice of this investigation was published in the Government Gazette on 15 March 1996 and all interested parties were invited to submit comments.

There is no doubt that with South Africa's changing trade policy and international economic relations, there will be greater anti-dumping activity. As repeatedly stated by the new Government, protection on demand is dead, and local producers can no longer expect to invoke the protectionist mechanisms that were so readily available in the days of sanctions and import replacement. Tariffs are reducing and local industries, nurtured on protection, will be facing serious threats from foreign competi-

---

11 (...continued)
    try and seek consensus on their resolution principally during the transition and potentially thereafter. It has subsequently been replaced by the National Economic Development and Labor Council (NEDLAC) which includes organizations of community development interests, in addition to the interests represented on the NEF.

12   Act No. 39 of 1995.

13   Section 4(1) of Act No. 107 of 1986.

tors. South Africa is a vulnerable economy and clearly attracting the attention of some major international players, who effectively ignored the South African market in the days of sanctions.

Anti-dumping actions can have a great impact on all parties, whether manufacturers, importers or exporters. Effective anti-dumping legislation is vital for South Africa in the new more liberalized trading order. At the same time, it should be clear and transparent and should not be used as a non-tariff barrier in the face of the dismantling of protectionism, with the potential to incur the wrath of our trading partners and inviting WTO complaints and retaliation.

The new Government of National Unity has committed itself to liberalization and GATT compliance. There is a clear recognition that South Africa has to abide by GATT principles and adhere to the Uruguay Round, including the AD and SCM Agreements. The problems of the current anti-dumping legislation and practice have been recognized, and there is a clear intention to amend the legislation and practice to comply with the AD Agreement.

VIII. Safeguard Actions

Safeguard duties may be imposed above GATT bindings when increased imports are causing or threatening serious injury to an industry in the importing country. In the case of safeguard duties, the GATT requires the country imposing such duties to make up for their imposition by granting tariff concessions to the exporting country or to suffer retaliation by the exporting country in the form of higher tariffs.

Although the Board Act enables the Board to investigate, report and make recommendations to the Trade Minister on "disruptive competition"[14] and the Customs Act allows for the imposition of a "safeguards duty"[15], these provisions have not been utilized and the Board has not yet conducted such an investigation. The legislation and administrative procedures clearly also need to be amended to ensure compliance with the requirements of the Safeguards Agreement, before South Africa could utilize these procedures in terms of the requirements of the WTO.

IX. Intellectual Property Rights

South Africa's laws for the protection of intellectual property are generally in conformity with industrialized nations. In particular, South Africa does not discriminate between domestic and international holders of intellectual property rights.

South Africa is a long-standing member of the Paris and Berne Conventions. It has also enacted the Patent Act No. 57 of 1978, as amended, and the Copyright Act No. 98 of 1978, as amended.

---

14   Section 4(1)(a)(i) of Act No. 107 of 1986.

15   Section 57 of Act No. 91 of 1964.

One of the major Uruguay Round agreements signed by South Africa is the Agreement on Trade-Related Aspects of Intellectual Property Rights (TRIPS). By virtue of the two conventions and two statutes cited above, South Africa is already in substantial compliance with the TRIPS requirements concerning patents and copyrights (including computer programs and compilations of data).

The new Trademark Act No. 194 of 1993, which came into force on 1 May 1995, generally follows the principles of the Paris Convention and TRIPS.

The new Designs Act No. 195 of 1993, which also came into force on 1 May 1995, will meet the TRIPS requirement for protecting integrated-circuit typographics and layout design. The Designs Act also introduces a registration system which provides protection for the proprietor of a functional industry design for 10 years, and for the proprietor of an aesthetic industrial design for 15 years, from the date of registration or issue, whichever is earlier.

X. Preferential Trade Relations

South Africa participates in a number of preferential trade relationships, both regional and bilateral. The most important is the South African Customs Union (SACU) of 1968, which consists of Botswana, Lesotho, Namibia, South Africa, and Swaziland.[16] With few exceptions, free and unimpeded trade takes place among the SACU members. There have historically been a number of political, economic and fiscal problems associated with the SACU, which are currently being addressed in the new political environment. The SACU is currently undergoing a major restructuring in the near future.

In 1994, South Africa became a member of the South African Development Community (SADC). The other members are Angola, Botswana, Lesotho, Malawi, Mozambique, Namibia, Swaziland, Tanzania, Zambia, and Zimbabwe. Mauritius has only recently become a member. The SADC agreement is phrased in terms of general objectives, rather than detailed obligations. However, more detailed obligations are envisaged in terms of protocols. The members are presently negotiating a trade protocol which will over time eliminate trade barriers among themselves.

South Africa has concluded bilateral preferential trade agreements with neighboring countries such as Malawi, Mozambique and Zimbabwe which grants bilateral trade preferences. The trade agreement with Zimbabwe, is currently being renegotiated, and is subject to some controversy, particularly in respect of the textile industry.

South Africa is also negotiating a preferential trade agreement with the European Union (EU). The EU's proposal envisages immediate duty-free treatment of South African exports to the EU and duty-free treatment of EU exports to South Africa that would be phased-in over 10 years. Finality has not, however, yet been reached by the parties. South Africa is particularly concerned about the EU's exclusion from the arrangement of about 40% of South Africa's agricultural exports to the EU.

XI. Exports

---

16   See Footnote 8 above.

The General Export Incentive Scheme (GEIS) was introduced on 1 April 1990 for an initial period of 5 years which ended on 31 March 1995. It was intended to counteract the anti-export bias in the South African economy. Inter alia, the scheme was intended to encourage high levels of beneficiation of products before export and the exports of products with a high South African content, taking into account fluctuations in the exchange rate of the Rand against the currency of South Africa's main trading partners, as well as the effects of inflation on the Rand.

It has been recognized that the GEIS is clearly in contravention of the GATT and the SCM Agreement, and South Africa committed itself to phase out the GEIS in three years. It was also recognized that GEIS, being open-ended, was a tremendous strain on the fiscus, and that the benefits would be reduced forthwith.

The first change was the announcement in the 1994/5 Budget that GEIS benefits would be taxable with effect from March 1995. At the end of 1994, after extensive deliberations in the National Economic Forum (now the National Economic, Development and Labor Council)[17], a revised general export incentive scheme was developed which entailed a downward adjustment of the GEIS benefit levels, the elimination of certain structural imbalances (eliminating relative primary products from benefits), and the eventual termination of the scheme on 31 December 1997 in compliance with South Africa's commitments.

Simultaneously with the announcements of these changes, the Trade Minister, stated his intention, to implement other WTO friendly "supply side" measures as GEIS is phased out. As recently as last month, it was announced that due to budgetary restraints GEIS would in fact be phased down quicker than previously announced.

There are, however, new opportunities for South African exports in the new trade environment. As a result of the Uruguay Round, tariffs are reducing world wide, opening up new markets for South African exports. A number of industrialized countries have made available their Generalized System of Preferences (GSP), giving access to South African exports with preferential or zero tariffs for a number of products. Although these GSP schemes are generally only made available to developing countries, the goodwill generated by South Africa's political transition led to a number of developed countries (such as, the United States, European Union, Canada, Japan and Norway) granting South Africa these benefits, despite its classification as a developed country.

It should also be realized, however, that South African exports are exposed to an increased risk of trade actions. South African exports are now possibly more vulnerable than ever for a number of reasons. Firstly, as tariffs are reduced in accordance with the Uruguay Round obligations, there is likely to be a worldwide increase in anti-dumping actions as it is one of the only GATT mechanisms that can be used against low-priced imports. Secondly, because of sanctions, there has been a culture of charging high prices on the domestic market, which is not yet a thing of the past. This increases the likelihood of anti-dumping actions against South African exports. Thirdly, although GEIS is being phased out, the exports still receiving benefits

---

17   See Footnote 11 above.

are "countervailable" in terms of the Uruguay Round Subsidies Agreement if they cause injury to another country.

XII. Conclusion

The Uruguay Round symbolizes the final movement away from the increasing trade protectionism of the 1930's and a movement towards a more open trading system. A failure to conclude the Uruguay Round could have unleashed protectionism on both sides of the Atlantic, with serious implications for the whole world. There is now no doubt that the trade winds are blowing favorably again. South Africa may be faced with many problems in coming to terms with dismantling protectionism. However, what must be remembered is that enormous opportunities and challenges will undoubtedly open up, particularly with South Africa's new political legitimacy. The only way forward for South Africa is towards GATT compliance and discipline and to become a more participative member of the international trade community.

Johannesburg, South Africa
May 1996

CHAPTER 9

COMPETITION LAW

By Pierre E. J. Brooks

I.   Introduction

Competition law is a crucial component of a country's overall competition policy which usually also encompasses other measures that enhance competition, such as economic deregulation, liberalized trade policies, and lenient foreign investment and ownerships requirements.

The rules governing competition have both a private (common) law and a public law dimension. The principal thrust of the common law is to protect what may be defined as a person's "right to attract custom." As a general rule, the effective exploitation of the right to attract custom requires a distinctive product, trade name, trademark, etc. It sometimes happens that the pursuit of the right to attract custom by one person could wrongfully impinge upon another's right to attract custom. There are various manifestations of such wrongful conduct, including passing off, the acquisition and use of a competitor's trade secrets, the undue influencing of a competitor's clients, disparaging a competitor's products or spreading falsehoods about his person, business or products, competition in breach of a statutory duty, and boycott actions. In cases of this kind, the remedial action is before the ordinary civil courts of the country where the recovery of damages is in accordance with the principles of aquilian liability.

In the public law domain, the Maintenance and Promotion of Competition Act of 1979 (the "Act") is the governing statute. Although South Africa has had legislation dealing with restrictive business practices for a long time, it was only when the Act came into force on January 1, 1980 that a more comprehensive competition law regime was established. This review deals solely with the salient features of that dispensation. However, it must be recognized that a particular set of facts could give rise to actions under either the common law or in terms of the Act.

II.   Exclusions

The Act expressly does not limit the rights acquired under intellectual (industrial) property statutes (trademarks, designs, plant breeders, patents, and copyright), provided that such rights are not used to enhance or maintain the price of commodities. Furthermore, the Act cannot be construed to prevent organizations of employees from protecting the interests of their members by entering into agreements or arrangements with employers in respect of matters covered by the applicable law governing labor relations. Subject to the qualifications mentioned below, the Act applies to all sectors of the economy.

Some statutes or other enactments contain provisions which are at variance with the provisions and underlying philosophy of the Act. In terms of the accepted canons of statute interpretation, they will, as a general rule, take precedence over the Act and may accordingly, either expressly or by necessary implication, exclude the Act's operation in certain sectors or in respect of certain activities.

III. Competition Board

The Act established the Competition Board (the "Board") as an autonomous statutory body with an investigative and advisory competence relating to matters regulated by the Act. It comprises a maximum of fourteen members who are either appointed by the Ministers of Trade and Industry, Finance, and Agriculture, or the nominee of the Governor of the Reserve Bank, or serve in an *ex officio* capacity. The chairman of the Board is a full-time member. At present, all the other members serve on a part-time basis. The Board is assisted in the performance of its functions by career civil servants who are collectively termed the Directorate: Investigations of the Competition Board.

The Board is empowered to undertake investigations into restrictive practices, acquisitions, and monopoly situations and, following the completion of such investigations, to make recommendations to the Minister of Trade and Industry (the "Minister") on what action, if any, he should take to remedy the situation. It must be emphasized that the Act does not specifically prohibit restrictive practices, acquisition or monopoly situations. However, in the appropriate circumstances, they could be prohibited by the Minister acting on a recommendation by the Board.

IV. Restrictive practices

A restrictive practice is defined in the Act to mean:
- (a) any agreement, arrangement or understanding, whether legally enforceable or not, between two or more persons; or
- (b) any business practice or method of trading, including any method of fixing prices, whether by the supplier of any commodity or otherwise; or
- (c) any act or omission on the part of any person, whether acting independently or in concert with any other person; or
- (d) any situation arising out of the activities of any person or class or group of persons,

which restricts competition directly or indirectly by having or being likely to have the effect of:
- (i) restricting the production or distribution of any commodity; or
- (ii) limiting the facilities available for the production or distribution of any commodity; or
- (iii) enhancing or maintaining the price of or any other consideration for any commodity; or
- (iv) preventing the production or distribution of any commodity by the most efficient and economical means; or
- (v) preventing or retarding the development or introduction of technical improvements or the expansion of existing markets or the opening up of new markets; or
- (vi) preventing or restricting the entry of new producers or distributors into any branch of trade or industry; or

(vii) preventing or retarding the adjustment of any profession or branch of trade or industry to changing circumstances.

"Commodity" encompasses both goods and services.

The definition of a restrictive practice may conveniently be divided into cause and effect components. It is only if the act, omission or situation mentioned in (a) to (d) restricts competition directly or indirectly by having one of the effects mentioned in (i) to (vii) that one has to do with a restrictive practice. "Restrict competition" is not a concept that is defined in the Act. Making a judgment in respect thereof requires identifying the relevant market as an important first step in that process.

Markets exist in two main dimensions, namely products (goods and services) and geographical area. Cognizance is also taken of the relevant functional market. This relates to the "level" at which a firm operates in the life cycle of a product, for example, the production, distribution (wholesale) or retail level. Furthermore, in demarcating the relevant product market, substitute products are also taken into account.

Competition is a process which manifests itself as independent rivalry between enterprises on a market in respect of all the dimensions of the price -- product -- service package offered to customers and consumers. If as a result of a particular transaction the market is obviously less conducive to inter-enterprise rivalry, or if the ability of one or more enterprises to compete effectively is significantly impaired, or if the barriers to entry become more onerous, it will be accepted that competition will be restricted.

In common with the practice in other jurisdictions, certain pernicious forms of anti-competitive behavior have been identified and outlawed. More particularly, following an investigation by the Board, Government Notice 801 of May 2, 1986 was promulgated by the Minister. It prohibits resale price maintenance, price fixing, market sharing, horizontal collusion on conditions of supply, and collusive tendering. The prohibition does not apply in respect of any agreement, arrangement, understanding, business practice or method of trading:

(1) between or among:
    (a) a holding company and its wholly-owned subsidiary, or between companies which are wholly-owned subsidiaries of the same holding company;
    (b) close corporations which have only the same person or persons as members;
    (c) companies of which all the shares are held by the same person or close corporation, or between such close corporation and such companies; or
    (d) persons in relation to goods which are exported to any country outside the Southern African Customs Union; or
(2) authorized by the provisions of any law.

The Act allows the Minister, acting on a recommendation of the Board in a particular case, to grant an exemption from one or more of the prohibitions set out in Government Notice 801. Parties seeking an exemption must convince the Board that an exemption is warranted. The greater the extent of the relevant market affected by the unlawful conduct in question and the more numerous the specific forms of such conduct for which exemption is sought, the more convincing the evidence and arguments on which the applicants seek to rely should be. Subjective and unsubstantiated opinions or speculation will not suffice to discharge the onus which rests with the applicants.

Although not restricted in respect of the factors it may take into account in assessing the merits of an application for exemption, the Board would usually be more inclined to do so where the conduct under scrutiny would:

(a) result in an appreciable quantifiable economic benefit for consumers over an extended period of time, or
(b) enhance competition in the relevant market, for example, where small firms can demonstrate that an exemption would enable them to compete more effectively with other large firms.

All complaints of restrictive practices other than those falling within the ambit of Government Notice 801 are dealt with on a case-by-case basis. In assessing the merits of such complaints, the Board follows what may be regarded as a rule of reason approach, which essentially entails forming a judgement about the competitive significance of the restraint. Factors which are taken into account in this process include the market power of the parties concerned, the extent of interbrand competition on the market, the extent of foreclosure resulting from the practice, the impact thereof on competitors, and any business justification arguments for the practice that may be advanced. Practices by firms having market power which have in the past been found to restrict competition include refusal to deal, discriminatory pricing policies, exclusive dealing, tying arrangements, boycott actions, and onerous restraint of trade clauses.

V. Acquisitions

The South African economy is characterized by high levels of concentration in a number of markets and extensive corporate conglomeration which places a substantial portion of the country's economic resources under the control of a few major groups. The relatively small size of the economy, sanctions, and disinvestment during the apartheid era, and stringent exchange control regulations have contributed to this state of affairs.

The Board has jurisdiction to scrutinize all takeovers and mergers in terms of which the holder of a controlling interest in any business acquires such an interest in any other business operating in the same relevant market, or in any asset of the latter business, provided the acquisition of such a controlling interest restricts competition to an appreciable extent.

Various factors are taken into account in determining whether competition in the relevant market has been, or is likely to be, appreciably restricted, including:

(a) the actual and potential level of import competition in the market;
(b) barriers to entry;
(c) the level of concentration in the market;
(d) the degree of countervailing power in the market;
(e) the likelihood that significant and substantially higher prices or profit margins would result;

(f) the extent to which substitute products are, or are likely to be, available;
(g) the dynamic characteristics of the market, including growth, innovation, and product differentiation;
(h) whether competitive parity among rival firms in the market would be unduly distorted; and
(i) the nature and extent of vertical integration in the market.

The degree of concentration in a market serves as a useful preliminary screening device in assessing whether a takeover or merger is likely to have an adverse effect on competition. For example, a combined post-acquisition market share of under 10 percent will not give rise to any concerns, and it will accordingly not be necessary to assess the impact of any of the other above-mentioned factors on the transaction. On the other hand, high market shares will not necessarily be determinative of the issue, in which case, the above-mentioned factors come into play.

Parties involved in a merger or acquisition may of their own volition, and shall when required by the Board to do so, provide the Board with the necessary information relating to the transaction in accordance with the Guidelines on Acquisitions of Control to enable it to make a meaningful appraisal of the transaction. Mergers or acquisitions can be cleared unconditionally or condoned subject to compliance with the conditions that may be imposed.

VI. Monopoly Situation

"Monopoly situation" means a situation where any person, or two or more persons with a substantial economic connection, control in the Republic or any part thereof, wholly or to a large extent, the class of business in which he, she or they are engaged in respect of any commodity. "Class of business" is not defined in the Act, but the Supreme Court, in a non-antitrust context, has held in regard to the sale of goods that there are different classes of business according to the difference in character of the goods sold and the varying manners in which business is conducted. If one utilizes this dictum in the interpretation of the definition of "monopoly situation," it is arguable that "class of business" is a more tightly delineated market than the traditional "relevant market."

A number of factors, any one of which, when taken separately, need not necessarily be determinative, have a bearing on whether a person controls a class of business, including

(a) the market share, technical knowledge, and access to raw materials and capital resources of the person whose situation is being assessed;
(b) the comparative strength of that person's competitors, if any, in the relevant class of business and the ease with which new competitors could enter such a business; and
(c) the extent to which that person is constrained by the suppliers or acquirers of goods or services in the relevant class of business.

Before it can be accepted that two or more persons control a class of business which none of the parties is able to do when acting unilaterally, it must be shown that there is a substantial economic connection between them. This is a question of fact to be assessed on a case-by-case basis. The relationship between a holding company and its subsidiaries, or between a controlling company and the companies it controls, points inexorably to such a connection. And so too, arguably, does a crossholding of shares of significant proportions coupled with interlocking directorates.

VII. Public Interest

The Act implicitly creates a rebuttable presumption that restrictive practices and acquisitions that restrict competition to an appreciable extent are against the public interest. On the other hand, unless the facts indicate otherwise, monopoly situations per se are not presumed to be against the public interest.

The position is that parties involved in restrictive practices or mergers and acquisitions could utilize the public interest factor as an escape mechanism justifying their actions. "Public interest" is an open-ended concept. The efficacy and credibility of competition law would be seriously undermined if unsubstantiated claims of alleged public interest benefits were routinely allowed to prevail over evidence that a particular transaction restricted competition on the relevant market. For this reason it is necessary for parties seeking condonation of a transaction having anti-competitive effects to produce cogent evidence that will satisfy the Board that the transaction can be justified on public interest grounds.

The assessment process entails the identification, weighting, and balancing of the detrimental (anti-competitive) and beneficial implications of the transaction. This most frequently occurs in the case of mergers and acquisitions. Improved utilization of capacity and resources, the promotion of research and development, minimizing the loss of employment opportunities, the rescuing of a failing company, enhancing the international competitiveness of domestic enterprises, and improvements in the country's balance of payment position are the public interest benefits cited most often by parties seeking clearance for a transaction.

VIII. Procedural aspects

Investigations are undertaken by the Board on its own initiative or in response to a complaint. The Minister can direct the Board to launch or terminate an investigation, but this rarely happens. Complaints are initially assessed on a preliminary basis in order to establish whether a formal investigation is warranted. A formal investigation requires official notification in the Gazette and is an essential procedural prerequisite for the remedial or preventative actions for which the Act provides that may subsequently be deemed necessary.

Interested parties are afforded 30 days from the date of publication of the notice in the Gazette to make written submissions to the Board. These could subsequently be supplemented by oral evidence. The Board is also empowered to summon and to interrogate any person who is able to furnish information on the subject of the investigation and may require such a person to produce to the Board any book, document or other object in his or her possession that may have a bearing on the matter.

There is no legal obligation on firms to give prior notice to the Board of an envisaged merger or acquisition. However, since a merger or acquisition that was not notified could subsequently be declared unlawful, most major firms will usually seek clearance from the Board before proceeding with the transaction. Applications for the condonation of a transaction are dealt with on an <u>ex parte</u> basis. Where clearance is given in such cases the Board will always reserve the right to reassess the transaction or to launch a formal investigation should it receive or uncover additional information necessitating such a course of action.

Once notification of a formal investigation has been published and before the Board's report on the matter is submitted to him, the Minister may, on the recommendation of the Board, prescribe by notice in the <u>Gazette</u>, for such period as may be specified in the notice, such action as in the opinion of the Minister needs to be taken to stay or prevent any restrictive practice which exists or may come into existence or any acquisition being made or proposed, as the case may be. At any time after publication of a notice of an investigation, the Board may negotiate with the appropriate person(s) with a view to making an arrangement which, in the opinion of the Board, will ensure the discontinuance of the restrictive practice, acquisition or monopoly situation which is the subject of the investigation, or will remove the anti-competitive features thereof. All such arrangements must be approved by the Minister and be published in the <u>Gazette</u>.

Following the completion of an investigation the Board submits a report to the Minister in which it findings and recommendations are set out. All reports may be published by the Minister in the <u>Gazette</u> or be made known by him in any other manner. They must also be tabled in Parliament.

IX. Remedies

The Minister has fairly extensive powers to deal with restrictive practices, acquisitions, and monopoly situations. More specifically, the Minister may declare the particular restrictive practice, acquisition or monopoly situation unlawful by notice in <u>Gazette</u> and require the person who is involved in the restrictive practice or monopoly situation, or who is a party to the acquisition, to take such action as the Minister may deem appropriate to remedy the situation. The dissolution of a body corporate or unincorporated, the termination of the membership of a member of a body corporate, and the suspension or termination of the voting rights attached to any shares are some of the measures the Minister may prescribe. In exercising his discretion in this regard, the Minister will adhere to the principle of proportionality. This entails that the measures announced by the Minister to counter anti-competitive transactions or situations must be effective without being excessive in the circumstances.

X. Appeals

There is a right of appeal by any person affected by a notice published by the Minister to counter anti-competitive conduct, transactions or situations. The appeal lies to a special court constituted for that exclusive purpose. The members of the special court consist of a judge of the Supreme Court, who is the president of the court, and two other appropriately qualified members appointed by the country's president.

The appeal takes the form of a de novo reappraisal of the relevant issue, following which the special court may confirm or set aside the Minister's notice to which the appeal relates or amend it in such a manner as it may deem equitable. The decision of the special court is not subject to appeal to or review by any court of law.

A peculiarity of the appeals procedure is that complainants have no right of appeal where the Minister decides that no action should be taken in respect of an alleged restrictive practice or a particular acquisition or monopoly situation.

XI. Enforcement

Contravention of certain provisions of the Act and of Government Notice 801 of May 2, 1986 and other notices issued pursuant to the Act is an offense. Prosecutions in respect thereof are accordingly instituted and conducted before the criminal courts. A person convicted of a contravention of Government Notice 801 could be imprisoned for a period not exceeding five years or be required to pay a fine not exceeding R100,000. Regrettably, the enforcement procedures have proved to be largely ineffectual and are one of the weak aspects of South African competition law.

XII. Prognosis

The Government recognizes the defects in the current competition law regime and has indicated that it intends introducing new legislation early in 1997. With many market dominant firms and the major conglomerates fearing that they may be adversely affected by the new law, one can anticipate that there will be some lively debates before Parliament eventually passes a new Act.

Some of the major issues which will come under close scrutiny are whether:

(a) the Government should be involved in the decision-making in competition cases;

(b) market dominant firms should be broken up or merely prevented from abusing their positions;

(c) the current criminal sanctions for contravention should be replaced by substantial administrative penalties;

(d) persons should be entitled to civil damages where they suffer loss as a result of anti-competitive behavior governed by the Act; and

(e) the Competition Board should be given increased powers.

CHAPTER 10

THE PROTECTION OF INTELLECTUAL PROPERTY

By David F. Sheppard

I. Intellectual Property - Conventions and Courts

South Africa has separate Acts for the protection of patents, registered designs (i.e. design patents in the U.S.A.), trade marks and copyright. South Africa is a member of the major Intellectual Property conventions, of which U.S.A. also is a member and, like the U.S.A., is a strong protector of Intellectual Property rights. Just as the U.S. Patent and Trade Mark Office is in Washington and is run by the Commissioner of Patents who is responsible to the Government, so the South African Patent and Trade Mark Office is in Pretoria and is run by the Registrar of Patents who is responsible to the South African Government. The South African Intellectual Property Acts have been amended to comply with TRIPS.

Infringement matters, generally speaking, are heard by a Judge of the Supreme Court who, in patent matters always sits in Pretoria and is known as the Commissioner of Patents while he is hearing that matter. In the case of other Intellectual Property infringement matters, the matter also usually is heard in Pretoria but can be heard in other jurisdictions in South Africa, e.g. Cape Town, Durban, Bloemfontein or Johannesburg in certain instances when it is convenient to do so.

The Judges who hear Intellectual Property matters normally have heard many such matters and have a good background of this special area of law. Most of them have acted as Counsel arguing Intellectual Property disputes in their younger days before being elevated to the bench, i.e. being appointed as a Judge. This specialist knowledge is of great assistance in speeding up Court hearings.

A U.S. Plaintiff or Defendant would act through a South African Attorney who specialized in Intellectual Property (and there are only about six firms and a number of single Practitioners who are members of the South African Institute of Intellectual Property Law). In Court matters, the South African Attorney will normally appoint a Counsel (i.e. a Specialist Advocate) who is experienced in Intellectual Property Law to argue before the Court on papers prepared by the Attorney and examine or cross-examine witnesses where oral evidence is appropriate.

A U.S.A. importer or investor wanting to do business in South Africa, may license a South African licensee under the Intellectual Property concerned, details of which are set out below. A South African Intellectual Property Attorney will be experienced in advising on, and the drafting of, all necessary agreements.

There are normally two levels of appeal from a single Judge if leave to appeal is granted. These are usually to an Appeal Court consisting of three Judges of the province where the matter was initially heard and finally to the Appellate Division which sits in Bloemfontein where five Judges of Appeal hear the matter.

II. Patents

The present Patents Act is Act No. 57 of 1978 which came into force on 1st January 1979. South Africa is a member of the Paris Convention, thereby enabling U.S.A. applicants to file patent applications in South Africa within one year of the date of filing of the original U.S.A. application in order to claim priority of the U.S.A. filing date. Patent applications can still be filed in South Africa after the expiration of the one year convention year provided by the Paris Convention if the invention, at the actual date of filing in South Africa, is still new and inventive. A patent application filed in South Africa more than one year after the earliest U.S.A. filing date has the South African filing date as the date on which the novelty and inventiveness of the invention are decided.

Patents are granted for any new invention which involves an inventive step and which is capable of being used or applied in trade or industry or agriculture. Matters which are excluded from patent protection in South Africa are similar to those excluded in Europe and include discoveries, scientific theories, mathematical methods, literary, dramatic, musical and artistic works, aesthetic creations, a scheme, rule or method for preparing a mental act, playing a game or doing business, a program for a computer or the presentation of information. Whereas a method of treatment of the human or animal body by surgery or therapy or of diagnosis practiced on the human or animal body is not deemed to be an invention in South Africa (unlike in the U.S.A.) a second pharmaceutical use can be protected in a similar manner to that adopted in the European Patent Office. Thus, claims are allowed to an invention consisting of a substance or composition for use in a method of treatment of the human or animal body by surgery or therapy or of diagnosis practiced on the human or animal body, notwithstanding the fact that the substance or composition forms part of the state of the art immediately before the priority date of any claim of the invention if the use of the substance or composition in any such method does not form part of the state of the art (i.e. meets the novelty requirements) at the priority date of the claim.

An invention is novel if it does not form part of the state of the art at the priority date of the claim. The state of the art comprises all matter (whether a product, a process, information about either or anything else) which has been made available to the public (anywhere in the world) by written or oral description, by use or in any other way. It is therefore essential for a U.S.A. applicant that there is no disclosure of details of an invention before the priority date, which would normally be the date of filing of the basic U.S.A. patent application. South Africa therefore follows many other countries in the world by determining novelty as of the date of first filing in a Patent Office (the priority date) whereas the U.S.A. is more lenient, e.g. in not allowing printed publications or public use or sale during the year prior to the application in the U.S.A. to destroy the novelty of the invention. For purposes of novelty, but not obviousness, the state of the art as defined in the South African Patents Act also includes matter contained in an application open to public inspection, on or after the priority date, if that matter was contained in that application both as lodged and as open to public inspection and the priority date of that matter is earlier than that of the relevant claims.

Whereas only the inventor may apply for a patent in the U.S.A. applications may be filed initially in South Africa in the name of the inventor or by any person (e.g. a company) acquiring from the inventor the right to apply, or by such an inventor jointly with a person who has acquired the right to apply. Patent specifications drafted according to the U.S.A. style are allowable in South Africa but must be on A4 size paper. U.S.A. type claims are acceptable. Documents required for filing are a Declaration and Power of Attorney, An Assignment of Invention (where the assignee, e.g. a company, applies), two copies of the specification and claims, two sets of drawings (where applicable) and an Abstract. Where priority is claimed from an earlier U.S.A. application under the International Convention, a certified copy of the U.S.A. application has to be provided. All documents apart from the specification, claims and drawings can be filed belatedly. Facsimile copies of a specification, claims and drawings can be utilized to provide a filing date in urgent instances and clear typed copies of the specification can be filed belatedly.

Unlike the U.S.A., there is no examination as to novelty and obviousness. Instead, the onus is on the applicant, on learning of invalidity of the original broad scope of the claims, e.g. from the U.S.A. prosecution or from another foreign application where novelty and obviousness are considered by a Patent Office, subsequently to amend the South African claims voluntarily by limitation in order to distinguish the invention in a new and inventive manner over prior art which would adversely have affected the earlier claims.

Unlike the U.S.A. where amendments of a granted patent are permitted by means of a reissue application within two years or a request for re-examination, South African patents, after grant, can be amended voluntarily by the patentee at any time provided that:

- The effect of the amendment is not to introduce new matter or matter not in substance disclosed in the specification before amendment, or
- The specification as amended would not include any claim not fairly based on the matter disclosed in the specification before amendment, or
- The specification as amended would not include any claim not wholly within the scope of a claim included in the specification before amendment.

Like Canada, South Africa provides for the filing of a supplementary disclosure, for matter which may fairly be associated with the matter described in the specification as framed. Provided that acceptance of the application has not been published, such matter may be introduced by way of a supplementary disclosure. South Africa does not provide for continuations or continuations-in-part (which are unique to U.S. law), but does provide for the possibility of filing a patent of addition in respect of any improvement in or modification of the original invention which meets the South African novelty requirements but for which there may be a problem of obviousness. A patent of addition cannot be attacked on the ground that the invention claimed does not involve an inventive step having regard to the invention of the parent application. Thus, the inventions of a U.S.A. continuation-in-part application may be protected by way of a basic South African application and a patent of addition application in respect of new matter.

A South African patent, after grant, can be attacked by filing an application for revocation on one of the grounds specified in the Patents Act. The most usual ground of attack is that the invention is not patentable under Section 25, i.e. that it lacks novelty or is obvious compared with the prior art at the priority date of the claims.

In an infringement action a successful patentee is entitled to relief by way of an interdict, delivery up of any infringing product or article or product of which the infringing product forms an inseparable part, and an award of damages which may be calculated as a reasonable royalty. In addition, the Court normally grants the successful party, in any litigation proceedings, an award of costs.

A South African patent has a maximum unextendible term of twenty years calculated from the date of filing of the complete specification, subject to the payment of renewal fees annually as from the third year.

A U.S.A. importer or new investor in South Africa would be well advised to have his South African Patent attorney carry out a subject matter search through all patents in force in the field in which the importer or investor is interested.

A South African Patent attorney must sign a complete specification. A list of South African Patent attorneys, most of which are members of half a dozen firms, can be obtained from the SAIIPL, P. O. Box 4685, Pretoria, 0001 or from the author whose address is given below.

III. Trade Marks

The present Trade Marks Act is Act No. 194 of 1993. South Africa, like the U.S.A. is a member of the Paris Convention.

To be registrable in South Africa, a Trade Mark must be capable of distinguishing the goods or services of one person from the goods or services of another person, either generally or subject to limitations. A Trade Mark is considered capable of distinguishing if, at the date of application, it is inherently capable of so distinguishing or it is capable of distinguishing by reason of its prior use.

A Trade Mark, other than a certification or collective mark, means a mark used or proposed to be used by a person in relation to goods or services (e.g. a U.S.A. importer or investor in South Africa) for the purpose of distinguishing the goods or services in relation to which the mark is used or proposed to be used from the same kind of goods or services connected in the course of trade with any other person. There is a broad definition in the Act for "a mark" which may consist of any sign capable of being represented graphically, including a device, name, signature, word, letter, numeral, shape, configuration, pattern, ornamentation, color or container for goods or any combination thereof. Collective marks also are registrable in South Africa and are marks capable of distinguishing, in the course of trade, goods or services of persons who are members of any association from goods or services of persons who are not members thereof. Geographical names and other indications of geographical origin may be registered as collective trade marks.

Certification marks are marks capable of distinguishing, in the course of trade, the goods or services certified by any person in respect of origin, material, mode of manufacture or performance, quality, accuracy or any other characteristic from goods which are not so certified.

Trade marks which are excluded from registration include:

- A mark which does not constitute a trade mark or is not capable of distinguishing or which consists exclusively of a sign or indication which designates various characteristics of the goods or services, or which has become customary in the current language or in bona fide established practices in the trade.
- A mark in respect of which the applicant for registration has no bona fide claim to proprietorship or in terms of which an application has been made in bad faith.
- A mark in respect of which the applicant for registration has no bona fide intention to use the mark as a trade mark by himself or through a licensee. Thus if a U.S.A. importer or investor in South Africa applies for registration of a mark, he must have the intention of using the mark and must use it within a period of five years.
- A mark which consists exclusively of the shape, configuration or color of goods where such shape, configuration or color is necessary to obtain a special technical result or which results from the nature of the goods themselves.
- A mark which constitutes, or an essential part of which constitutes, a reproduction, imitation or translation of a "well-known" foreign trade mark in terms of the Paris Convention in respect of goods or services similar or identical to the goods or services in question.

A "well-known" foreign trade mark is one which is well-known in South Africa as being the mark of a person entitled to convention benefits whether or not such person carries on business or has any goodwill in South Africa. Protection is therefore available in South Africa for well-known U.S.A. Trade Marks provided that the owner submits full evidence to justify such protection.

South Africa follows the International Convention on classification of trade marks, and a trade mark has to be filed in each class in which protection is desired. After filing, the application for registration is examined by the Trade Marks Office to determine the inherent registrability, as well as possible conflict with prior registrations or applications. Like most countries, the Trade Mark Office will issue official actions either accepting a trade mark or, preliminarily refusing it or indicating the conditions subject to which it may be accepted. Once a trade mark has been accepted, it is advertised in the Trade Marks part of the Patent Journal. In the absence of objections by third parties within three months of the advertisement date, the application proceeds to grant and a certificate of registration is issued.

A U.S.A. importer or investor is well advised to ask his South African Trade Mark attorney to carry out a search for a mark or marks and, if the search is negative, to request the filing of the mark(s) in those classes which are relevant. This advisably is done at an early date.

Trade Marks may be removed from the register by an interested person if:
- The trade mark does not comply with the requirements of the Act relating to registrability;
- The use of the trade mark has not complied with any condition entered in the register in relation thereto;
- There is a lack of bona fide intention to use the mark at the time of application for registration and there has in fact been no bona fide use of the mark in relation to relevant goods or services by the proprietor or a person permitted by him to use the mark, up to the date three months before the date of application for its removal. A U.S.A. importer or investor who intends doing business in South Africa must intend to use a mark and actually use it in relation to the goods for which it is registered;
- Up to the date three months before the date of application for removal, a continuous period of five years or longer has elapsed from the date of issue of the certificate of registration during which the trade mark was registered and during which there has been no bona fide use of the mark in relation to relevant goods or services by the proprietor or a person permitted by him to use the mark; or
- If, in the case of a mark registered in the name of a body corporate, or in the name of a natural person, such body corporate was dissolved, or such natural person has died, not less than two years prior to the date of application and there has been no application for registration of an assignment of such trade mark.

There are three types of trade mark infringement, namely:
- The unauthorized use in the course of trade in relation to goods or services in respect of which the trade mark is registered, of an identical mark or of a mark so nearly resembling it as to be likely to deceive or cause confusion.
- The unauthorized use of a mark which is identical or similar to the trade mark registered, in the course of trade in relation to goods or services which are so similar to the goods or services in respect of which the trade mark is registered, that in such use there exists the likelihood of deception or confusion, or
- The unauthorized use in the course of trade in relation to any goods or services of a mark which is identical or similar to a registered trade mark, if such trade mark is well-known in the Republic and the use of the said mark would be likely to take unfair advantage of, or will be detrimental to, the distinctive character or repute of the registered trade mark, notwithstanding the absence of confusion or deception.

Remedies for infringement of a registered trade mark are an interdict, an order for the removal of the offending trade mark from the infringing goods or alternatively delivery up of the infringing goods, an award of damages which is calculated from the date of advertisement of acceptance of the application for registration or, *in lieu* of damages, a reasonable royalty which would have been paid by a licensee for the use of the trade mark concerned and, usually, an award of costs to the successful party.

South Africa is a country whose inhabitants usually ask for goods by the name they have seen in advertisements. Thus, a registered trade mark accompanied by appropriate media advertising are very useful marketing tools in South Africa. Since much of South Africa's goods and commodities are exported northwards through English and Portuguese speaking Africa as far as the Sahara, South African Trade Mark attorneys often file applications for the person doing business in South Africa, not only in South Africa, but in the many countries of sub-Saharan Africa including Zimbabwe, Zambia, Angola, Mozambique, Botswana, Lesotho, Swaziland, Kenya, Tanzania, Uganda and others.

The duration of a registered trade mark is a period of ten years calculated from the date of the original application and may be renewed in perpetuity for like periods on application and payment of renewal fees.

IV. Registered Designs

Registered Designs are protected by means of the Designs Act No. 195 of 1993 which came into force on 1st May 1995. It enables, e.g., a U.S.A. Applicant of a Design patent to protect that design or a substantially similar design in South Africa.

The design to be protected may be an aesthetic design which is registrable in part A of a register or a functional design which is registrable in part F of the register. Alternatively, the design may have both aesthetic and functional features in which case it can be registered in both part A and part F of the register. A U.S.A. importer or investor doing business in South Africa can also protect integrated circuits and mask work under the South African Designs Act, as is explained below.

An aesthetic design means any design applied to any article whether for the pattern or the shape or the configuration or the ornamentation thereof, or for any two or more of those purposes, and by whatever means it is applied, having features which appeal to and are judged solely by the eye, irrespective of the aesthetic quality thereof. Features which are necessitated solely by function and a method or principle of construction are excluded from protection of an aesthetic design. On the other hand, a functional design means any design applied to any article whether for the pattern or the shape or the configuration thereof, or for any two or more of these purposes, and by whatever means it is applied, having features which are necessitated by the function which the article to which the design is applied, is to perform, and includes an integrated circuit typography, a mask work and a series of mask works.

Integrated circuit typography means a functional design which consists of a pattern, shape or configuration of the three-dimensional disposition of the electrical, electromagnetic or optical elements and circuitry of an integrated circuit. A mask work means a functional design which consists of pattern or an image however fixed or encoded having or representing at least part of an integrated circuit. A series of mask works means a related group of mask works which together represent the three-dimensional disposition of the electrical, electromagnetic or obstacle elements and circuitry of an integrated circuit. Thus, the South African Designs Act gives these very wide definitions of protectable items broader, it is believed, than in the U.S.A. However, the South African Designs Act specifically excludes spare parts for a machine, vehicle or equipment from protection.

A U.S.A. applicant can file an application for a South African design, through his South African attorney if it meets the novelty requirements.

An aesthetic design must be new and original, and a functional design must be new and not common place in the art in question. A design is deemed to be new if it is different from and does not form part of the state of the art immediately before the effective date. The effective date denotes the date of filing of a non-convention application in South Africa, or the priority date (e.g. the date of application of the U.S.A. design patent) if the application is filed as a convention application, or the "release date" whichever is the earlier. The release date is the date on which the design was first made available to the public (anywhere in the world) with the consent of the proprietor or any predecessor in title. Care must therefore be exercised in not publishing details of a design preferably before applying for protection in the U.S.A. and, within six months, for protection in South Africa.

The state of the art, on which novelty is decided, comprises all matter which has been made available to the public (anywhere in the world) by written description, by use or in any other way as well as all matter contained in an application for registration of a design in South Africa or an application in a convention country for the registration of a design which has subsequently been registered in South Africa as a convention application.

Applications for registration of a design are made by the proprietor who is the author of the design; or where the author executes the work for another person, by that other person; or where a person or his employee acting in the course of his employment makes a design for another person in terms of an agreement, such other person; or where the ownership in the design has passed to any other person, such other person.

For filing a design application claiming priority from an application filed in the U.S.A., the South African design must be filed within six months of the date of a basic U.S.A. design and the documents required comprise a Declaration and Power of Attorney, an Assignment document where the applicant has acquired the right to apply from a predecessor in title, representations of the design, a definitive statement of the feature of the design in which the applicant claims protection and a certified copy of the basic U.S.A. application.

In the case of a functional design for an integrated circuit typography or a mask work or a series of mask works, an explanatory statement referring to the function and operation thereof must be furnished. For other functional designs and for aesthetic designs, an explanatory statement is optional.

Designs are registrable in thirty-two classes which follow those specified under the International Convention.

The duration of registration of an aesthetic design is fifteen years and of a functional design is ten years from the effective date, subject to the payment of renewal fees.

Amendment of a registered design is possible but no amendment shall be allowed if:

- The effect of the amendment would be to introduce new matter or matter not in substance disclosed in design application or the design registration before amendment;
- Registration of the design as amended would include any matter not fairly based on matter disclosed in the document before amendment;
- The effect would be to alter a registration in terms of the repealed Act No. 57 of 1967 from a part A to a part F registration, or
- The scope of the registration after amendment would be wider than that before amendment.

As with the case of an article that can be patented, a U.S.A. importer or investor wishing to do business in South Africa would be well advised to have a subject matter search carried out in the class or classes or relevance by his South African Patent Attorney.

In proceedings for infringement, a successful Plaintiff shall be entitled to an interdict, surrender of any infringing product or any article or product of which the infringing product forms an inseparable part, an award of damages or, in lieu thereof, a reasonable royalty which would have been paid by the licensee in respect of a registered design and, usually an award of damages to the successful party.

V. Copyright

The present Copyright Act is Act No. 98 of 1978 as amended. South Africa is a member of the Berne Convention on Copyright.

Unlike the U.S.A., copyright in terms of the Copyright Act exists de facto and no registration is required or possible, except in respect of cinematographic films. The Copyright Act applies equally to copyright originating in the U.S.A. since 1990. A U.S.A. owner of copyright therefore obtains South African rights easier than he or she obtains U.S.A. rights.

Copyright is conferred in a work for which the author or, in the case of a work of joint authorship, any one of the authors who is at the time of work (or a substantial part thereof) was made, a qualified person. For copyright originating in the U.S.A., a qualified person would be a person who is a U.S. citizen or who is domiciled or resident in the U.S.A. or, in the case of a juristic person, a body incorporated in the U.S.A.

Works which are eligible for copyright are literary works, musical works, artistic works, cinematographic films, sound recording, broadcasts, program carrying signals, published editions and computer programs. Thus, South Africa specifically provides protection under the Copyright Act for computer programs, an area of protection which is not provided for in some other countries.

An owner of copyright should make it known what he is protecting. Thus, marking of any work with the copyright sign ©, the name of the author and the date is strongly recommended for all literary, musical or artistic works. A presumption then exists, unless the contrary is proved, that the person so named is the author of the work. Even where transfer in the copyright in a literary, musical or artistic work or in a cinematographic film has occurred, the author shall have the right to object, as author, to any distortion, mutilation or other modification of the work where such action is or would be prejudicial to the honor or reputation of the author even though the author is not, at that time, the owner of the copyright.

The term of copyright in respect of literary, musical or artistic works, other than photographs, is the life of the author plus fifty years from the year in which the author dies provided that, if before the death of the author, there has been no publication or public performance or offer for sale to the public or records or broadcasting, the term of copyright continues to subsist for a period of fifty years from the end of the year in which the first of these acts is done. With respect to cinematographic films, photographs and computer programs, the period of copyright is fifty years from the end of the year in which the work was lawfully made available to the public or, failing this, fifty years from the end of the year in which the work was made. In respect of sound recordings, the period of copyright is fifty years from the end of the year in which the recording is first published. In respect of broadcasts, the term is fifty years from the end of the year in which the broadcast first takes place. In respect of program-carrying signals, the period of copyright is fifty years from the end of the year in which the signals are emitted to a satellite.

Proceedings for relief of infringement of copyright can be instituted either by way of application on affidavit evidence or by way of an action which would lead to oral evidence being heard. Relief may be granted by way of damages, an interdict, delivery of infringing copies or plates used or intended to be used for infringing copies, as well as usually an award of costs. The Court has power to award additional damages depending on the flagrancy of the infringement and any benefit shown to have been accrued to the Defendant by way of the infringement. Furthermore, a person who knowingly infringers existing copyright can also be liable for a criminal punishment.

Pretoria, South Africa
April 1996

Bibliography:

The Patents Act No. 57 of 1978

The Trade Marks Act No. 194 of 1993

The Registered Designs Act No. 195 of 1993

The Copyright Act No. 98 of 1978 as amended

CHAPTER 11

SOUTH AFRICAN EMPLOYMENT LAW

By Puke Maserumule

I. Introduction

There are a number of statutes in South Africa which regulate employment law, such as those which deal with health and safety, minimum employment standards, collective bargaining and industry specific legislation. An understanding and appreciation of these statutes is important for all employers carrying on business in the country because it avoids contravention of the law and conflict with employees and their trade unions.

As a result of the change to a democratic system in the country, changes have been introduced in order to bring the South African statutes in line with internationally accepted standards. As a result, there are statutes which although current and in force at the moment, are likely to undergo major changes in the near future. Where appropriate and practical, this article will deal with both the current statutes and the proposed new statutes, so as to place the reader in a position to assess both the current law and the possible changes to the law.

In so far as affirmative action is concerned, this is currently dealt with in the interim constitution. Parliament has yet to enact an affirmative action (employment equity) statute and it is not certain at the moment whether and when this will happen. This topic will be dealt with on the basis of what is currently provided for in the interim constitution, taking into account the views of other commentators who have aired their views on the subject.

The format that is adopted herein is to give a summary of the provisions of statutes with which employers will be confronted with on a daily basis. Thereafter will follow a discussion on affirmative action and how this will impact on employers who invest in the country.

II. Basic Conditions of Employment Act 3 of 1983

This is the statute which currently lays down minimum employment standards for the majority of employees in the formal sector. It is important to emphasize that these are indeed minimum standards as in most cases, especially where the employees are unionized, the terms of employment will be different depending on what is agreed during collective bargaining.

The statute covers all employees except that those who earn between R 34 500-00 and R 40 500-00, depending on the areas where they work, are excluded from certain provisions of its provisions.

It is also important to bear in mind that this statute is likely to be repealed and replaced by an Employment Standard statute. However, at present there is only a green paper setting out in general terms perceived shortcomings in the present statute and general proposals as to the policy which should underlie the proposed new statute.

This statute regulates the following important aspects:

A. Maximum Working Hours

The statute limits the number of hours that an employee may ordinarily work to 9 hours and 15 minutes per day, with the exception of security guards who may work up to 12 hours per day and farm workers up to 8 hours and 36 minutes per day. The limitation per week is 46 hours for all employees, save that those who work as security guards may work for 60 hours per week and those engaged in the farming industry, 48 hours per week.

B. Overtime

The statute limits overtime worked to a maximum of 3 hours per day and 10 hours per week for most employees. Farm workers' overtime is limited to 2.5 hours per day and 6 hours per week. Payment for overtime is fixed at a minimum of time and one third for normal overtime worked during the week which increase to double time for overtime worked on a Sunday or public holiday.

C. Sunday Work

Work on Sunday is generally prohibited save where an exemption has been granted or the employers operation are deemed to be continuous operations in terms of this statute.

D. Annual Leave

Employees are entitled to a minimum of 14 days paid leave per annum, i.e. for each completed cycle of 12 consecutive months of employment.

E. Sick Leave

Employees are entitled to a total of 36 days paid sick leave for each completed cycle of 36 months of employment with the one employer. An employee may not be given notice of termination of service while on sick leave.

F. Termination of Service

During the first four weeks of employment, the employment contract may be terminated on giving 24 hours' notice by either the employee or the employer. Thereafter, one week's notice is required from a weekly paid employee and two weeks' notice from a monthly paid employee. These provisions are, however, subject to the provisions of the Labor Relations Act which require that an employee may only be dismissed for misconduct, incapacity or operational requirement. It is not advisable to rely on the provisions relating to termination on notice as such termination may be held to be unfair under the Labor Relations Act.

G. Certificate of Service

Upon termination of an employee's services for whatever reason, the employer is obliged to provide that employee with a certificate setting out that employee's date of employment, occupation, wage and date of termination of service.

H. Records

All employers are required to keep records containing information such as the time worked by an employee, his wage and all other information which may be required.

I. General

It should be noted that a breach of the important provisions of the statute constitute a criminal offence for which an employer may be prosecuted. There are inspectors whose duty it is to ensure that the statute is complied with and who regularly and on a random basis visit employers' premises for this purpose.

III. Employment Standards Bill

The government has published a green paper on employment standards to replace the Basic Conditions of Employment Act and the Wage Act. The new legislation which is likely to follow will in part be a product of the new labor regime. The proposed statute has been the subject of negotiation at the National Economic, Development and Labor Council (NEDLAC).

In summary, some of the major proposals contained in the green paper are the following:

- A reduction of ordinary weekly hours from the present 46 hours to 45 hours and ultimately, 40 hours and in the case of security guards from the present 60 hours to 48 hours per week;
- The introduction of 4 months maternity leave during which employment is guaranteed and 3 days paid paternity or child care leave;
- The removal of inappropriate restrictions on working time and other employment conditions to allow for greater market flexibility;
- The extension of scope of the statute to cover all employees, including farm and domestic workers and part-time who are currently either wholly excluded or only partially covered;
- The establishment of an Employment Standards Commission which will replace the Wage Act (which is discussed below);
- Abolish the prohibition on Sunday work, save that employees may not work for more than three consecutive Sundays;
- Increase annual leave to three weeks' paid leave for all employees;
- Increase the notice period for all employees, save during the first four weeks of employment, to four weeks' notice of termination. This provision will not apply to termination of service for misconduct;

- Decriminalize non-compliance with the statute and authorize inspectors to levy penalties on employers and issue notices to employers to comply with the statute.

IV. Wage Act No. 5 Of 1957

This statute is mainly concerned with the setting of minimum wages and other terms and conditions of employment in specific sectors of the economy. It has been used to set minimum wages in such industries as catering, chemical and textile and clothing. Its main target is those areas where there are no industrial councils and hence no industrial council agreement to regulate minimum wages and other terms and conditions of employment.

The statute is implemented through a wage board made up of three persons appointed by the Minister of Labour. This board investigates conditions in certain trades or industries and makes recommendations to the Minister with regard to wages and other terms of employment. Once accepted, the recommendations are then published in a government gazette as wage determinations and are binding on all employers specified in that determination unless exempted. The wage determinations remain in force until amended or cancelled by the Minister by notice in the government gazette.

Failure to comply with the provisions of a wage determination constitutes a criminal offence for which an employer may be prosecuted.

This statute is likely to be repealed and replaced by the proposed Employment Standards statute.

V. Occupational Health And Safety Act 85 Of 1993

This statute regulates the working environment at the workplace, save for the mining industry which has its own legislation and which is dealt with elsewhere in this chapter.

The statute requires employers to maintain safe and healthy working environments, free of hazards, for both their employees and members of the general public.

Health and safety representatives must be elected in all businesses where there are more than 20 employees. In the case of an office or shop, there should be at least 1 health and safety representative for every 100 employees and in any other workplace, 1 health and safety representative for every 50 employees. These representatives' main duties are to ensure that appropriate health and safety measures are in place and to make representations to the employer with regard to health and safety matters. They are also entitled to visit scenes of accidents at the workplace and to take part in any investigation or enquiry following an accident.

The statute also makes provision for the establishment of health and safety committees where there are two or more health and safety representatives. The employer is to be represented on that committee by the same number of persons as there are representatives. These committees are empowered to make recommendations to the employer with regard to health and safety matters or to an inspector appointed under the Act where the employer does not accept the recommendations so made. They also have to discuss incidents which have taken place at the workplace.

An employer is, in terms of this statute, required to report any major incident at the workplace which causes serious injury to an inspector appointed in terms of this statute. Inspectors appointed in terms of this statute are entitled, without prior notice, to enter upon an employer' premises, question any person thereon on matters relating to the statute, inspect books and records, substances and machinery or to seize same.

Employers are required to have a copy of the statute and regulations made thereunder available for perusal by any persons on its premises.

There are a number of specific regulations promulgated in terms of this statute with which an employer must familiarize himself. These range from general safety regulations, environmental regulations, facilities regulations, certificates of competency with regard to the carrying on of certain functions, asbestos and lead and machinery and electrical regulations.

It is imperative that each employer familiarize himself/herself with the regulations applicable to his/her business. These regulations are very detailed and in many instances very prescriptive and cannot be discussed in any detail here. The regulations are deemed to form part of the statute and non-compliance therewith constitutes non-compliance with the statute itself.

Failure to comply with the provisions of this statute constitutes a criminal offence for which an employer may be prosecuted.

VI. Compensation For Occupational Injuries and Diseases Act 130 Of 1993

This statute regulates the payment of compensation to employees injured during the course of their duties or who suffer from diseases due to the nature of the work performed.

The funding for payment of compensation is through a levy payable by the employer and whose calculation is based on a percentage of the total earnings of the employees employed by each employer.

An employer may be exempted from payment of the levy if he/she has, with the approval of the commissioner, obtained a policy of insurance for the full extent of his potential liability in terms of this statute to his/her employees from a mutual association.

Should an employee be injured at work and in claiming compensation under the statute, allege and it is proved that the injury sustained was due to the negligence of the employer, the commissioner appointed in terms of the statute may raise the levy payable by the employer.

VII. Unemployment Insurance Act 30 Of 1966

The statute requires an employer to provide the Director-General of Labour with his/her full particulars within 14 days after commencing business in the country.

Every employer is obliged to contribute 1.0% and every employee also 1.0% of the latters' monthly earnings to the Unemployment Insurance Fund.

After taking an employee into employment, the employer must apply for a contributor's card (commonly referred to as a "blue card") for that employee from the Director-General of Labor unless the employee already has such a card. This card is kept by the employer for as long as the employee remains in his/her employ. Upon termination of that employee's services, the employer is required to enter on the card the date of commencement of employment, weekly or monthly pay and the date of termination of service. The card is then signed by the employer and given to the employee to enable the latter to claim unemployment pay should this be necessary.

VIII. The Labour Relations Act 66 of 1995

This is perhaps the most important statute with which employers must familiarize themselves and about which legal advice will most frequently be required. It is the statute which primarily regulates the employer's relationship with his/her employees with regard to collective bargaining, strikes and lock-outs, and termination of employment.

A new Labour Relations Act is to come into effect, probably from 1 June 1996 which replaces a similar statute which has been in operation for the past few decades. The new statute is a product of negotiation between employers, labor and government which was agreed upon at NEDLAC. Because the statute is still new, some of the views expressed herein may not necessarily coincide with the way in which it will in practice be implemented.

It is not possible to discuss in detail all the provisions of this statute in this chapter and only the most important provisions will be dealt with herein.

The essence of the statute is to provide a regulatory framework for employers and employees with a view to minimizing industrial conflict and disputes and to provide procedures to deal with disputes which may arise. What follows hereunder is a discussion of the relevant and important chapters in the statute.

A. Freedom Of Association

Employees are granted the right to join trade unions of their choice and to participate in the activities of such unions and the federation of trade unions of which such unions are affiliates. This right flows from the constitutionally guaranteed right of employees to organize and bargain collectively.

The statute prohibits an employer from interfering with employees' right to join unions and participate in their lawful activities, either by way of victimizing them for their membership of a trade union or seeking to prevent them from becoming members of a trade union or refusing to employ them because of their membership of a trade union. This right cannot be limited by a contractual agreement and any purported limitation is deemed to be invalid.

The statute equally protects an employers right to join or form an employers' organization and to participate in its lawful activities. There are a number of such employers' organizations in the country, usually those in the same industry, such as textiles, steel and engineering, motor (automotive) and mining. These employers' organizations have in many instances formed industrial councils which bargain with trade unions at a central level for minimum wages and other terms and conditions of employment.

B. Organizational Rights

Trade unions are entitled to have access to employers' premises for the purpose of recruiting members, hold meetings with the employees on the premises outside working hours and hold ballots of union members on the premises.

Employers are also obliged to deduct union dues from wages of members of a representative union and pay over the money so deducted to the union on a monthly basis. Employees are also entitled to elect union representatives (shop stewards) who will represent the union members in their dealings with the employer. The statute also provides for agency shop and closed shop agreements with representative unions (i.e. unions having as members the majority of the employer's employees).

An employer is obliged to disclose all relevant information, including financial information, to a representative union for purposes of collective bargaining. If the employer refuses to disclose information so requested, a dispute which arises as a result thereof is to be submitted to arbitration.

C. Bargaining Councils

These may be formed by one or more registered trade unions and one or more registered employers' organization. The bargaining councils may conclude and enforce collective agreements, resolve labor disputes, establish and administer provident or pension funds for employees.

D. Strikes and Lock-Outs

All employees have a constitutionally protected right to strike for purposes of collective bargaining. Employees may take part in strike provided that the dispute giving rise to the strike has been referred to the Commission for Conciliation, Mediation and Arbitration (" the Commission") which has failed to resolve the dispute and the employer has been given at least 48 hours' notice of the commencement of the strike. Employees may not strike where:

- There is a binding collective agreement;
- There is an agreement to refer such dispute to arbitration;
- The dispute is one which in terms of the statute must be referred to arbitration by the Commission or to a Labour Court;

- The employees are engaged in essential services or maintenance services; or
- There is a wage determination that regulates the issue in dispute during the first year of that determination.

Secondary strikes, i.e. a strike by employees in support of a strike by employees of another employer provided that the employer of the secondary strikers has been given 7 days notice of the strike and the nature and extent of the strike is reasonable in relation to the effect that the secondary strike may have on the employer of the primary strikers. At this stage, it is not clear as to what will be regarded as "reasonable" in relation to the nature and extent of the secondary strike.

The statute further provides that a strike which complies with its provisions will be regarded as a protected strike and as result, such a strike will not be regarded as a breach of contract nor a delict giving rise to a claim for damages by the employer affected by such a strike. Employers are also precluded from dismissing such employees for striking, save that such employees may be dismissed for misconduct committed during the strike (such as assaults, intimidation of other employees, customers or suppliers) or for reasons based on the operational requirements of the employer, i.e. if the employer is faced with financial ruin due to the prolonged effects of the strike. Where dismissal is permitted by one of the two exceptions, the employer is still obliged to comply with fair procedures before effecting such dismissals.

Where the employees have not complied with the provisions of the statute prior to embarking on strike action, the employer may:

- Seek and obtain an interdict (an injunction) from the Labour Court to restrain the employees from continuing with the strike;
- Seek and obtain an order form the Labour Court for the payment of compensation for any loss arising out of such a strike.

Employees whose strike complies with the provisions of the statute may also take part in a lawful picket in support of such a strike.

Employers are likewise entitled to lock-out employees in pursuance of a collective bargaining dispute provided that the dispute has been referred to the Commission for conciliation and 48 hours' notice has been given to the trade union prior to the commencement of the lock-out. The same limitations which apply to a strike as set out above also apply equally to a lock-out, as does the protection afforded to a strike. There is no corresponding provision in respect to secondary strikes and as such a purported secondary lock-out will be illegal.

It is important to note that the statute prohibits an employer from employing replacement labor during a lock-out where such a lock-out is an "offensive lock-out", i.e where the employer locks out the employees first before such employees have embarked on strike action. However, where the lock-out is in response to a strike, an employer may employ replacement labor to perform the functions of the striking employees.

E. Work Place Forums

This is one of the most important sections of the statute and is an innovation introduced to limit workplace conflict and to introduce some kind of co-operative relationship between employers and employees and reduce industrial unrest.

These forums are established where a representative trade union makes application for one to be established, provided that the employer employs 100 employees or more. If the employer employs less than 100 employees, there is no legal obligation for the employer to agree to the establishment of such a forum.

A work place forum must have a constitution to regulate its operation and the statute provides for matters which it is obligatory to include in such a constitution. Where the employer and the trade union cannot agree on the constitution of the forum, a commissioner is appointed to fashion out a constitution for the parties. It is obviously preferable that the employer and the union should draw up their own constitution rather than have one imposed by a commissioner who may not be alert to the peculiar interests of the parties.

Although a workplace forum is initiated by a trade union, its membership is open to all employees who are entitled to take part in the ballot to elect its members. Further, the forum represents the interests of all employees of the employer and not just those of the union's members.

Workplace forums are entities made up of employees elected by other employees of the employer. Workplace forums must be consulted by the employer with regard to matters such as the restructuring of the workplace, partial or total plant closures, mergers and transfers where such affect the employees, dismissal for operational reasons (redundancies and retrenchments), job grading, product development plans and export promotion. Such consultations need not result in agreement and if none is reached, the employer may implement the measures contemplated.

An employer is obliged to consult and reach consensus with a workplace forum (joint decision making) with regard to the following matters:
- Disciplinary codes and procedures;
- Rules at the workplace which do not relate to the work performance of employees (This will probably cover such issues as dress codes);
- Affirmative action measures; and
- Changes to social benefit schemes initiated by the employer.

In so far as the issues enumerated above are concerned, the statute requires that agreement be reached with the workplace forum before implementation thereof. In the event that agreement cannot be reached and the employer wishes to implement such measures, the employer must refer the matter to private arbitration or arbitration by the Commission.

It is important to bear in mind that the workplace forum exists and operates alongside any union structure such as a shop stewards committee. What the statute does is to limit conflict between these two structures by excluding from the ambit of the workplace forum those matters which, although falling within the competency of the workplace forum, are covered by a collective agreement between a trade union and the employer.

A workplace forum may be dissolved upon a request made by the representative union (which would have applied for its establishment) provided that more than 50% of the employees who take place in a ballot for that purpose vote in favour of such a dissolution. No provision exists entitling the employer to request that a ballot be held to vote for or against the dissolution of a workplace forum and such a request, if made, and any subsequent ballot in favor of dissolution would therefore be invalid.

F. Dispute Resolution

The statute provides for disputes to be resolved either by way of private arbitration where same is provided for in a collective agreement, arbitration by the Commission and the Labour Court.

Most disputes which will be dealt with are those arising from the dismissal of employees for misconduct, which must be referred to compulsory arbitration or dismissal for operational reasons (redundancies and retrenchments) which must be referred to the Labor Court. A decision or award by an arbitrator is final and binding, with no recourse to appeal although such decision or award may be taken on review to the Labour Court or Supreme Court. Decisions of the Labour Court may be taken on appeal to a Labour Appeal Court, which is a final court of appeal, established under the statute.

Where a dispute is referred to arbitration in terms of the statute, as a general rule, parties, i.e. the employer and the employee/trade union, are not permitted to be represented by a legal practitioner. The commissioner hearing the dispute does, however, have a discretion to allow legal representation. It is likely that the exclusion of legal representation may be challenged in the Constitutional Court and there have been comments by some labor law practitioners that this will in effect be done. There is no limitation on legal representation in matters referred to the Labour Court.

G. Code of Good Practice

The statute also contains a code of good practice for dismissals. It sets out guidelines for dismissal for misconduct and incapacity (poor work performance, ill health or injury). These include the substantive requirements and fair procedures to be followed prior to dismissal. The commissioners who are to adjudicate dismissal disputes for misconduct and incapacity are entitled to take into account the extent to which the employer has complied with the code in determining what award to make. It is worth noting that in cases where the commissioner finds a dismissal to have been procedurally unfair, he/she may then order the employer to pay the costs of the arbitration.

IX. Affirmative Action

There is currently no legislation which regulates affirmative action as such. Provisions relating to affirmative action are presently those contained in section 8(3) of the South African interim constitution which has been retained in the draft of the final constitution. The section deals with equality of all citizens before the law and outlaws discrimination on a number of grounds. The proviso in section 8(3) permits the enactment of measures to redress the imbalances created by discriminatory legislation and practices under the former apartheid regime.

The generally accepted view amongst South African commentators is that the provisions of this section and the chapter under which it falls in the constitution only bind the state and its institutions and accordingly do not apply to private persons, including private sector employers. This has left the issue of affirmative action to be dealt with by civil society and its organs.

The debate on affirmative action has been a heated and emotional one. Generally, the trend in industry has been to give qualified support to the implementation of affirmative action, provided that there are no set quotas and employers are left to design their own programs and the implementation thereof. On the other hand, the majority of blacks have called for the enactment of an affirmative action statute, arguing that employers are failing to implement any sustainable programs in this regard. Government has taken the view, for the moment, that employers should be given the opportunity to fashion and implement their own programs with the rider that should there be no visible progress, it will consider enacting legislation to deal with the matter.

There has been a call, supported by government (through its departments) that companies which tender for government contracts must be able to show that they have in place a working affirmative action program. With the establishment of Tender Boards at Provincial level, this policy is now implemented by provincial governments.

It can safely be stated that unless government is satisfied that companies are genuinely pursuing affirmative action policies, it is conceivable that affirmative action statute will be introduced to speed up the process.

The debate on affirmative action is also closely linked to the call for black economic empowerment. It will be expected of companies in the country not only to implement affirmative action, but to also bring on board black shareholders in a significant way, including the appointment of both executive and non-executive black directors on the boards of companies.

Finally, all companies doing business in South Africa will be well advised to have an affirmative action program if they are to succeed in their operations.

X.   Conclusion

As can be seen from the above discussion, there is a myriad of statutes that employers in South Africa have to familiarize themselves with so as not to fall foul of the law. This summary is by no means meant to be a substitute for good legal advice and all employers will be well advised to seek appropriate legal advice for a much more comprehensive understanding of the applicable laws.

There are also other industry specific statutes, such as those relating to mining and agriculture which are not dealt with herein. These statutes by and large deal with the peculiar and specific characteristic of these industries and their history. However, for the most part, the statute cited herein also apply to these industries save where the specific statute expressly exclude their operation.

Johannesburg, South Africa
May 1996

Bibliography:

Industrial Law Journal, published quarterly by Juta & Co. Ltd.

Employment Law, published bi-monthly by Butterworths Publishers (SA)

Contemporary Labour Law published monthly by Calvin Brown & Associates

Labour Legislation Service, a looseleaf publication containing most of the relevant employment legislation, published by Butterworths Publishers (SA)

South African Labour Law, a looseleaf publication edited by Clive Thompson and Paul Benjamin, published by Juta & Co. Ltd.

The Labour Relations Act of 1995, edited by du Toit, Woolfray et al.

CHAPTER 12

PRIVATIZATION IN SOUTH AFRICA

By Tiego Moseneke

I. Introduction

Beginning in the 1970s and accelerating markedly in the eighties, the world's industrialized and emerging markets experienced waves of transactions broadly designed to terminate or restructure the nature and scope of the states' participation in national economies. Such developments have sometimes (e.g., Eastern Europe) been part of a far reaching process of social and political reform. Elsewhere (e.g., the United Kingdom), these processes have significantly been driven by ideology. In yet other countries (principally the Asian markets), privatization initiatives have -- paradoxically -- been tightly linked to state-driven industrial strategies: the state privatizes so as to exit certain sectors after having completed its "priming role," intending immediately to enter and boost new sectors of "sunrise industry."

South Africa's evolving privatization approach is potentially a significant reinvention of the concept, combining aspects of these existing approaches with innovative amendments designed to accommodate peculiarly South African circumstances. The South African government speaks not of "privatization" (which might seem to suggest a goal of transferring ownership as an end in itself) but rather of "state asset restructuring," which is meant to place the emphasis on efficient reform of industry structure (public and private alike). The distinction might seem, superficially, like no more than another of the familiar euphemisms that have abounded as synonyms for privatization in emerging markets. But it would be a serious mistake to approach the South African debate in this way.

The South African case is intended to be an interesting hybrid of, and in some ways an improvement on, existing approaches. Relative to experience elsewhere, "privatization" in South Africa will be less about rushing assets into private hands (a transaction-driven and banker-driven process) and much more about developing effective regulatory channels within which to mobilize local and international private finance and expertise. The latter task -- the South African task -- is one of designing effective regulatory frameworks and institutional models for incoming investment, a task to which the international legal community can bring valuable resources of comparative expertise. The goal of the present contribution is to convey the texture of the South African debate as well as the conflicting priorities and legal issues that have arisen in the ongoing South African privatization initiative.

II. Privatization And Socio-Political Reform

South Africa is, manifestly, a society in significant political transition. Yet it has always had a well developed and fairly sophisticated (albeit internationally isolated) private sector, including a secure, highly developed and substantially deregulated financial services sector and a mining industry that is a world leader. South Africa's retail sector is highly sophisticated, containing for instance a per capita concentration of opulent shopping malls that is among the world's highest. The country's physical infrastructure (roads, electrification, telephones, etc.) served well those whom they were historically intended to serve, but neglected the country's majority.

So the South African task is not one of "shock therapy" designed to introduce market mechanisms where they previously were wholly absent. The substantial falloff in industrial output that accompanied this strategy in every Eastern European economy in which it was applied is highly unattractive in South Africa, where unemployment rates approach 40% and joblessness is highly concentrated among the intended beneficiaries of the political transition. In these circumstances, a principal focus of the South African privatization process will be the efficient expansion of social services, and of infrastructure to previously excluded areas.

III. The South African Ideology Of Privatization

In short, there is no governing ideology underneath the South African state asset restructuring process. The new government is committed to implementing mechanisms that will be practically useful in attaining social goals, rather than in advancing any of the range of available ideologies (running the spectrum from nationalization to big bang sell-offs) as an end in itself.

In part, this pragmatic approach is a response against the previous South African government's unattractive ideological priorities in this area. In South Africa, privatization was originally advocated by apartheid hardliner apartheid President PW Botha who was concerned, in 1988, to find ways to offset the revenue losses inflicted by international sanctions against apartheid. And in neighboring Namibia, a region that South Africa had occupied for decades despite contrary directives from the International Court of Justice and the United Nations, the South African government's attempted sales of state assets in 1989 were seen as part of a preemptive strategy to tie the hands of the incoming democratic government. Today, these dubious origins still cast a shadow over popular perceptions of privatization, so that the new government is constrained to ensure that its own restructuring initiatives are sharply distinguishable, in goals and substance, from what went before.

IV. Privatization And Industrial Strategy

South Africa's public and private sectors alike are widely perceived to be overreliant on government cash and noncash supports. The broad thrust of the new government's economic policy is towards market liberalization, reduction of tariff and other trade barriers, reduction of export and other subsidies and increased domestic competition. The government takes its World Trade Organization (WTO) obligations very seriously and, in several areas, its voluntary reforms actually exceed the letter of its WTO obligations.

Conversely, privatization initiatives are very much seen within the context of a coherent industrial strategy. The South African government accepts the balance of international opinion which (contrary to Thatcherite ideology) holds that the privatization of certain state assets and enterprises need not -- and optimally ought not -- to reduce the overall role of the state as an economic actor. In South Africa, an influential policy view holds that an optimal balance of state-private participation may mean a significant reduction of state involvements in certain sectors and stability, or even increased participation, in others. In sectors such as telecommunications, there is already a balance of state and private participation, including a well-developed cellular telephone market. Even if -- as has been widely speculated -- the principal South African fixed line provider, state-owned Telkom, introduces a strategic equity partner or some other form of private investment, a well developed regulatory regime will mean significant continuing public interest oversight (unlike some of the Latin American examples, where postprivatization telecom operators had effectively free rein at consumer expense).

The Asian model of "rolling privatization," wherein the state exits maturing or nonstrategic sectors in order to pioneer new sunrise industries, has received much attention in South Africa. In this approach, the state's role is less one of ownership than of assisting sunrise industries through preferential access to credit, expertise, marketing facilities, etc. On this approach, government would identify sectors where the national economy ought to have sustainable competitive advantages and would target incentives towards all enterprises in that sector. The benefits are thus not confined to state-owned or specifically earmarked companies. Added benefits can be achieved by setting intra-sectoral criteria for eligibility (e.g., export performance) so that firms earn support for actions and executive decisions consistent with long-term sectoral strategy. Such an approach may best enable the country as a whole to achieve its policy and economic objectives. This approach, as part of a broader set of supply side incentives to boost South African industry, is an important part of the ongoing privatization debate.

V.   **Privatization And Antitrust Reform**

Because the South African private and public sectors alike are overconcentrated, a large part of the regulatory reform associated with privatization relates to antitrust issues. South Africa's current antitrust law, the 1979 Promotion and Maintenance of Competition Act, is currently under review and significant changes are expected. The 1979 Act is widely criticized for its perceived toothlessness. The relevant concern, in a privatization context, is that the simple sale of state monopolies into the hands of private monopolists or dominant conglomerates would defeat the otherwise expected efficiency gains from privatization. The overconcentration of ownership in the South African economy has attracted much adverse attention internationally. Elaborate webs of cross-ownership, interlocking directorships and spirals of subsidiaries which control subsidiaries which in turn control further subsidiaries -- all these ingredients are perceived to inhibit useful dynamism in the South African economy and, specifically, to deter or even exclude incoming investment. New antitrust legislation, currently being keenly debated, is expected to be enacted this year.

VI. **Privatization And Worker Concerns**

One aspect of the nonideological approach to privatization in South Africa is that the process is not viewed, as it was in Thatcherite Britain, as a means of reducing the political power and influence of trade unions as an end in itself. As in many emerging markets, the concerns of labor are perceived to be legitimate and successful privatization proposals will require a strong workers' rights component. A variety of models are under discussion in South Africa, ranging from short-term job security arrangements to actual equity participation in privatized assets by the well-funded labor union pension funds. In addition, the labor movement has insisted that the societal gains of particular privatization proposals should be clearly articulated and carefully verified. This has brought some balance to a debate in which, too often, those on the opposite side of ideological spectrum from labor present privatization as a panacea.

VII. Potential Mechanisms For Privatization In South Africa

Based on prior international experience, a number of privatization mechanisms are available, several of which are under consideration in South Africa. These include:

A. Mass Privatization

This involves the distribution to the general population of shares in a state corporation or of vouchers that enable their holders to bid for state corporations within auction-type structures. While such a model might seem to have obvious benefits as a wealth redistribution mechanism in South African circumstances, the South African debate over mass mechanisms has also been characterized by some caution. The fear is that the broad spread of ownership ostensibly achieved by such schemes can be more illusion than reality. This problem of hollow benefits is potentially acute where voting rights attaching to mass shares or vouchers in a privatized entity are diluted in proportion to the discounted economic value offered in exchange for them, or if the beneficiary population is relatively unsophisticated, or if the schemes fuel an indiscriminate short-term popular enthusiasm that serves to cloud the adverse overall socio-economic impact of particular privatizations.

B. Small Privatization

As an alternative to mass schemes, the sale or outsourcing of government-owned properties or services has the advantage of conferring genuine and unambiguous ownership rights on purchaser-beneficiaries. However, while there is real scope for such a process in South Africa, the availability of state owned enterprises of this scale is more constrained than in, say, the Eastern European markets where, unlike South Africa, state ownership was all pervasive prior to the political transition. Such processes are anyway generally of most interest to domestic, rather than international, players.

C. Conditional Privatization

This involves an offer to sell state assets or concessions, but only if a qualifying purchaser (e.g., from a historically disadvantaged group) emerges. In theory, there is no necessary size limitation on the sorts of assets that can be marketed in this way. One variant on this method is for government to make a general statement of its intention to entertain bids or proposals in respect of broad categories of assets, leaving the initiative with would-be purchasers to devise socially beneficial schemes. This approach is most appealing in nonstrategic sectors of little urgency or sensitivity.

D. Negotiated Transactions

These involve direct negotiation and contracting between the state and an incoming private investor. They may embrace joint ventures, including direct foreign investment, and the state may retain an appropriate stake in the company. The primary advantage here is flexibility. Strategic investment in assets like South African Telkom or South African Airways might proceed by this path.

E. Build-Operate-Transfer (BOT)

This is more a technique to finance future large scale projects than a means for the disposition of existing state assets. It is highly relevant to South Africa's infrastructure expansion plans, and so is discussed in more detail in the Project Finance section below.

F. Public Offerings

This refers to the straightforward process of floating on a stock exchange the shares of a state enterprise. The flotation may be placed on the Johannesburg Stock Exchange or -- by devices such as American Depositary Receipts -- on overseas markets. Small stock quantities should be available in all offerings to enable the participation of small and medium sized investors.

G. Auctions

This familiar process of selling state assets to the highest bidder has advantages of transparency and, often, of low transaction costs. However, auctions often make it more difficult to attend to long term strategic concerns since there is reduced scope for negotiations. Additionally, auction procedures are generally biased towards cash-maximization priorities which (as emerges below) will not be the South African government's only goal in every case.

H. Leasing

In circumstances where outright disposition of the state's ownership interest in property might be particularly politically sensitive (e.g., landmark real estate), an attractive idea in South Africa is to lease the asset. Leasing is functionally similar to partial privatization through selling some shares in a private entity. Partial share ownership requires the state to exercise shareholder monitoring functions which allow it flexibility in managing its relationship with the part-privatized entity. Conversely, negotiation of a lease will formalize the specific obligations of the incoming private investor to the state. The state loses some flexibility but can expect to expend less by way of ongoing monitoring costs. The method can also work in reverse, with the private party building and then leasing the property to the state.

I. Sale and Leaseback

Where the state remains a partial shareholder, investors may remain nervous about the risk of state intervention in postprivatization business operations, and this will affect the state's revenues from the sale. One remedy is to execute an outright sale while binding incoming management to continue to cater to specified government needs on stated payment terms. This approach captures the efficiencies of private asset management while allowing the state to dictate (by terms included in the lease) the overriding goals.

J. Sale of Tangible Assets

This is the straightforward disposition of assets such as real estate or vehicles. This may be part of the liquidation of a non-viable enterprise, or it may represent a rationalization of an ongoing enterprise. The overriding goal may be to raise money.

K. Tender

Given historical imbalances in South Africa, the principle of tenders restricted to specified participants, or groups of participants, is likely to be an important part of the unfolding privatization program. In addition, tender requirements can play a role in mobilizing policy ideas, by requiring bidders to present functional solutions for stated problems, or paths towards attainment of specified goals. In lay terms, the state can define the cart, and require investors to propose the horse -- the engine that will drive the project towards achievement of its end result. Certain South African governmental and state enterprise information technology (IT) contracts have already been framed in this way.

L. Self-Privatization

In some parts of the world, governments have permitted or encouraged state enterprises themselves to generate detailed privatization proposals. However, this method increases the incentives for enterprise insiders to hoard information and selectively to release that which laces their own proposal in a favorable light. Moreover, since the method is essentially a form of management buyout, it disproportionately favors incumbent bureaucrats who, in transitional societies such as South Africa, tend to be holdovers from the prior regime. This approach has thus been firmly rejected by the South African government.

M.   Debt-Equity Swaps

Some governments have allowed sovereign creditors to bid the value of the their debt in exchange for ownership of former state enterprises. Inevitably, such transactions result in large discounts in favor of creditors, raising little cash for government and allowing little room for negotiation of extraneous social obligations. While the South African sovereign debt situation is a matter of significant concern, it is not a crisis issue, so the need for the relatively drastic approach of debt-equity swaps has not arisen.

VIII.   Project Finance Initiatives

Because it involves the materialization of new assets rather than the alienation of existing ones, private finance of public infrastructure has not attracted as much political attention and debate as has the sale of South African state assets. Yet, in economic terms, the dollar volume of the financing involved in attempts to expand South Africa's road, water, housing, electricity and other social services networks is of immense significance. The South African government's infrastructure expansion plans must rank as among the most private-sector driven programs in the emerging markets today. The challenge for investors and their advisors is to be imaginative in assembling aggressive proposals involving risk-layered debt instruments and flexible securities that, in general, transport cutting edge corporate finance techniques into the more solid project finance arena. The fact that there is a vibrant domestic South African financial services sector -- large chunks of which are now owned by incoming international investments banks -- ensures that there will be (as there indeed already is) world class project finance talent chasing these lucrative projects. One concern on larger projects involving foreign money is the continuing existence of exchange control restrictions in the South African market. These are being phased out gradually -- a commitment which government has recently renewed -- but the exact timing of outright abolition remains unclear.

IX.   Competing Goals Of Privatization In South Africa

To a large extent the chosen method(s) of privatization will depend on the government and societal goals that underlie the process. Many conflicting goals have ben discussed as potential priorities in the South African privatization debate. Different constituencies have variously argued that privatization should be undertaken in order:

- To foster a more even distribution of private wealth to workers and to citizens generally;
- To free government of the burdensome day-to-day management of event profitable commercial concerns;
- To speed reform of inefficient state bureaucracy through (e.g.) "contracting out" various parts of their work;
- To avoid or end the fiscal drain of money-losing state enterprises;
- To tease underground money into the legitimate economy, as in China;
- To induce repatriation of capital currently held overseas;

- To enhance the efficiency of state enterprises;
- To improve the regulatory environment by separating the commercial and regulatory functions of government-owned enterprises;
- To raise revenue through the sale of state assets;
- To raise money from overseas donors by conforming to their real or perceived ideological preferences;
- To show a commitment to economic liberalization, thereby reducing perceived "country risk" and so attracting favorable overseas financing terms;
- To attract foreign direct investment;
- To form strategic public-private joint ventures;
- To broaden participation in the local capital markets through mass share ownership;
- To enhance the liquidity of the local capital markets through placing large and attractive share offerings;
- To reduce the role of government in the economy as an end in itself;
- To speed the introduction of pricing mechanisms in previously market-sheltered sectors of the economy;
- To foster a culture of entrepreneurship;
- To boost the small business sector;
- To increase export earnings.

Clearly this vast array of potential objectives is not all achievable at once. Nor even are all these goals mutually compatible. One trade-off that has been particularly well-ventilated in South Africa is that between cash maximization (for sovereign debt reduction or other purposes) versus competing goals such as enhancing competition, expanding service provision networks, or ensuring consumer welfare. The latter goals require regulatory or other constraints that may adversely affect price, so that if the success of privatization that aims at the latter goals is judged solely by reference to the former criteria (cash maximization and or debt reduction), it might wrongly seem merely a mild or negative success. Fortunately, the task of navigating these priorities and, where necessary, choosing among them is somewhat advanced in South Africa.

X. South African Priorities And The Current State Of Play

On 31 August 1995, governmental guidelines on state asset restructuring ("The August Guidelines") significantly clarified South Africa's priorities. These are:
- Facilitating economic growth;
- Funding the Reconstruction and Development Program (the new South African developmental agenda);
- Creating wider ownership in the economy;
- Mobilizing private sector capital;
- Reducing state debt;
- Enhancing competitiveness;
- Promoting fair competition; and
- Financing growth and requirements for competitiveness.

With the release of the August Guidelines, six sectoral task teams were established by government in each of the areas of the economy where the state holds assets. These are:
- Post and Telecommunications;
- Energy (electricity and fuels);
- Transport (ports, harbor, roads, airlines, etc.);
- Defence (arms manufacture, procurement and marketing);
- Development financing institutions (Industrial Development Corporation, Development Bank of South Africa, etc.); and
- Other assets (e.g., state forestry company; state-owned holiday resorts and various scattered assets).

Each of these government task teams generally comprises the Minister of Public Enterprises (which generally holds government's shares in its enterprises), the Ministry of Finance, and any relevant regulatory Ministers (e.g., the Minister of Transport on that task team; the Minister of Forestry on that one). On certain task teams the Ministry of Trade and Industry is also represented (principally Defence and development finance institutions).

In February 1996, as a further step forward, the South African government and the trade union movement concluded a National Framework Agreement, designed to ensure adequate consultation throughout the state asset restructuring process.

The selection and appointment of sovereign advisors is imminent.

XI. Conclusion

A key feature of the South African state asset restructuring process is the emphasis on transparency. The complex social goals involved will not be successfully attained unless these goals, rather than extraneous and potentially self-interested influences, determine the course of events, the design of proposals and the evaluation of competing bids.

In summary, the South African state asset restructuring debate, like so many legal and policy debates in transitional societies, is one in which strict legal (or legalistic) considerations jockey for attention alongside large questions of societal reform. It is an exciting time for lawyers, one in which legal practice and legal reform are in a period of mutually reinforcing ferment.

Johannesburg, South Africa
May 1996

CHAPTER 13

DEVELOPMENTS IN CURRENT SOUTH AFRICAN ENVIRONMENTAL LAW

By Robyn Stein

South Africa has sometimes been considered a polluter's nirvana – a state where relative environmental lawlessness reigns. The supposition that South African law ignores the environment is both incorrect and unfounded. The South African statute books are, in fact, replete with Parliamentary legislation, Provincial ordinances and local government by-laws which provide for environmental protection and control. The problem, however, is that these laws have often been inadequately enforced.

Over the last two decades, public awareness of environmental matters has been stimulated in South Africa by increased media coverage. Environmental groups have become more and more active both in South Africa and abroad. Important developments in the environmental law context have simultaneously taken place during this period. With the advent of a democracy in South Africa, the protection of the environment is now engaged at a political level and is recognized in the Reconstruction and Development Program. This is because of the urgent need to build a developing economy against a background of limited natural and fiscal resources. This chapter will show that the pace of recent developments with regard to environmental law places added responsibility on the individual and the corporate sector to not only comply with the legislation but also to plan strategically for the future.

I. A Multitude Of Laws

The enactment of environmental laws is not a new phenomenon in South Africa. By the late 1600's, a number of measures were introduced to address environmental issues such as protection of drinking water from contamination as well as the protection of wild animals. In the two centuries that followed, a number of statutes directed at conservation of wildlife resources were introduced.

During the post-World War II period, increased environmental awareness was associated with the intensification of industrial growth and development. Between 1940 and 1969, a number of important environmental statutes were enacted and still remain on the statute books. The introduction of the Water Act and the Atmospheric Pollution Prevention Act were amongst the first legislative measures in South Africa designed to address and control pollution emanating from the growing number of industrial enterprises.

Legislating in the environmental arena has gained momentum over the past three decades and will continue to do so. Set out below are some examples of the principal South African laws pertaining to environmental protection and control.

A. The Environment Conservation Act 73 Of 1989

In 1989, South Africa's second dedicated environmental statute was promulgated in the form of the Environment Conservation Act. This Act repealed and replaced the first Environment Conservation Act which was promulgated in 1982. The 1989 Environment

Conservation Act does not constitute a codification of South African environmental law, but can be categorized as enabling legislation in that it provides the framework for the promulgation of policy and regulations, thus giving more content to the Act itself. The rationale underlying the Environment Conservation Act stressed the need for a flexible parliamentary approach toward the protection of the environment which simultaneously guards against inhibiting the development of industry.

The Minister of Environmental Affairs and Tourism (the "Minister") may determine policy under the provisions of the Environment Conservation Act, which policy thereby gains the force of law. Each minister, competent authority of a Provincial government, local authority or government institution which lawfully exercises powers affecting the environment is obliged to exercise such powers in accordance with policy as determined by the Minister.

On January 21, 1994, the Minister of Environment Affairs (now Environmental Affairs and Tourism) published a General Environmental Policy which he determined pursuant to the provisions of the Environment Conservation Act. The General Environmental Policy adopts the concept of "sustainable development" as the guiding principle for environmental management in South Africa. It states that developmental and education programs are necessary to provide economic growth, social welfare and environmental awareness and that such programs are to be formulated.

With regard to general land use and environmental management, the General Environmental Policy states that a balance must be achieved between environmental conservation and essential development. It provides that before embarking on any large-scale or high impact development project, a planned analysis must be undertaken in which all interested and affected parties must be involved. Furthermore, it provides that in order to attain a sustainable utilization of resources, the principles of integrated environmental management are accepted as one of the management mechanisms. The latter, it is submitted, is an indication of a trend in environmental legislation to require environmental impact assessments, in appropriate circumstances, as a matter of law. As far as pollution control is concerned, the General Environmental Policy provides that a national strategy for integrated waste management and integrated pollution control will be developed in which elements of responsibility, accountability, minimization, treatment and re-use will enjoy priority.

The "polluter pays" principle is incorporated into the Environment Conservation Act by way of "clean-up" obligations resulting from damage to the environment. Such obligations may be imposed by the Minister, the competent authorities of the nine Provincial governments as well as by local authorities. For example, Section 31A provides that, in circumstances where a company or person performs an activity or fails to perform any activity with the result that the environment is or may be seriously damaged, endangered or detrimentally affected, the aforementioned governmental authorities are empowered to direct an offender to (i) cease an activity which in their opinion in fact does or may seriously damage or detrimentally affect the environment or (ii) take steps as such authority deems fit. These directions may require the offender to take those steps which will be necessary to rehabilitate any damage caused to the environment at the offender's expense. Failure to comply with such a direction may lead the authority itself to undertake the necessary steps and to thereafter recover the costs from the offender.

As stated above, the Environment Conservation Act can generally be described as enabling legislation in that it provides the framework for the promulgation of regulations. A number of these regulations have been promulgated in terms of the Environment Conservation Act, which deal with, among other things, noise pollution and the identification of activities which may have a detrimental effect on the environment.

Waste management, including the disposal of hazardous waste, is also controlled under the provisions of Section 20 of the Environment Conservation Act. Pursuant to the Environment Conservation Act, no person may establish, provide or operate any disposal site without a permit issued by the Minister of Water Affairs and Forestry. A "disposal site" is defined in the Environment Conservation Act as a site used for the accumulation of waste and for the purposes of disposing or treatment of such waste. "Waste," in turn, is defined in the Environment Conservation Act (read together with a Government Notice published under the Act which expands the definition) as any matter, whether gaseous, liquid or solid or any combination thereof, which is an undesirable or superfluous by-product, emission, residue or remainder of any process which originates from any residential, commercial or industrial area and which is (i) discarded by any person, (ii) accumulated and stored by any person with the purpose of eventually discarding it (with or without prior treatment connected with the discarding thereof) or (iii) stored by any person with the purpose of recycling, re-using or extracting a usable product from such matter. Hazardous waste is not defined under the Environment Conservation Act or under the regulations promulgated under that statute. Certain matter is, however, excluded from the definition of "waste." For example, water used for industrial purposes or any effluent produced by or resulting from such use which is discharged in compliance with the provisions of the Water Act is deemed not to be waste.

The Environment Conservation Act also has important consequences for waste generators. It provides that, subject to the provisions of any other law, no person shall discard waste or dispose of it in any manner, except (i) at a disposal site for which a permit has been issued or (ii) in a manner or by means of a facility or method, and subject to such conditions, as the Minister may prescribe.

B. The Water Act 54 Of 1956

The Water Act is aimed at the control, conservation and use of water for domestic, agricultural, urban and industrial purposes. The Water Act is administered by the Minister of Water Affairs and Forestry. Although water law in South Africa is primarily regulated pursuant to the Water Act, together with the regulations promulgated under Section 26D thereof, a large number of statutes currently in force also deal directly with water. These statutes mainly concern particular water schemes in South Africa and are likewise administered by the Minister of Water Affairs and Forestry.

The Water Act makes a distinction between public and private water. This is because, under the Water Act, water (whether public or private) is never owned. The distinction between public and private water is employed as a method of allocating water to different users. The purpose of this distinction is to determine who has the right to use water and the manner in which it can be used.

Public water may not be used for industrial purposes except with the permission of a Water Court or pursuant to a permit issued by the Minister. However, the permission of a Water Court will not be required, among other things, where water is supplied by the Minister of Water Affairs and Forestry from a Government water work or by a local authority. The permission of a Water Court will also not be required where the quantity of public water used for industrial purposes in connection with any undertaking does not exceed, during any month, the largest quantity of such water lawfully used in connection with that undertaking during any month within the period of twelve months immediately preceding the commencement of the Water Act. No person may use a quantity of water (from whatever source) for industrial purposes in excess of 150 cubic meters during any day, except under the authority of a permit issued by the Minister of Water Affairs and Forestry and in accordance with any conditions attached to such permit.

The Water Act does not require permission of a Water Court to use subterranean private water for industrial purposes because the owner of the land on or under which it is found generally has a right to use such water. The quantity used is subject to control only in the case of subterranean water control areas. Under Section 21 of the Water Act, a person using water for industrial purposes is obliged to purify any effluent produced by such use in accordance with the requirements which the Minister of Water Affairs and Forestry may from time to time prescribe.

An essential feature of the Water Act is the regulation and control of water pollution. The Act seeks to control pollution and encourages the return of treated water to the source from which it is taken. Fairly wide-ranging "polluter-pays" provisions are incorporated into the Water Act whereby the Minister of Water Affairs and Forestry may recover the costs associated with the clean-up of water pollution under defined circumstances.

Under Section 23 of the Water Act, it is an offense to willfully or negligently commit any act that could pollute any public or private water in such a way as to render it less fit for, among other things, its ordinary use by other persons, the propagation of fish or other aquatic life or recreation or other legitimate purposes. No other pollution standard is given in the Water Act. Although the constitutionality of this provision of the Water Act is questionable, unless an accused brings proof to the contrary, willfulness or negligence is presumed if it is proved by the prosecution that an accused committed any act which could pollute water.

C. The Atmospheric Pollution Prevention Act 45 Of 1965

The Atmospheric Pollution Prevention Act regulates air pollution at the national government level. The Health Act, discussed below, also deals with limited aspects of air pollution.

Part II of the Atmospheric Pollution Prevention Act sets out controls for noxious or offensive gases, which include a wide range of groups or compounds when in a gaseous form. The Atmospheric Pollution Prevention Act controls noxious or offensive gases resulting from the operation of what is referred to in the Act as a "Scheduled Process." Sixty-nine Scheduled Processes have so far been listed in the Second Schedule to the Act.

Under the Atmospheric Pollution Prevention Act, it is an offense to carry out any of the Scheduled Processes in the absence of a registration certificate. It is also an offense to erect or alter buildings intended to be operated as a Scheduled Process in the absence of a registration certificate. The registration certificate may be canceled or suspended if the holder fails to comply with its conditions or fails to take steps laid down by the Chief Air Pollution Control Officer of the Department of Health to ensure the more effective operation of the appliances provided for in the registration certificate or to ensure the more effective prevention of air pollution.

A registration certificate is granted by the Chief Air Pollution Control Officer if he or she is satisfied that the "best practicable means" are being adopted for the control of air pollution caused or to be caused by the Scheduled Process concerned. The concept of "best practicable means" is defined in the Atmospheric Pollution Prevention Act and includes use and maintenance of pollution control equipment and the adoption of any other control methods, taking into account local conditions, costs, the prevailing extent of technical knowledge and the well-being of people in close proximity to the plant concerned.

The control of smoke (which includes soot, grit and gritty particles) is dependent upon the declaration of a controlled area by a local authority under the provisions of the Atmospheric Pollution Prevention Act. The manufacture, importation, installation and placement of fuel burning appliances and the construction of chimneys is regulated by the Atmospheric Pollution Prevention Act and requires the approval of a local authority or the Chief Air Pollution Control Officer.

Nuisances arising from smoke emissions are controlled under the Atmospheric Pollution Prevention Act through a notice abatement procedure. Failure to comply with a notice from a local authority to abate a nuisance caused by smoke or any other product of combustion emanating from any premises amounts to a criminal offense. If non-compliance continues for more than one month after conviction, Section 17 of the Act provides that the local authority can take whatever action it considers necessary to abate the smoke and recover costs incurred from the polluter.

Vehicle emissions are also controlled under Part V of the Atmospheric Pollution Prevention Act. The provisions of the Atmospheric Pollution Prevention Act controlling vehicle emissions are applicable to areas specifically designated by the Minister. The control of vehicle emissions under the Atmospheric Pollution Prevention Act only applies to an area falling under the jurisdiction of a local authority.

D. The Health Act 63 Of 1977

The Health Act provides measures for the promotion and protection of the health of the inhabitants of South Africa. The Health Act is principally directed at the human environment.

Pursuant to Section 27 of the Health Act, where in the opinion of a local authority, a condition has arisen in a district which is of such a nature as to be offensive or a danger to health unless immediately remedied (and to which the provisions of the Atmospheric Pollution Prevention Act are not applicable), a local authority may serve a written notice on the person responsible for such condition having arisen or on the occupier or owner of the premises on which the condition exists, calling upon the person responsible or owner/occupier to remedy the condition within such period as may be specified in the notice. Failure to comply with any such notice constitutes a criminal offense.

The Health Act also contains a "polluter pays" provision, in that if a person on whom a notice is served failed to comply with that notice, the local authority may enter the premises in question and take all such steps as may be necessary to remedy the condition. Once this has been done, the local authority may recover the costs of remedying the condition from the person on whom the notice was served or from the owner or occupier of the premises in question.

E. The Occupational Health And Safety Act 85 Of 1993

In South Africa, the Occupational Health and Safety Act constitutes the principal statute regulating occupational health and safety in the industrial workplace. Regulations promulgated under the now repealed Machinery and Occupational Health and Safety Act have been retained. These relate to noise, asbestos, environmental safety, lead, hazardous substances, temperature and lighting in the workplace. Compliance with the requirements of the Occupational Health and Safety Act forms part of the mandatory duties of an employer who intends to operate a workplace. Pre-existing conditions on a property which are unsafe or a danger to health may require improvements to the extent that they do not comply with the provisions of the Occupational Health and Safety Act.

Pursuant to the Occupational Health and Safety Act, an employer also has wide-ranging obligations to third parties other than its employees. An employer is obliged to conduct an undertaking in such a manner as to ensure, as far as is reasonably practicable, that persons (other than employees) who may be affected by the employer's activities are not thereby exposed to hazards to their health and safety.

F. The Hazardous Substances Act 15 Of 1973

The Hazardous Substances Act applies to substances declared by the Minister of Health to be a Group I, II, III or IV hazardous substance. Groups I and II relate to substances of a toxic, corrosive, irritant, strongly sensitizing or flammable nature. Groups III and IV relate to electronic products and radio-active materials, respectively.

Under Section 3 of the Hazardous Substances Act, no person may "sell" (which includes offer, advertise, keep, display, transmit, consign, convey, deliver for sale, dispose of, exchange, manufacture or import for use in South Africa) a Group I or Group III hazardous substance without a license, and then only pursuant to the terms and conditions of that license. Regulations promulgated under the Hazardous Substances Act also impose conditions on activities involving Group I hazardous substances, including their manner of supply or sale, the records kept, permissible purchasers, the labelling of containers and the disposal of empty containers. The transportation of Group I and II hazardous substances by means of road tanker is also governed by regulations promulgated under the Hazardous Substances Act.

G. Ordinances And By-Laws

Provincial ordinances emanated from the Provincial of the four previous provinces of South Africa. Under the Interim Constitution, South Africa now comprises nine Provinces, each with their own legislature and defined legislative powers. Until repealed, the ordinances promulgated by the former Provincial Administrators remain in place.

Legislation promulgated by a local authority in South Africa is referred to as a "by-law." By-laws are examples of delegated legislation which may, among other things, be tested for reasonableness and certainty by the Supreme Court of South Africa under the process of judicial review. Pollution is commonly regulated by local authorities through by-laws which prohibit littering of, for example, public places and streams. Failure to comply with the provisions of these by-laws is generally a criminal offense. By-laws differ from local authority to local authority as far as pollution and environmental control and protection are concerned.

Another common method used by local authorities to control pollution is the notice abatement procedure prescribed for dealing with nuisances. Under this procedure, a notice is served on the author of a nuisance calling upon him, her or it to remove or abate the nuisance within a specified time. Failure to comply with the notice is an offense and entitles the local authority concerned to remove or abate the nuisance itself and to recover costs incurred from the party causing the nuisance.

II. The Fragmented Administration Of The Laws

The existence of a myriad of environmental statutes in South Africa has had the net effect that their administration has been placed in the hands of a multitude of public authorities. Under the statutes, various government departments have wide-ranging inspection and control powers.

Pursuant to the Interim Constitution, South Africa's nine Provincial legislatures have legislative competence in respect of environmental matters. These legislatures have the power and function to administer certain environmental statutes which have been assigned to the Provinces under the Interim Constitution. Furthermore, the nine Provincial legislatures also have the competence to make laws which are reasonably necessary for or incidental to the effective exercise of their legislative competence in respect of environmental matters. Under the Interim Constitution, an Act of Parliament and a Provincial statute are construed as being consistent with each other, unless and only to the extent that they are expressly or by necessary implication inconsistent with each other. Under the New Constitution (which is expected to come into operation in late 1996 or early 1997 and which will replace the Interim Constitution), the nine Provincial legislatures will have exclusive competence to pass legislation in respect of, among other things, control of public nuisance, noise pollution, refuse removal, refuse dumps and solid waste disposal. The nine Provincial legislatures will continue to share concurrent legislative competence with the National government in respect of, among other things, the environment, pollution control and regional planning and development.

Local authorities will also have the power to administer the control of public nuisance, noise pollution and refuse removal, refuse dumps and solid waste disposal. The New Constitution reserves the right of the Provincial legislatures to monitor and oversee the effective performance by the municipalities of these functions.

On the face of it, the New Constitution lays to rest any fear of yet another administrative and legal minefield. The powers of the Provinces are checked by provisions of the New Constitution which deal with conflicting National and Provincial legislation. Under the New Constitution, National legislation that applies uniformly throughout the whole country prevails over Provincial legislation if it is necessary for the protection of the environment.

Integration of the various spheres of government is an imperative of the New Constitution. Chapter 3 is dedicated to what is referred to as "Co-operative Government." Chapter 3 confirms that National, Provincial and local spheres of government are not only distinct but are also interdependent and interrelated. All spheres of government and all organs of State within each tier of government are enjoined by Chapter 3 to co-operate with each other in mutual trust and good faith. They are obliged to co-ordinate their actions and legislation with each other. An Act of Parliament must establish or provide for structures and institutions to promote and facilitate intergovernmental relations.

The Department of Environmental Affairs and Tourism, through the Minister, is principally charged with the administration of the Environment Conservation Act, although the Department of Water Affairs and Forestry also has certain functions in respect of waste management under that statute. The Water Act is administered, through the Minister of Water Affairs and Forestry, by the Department of Water Affairs and Forestry. Both the Health Act and the Hazardous Substances Act are administered, through the Minister of Health, by the Department of Health. The Atmospheric Pollution Prevention Act was previously administered by the Air Pollution Control Directorate of the Department of Health but now falls under the auspices of the Department of Environmental Affairs and Tourism's Air Pollution Control Directorate. The Occupational Health and Safety Act is primarily administered, through the Minister of Labor, by the Department of Labor. Each of the statutes discussed above contains delegation powers pursuant to which the administration of various provisions of the respective statutes may be delegated to local authorities and the Provincial governments. Various other government departments, such as the Department of Transport and the Department of Mineral and Energy Affairs, also have responsibility for environmental and related matters.

Criminal penalties are imposed in South Africa for a breach of a statutory provision. Such punitive measures may include fairly substantial fines and imprisonment in appropriate circumstances. In addition to any contravention of a statutory provision, liability may also arise in the common law by way of delictual (tort) liability. A breach of any statutory duty or prohibition contained in legislation will be regarded as constituting a wrongful act or omission and, provided that the other elements of a delict are proven (namely, wrongfulness, negligence, causation and patrimonial loss), the courts will award damages for any harm or injury to persons or property caused by the contravention of a statutory provision. However, if the relevant legislation makes it clear that it was the intention of the legislature that the penalty imposed in the legislation for contravention of the relevant provisions is to be the sole remedy, then the contravention in question will not constitute grounds for recovery of damages in terms of the law of delict. It should also be pointed out that the mere fact that a person has been granted a permit to carry out a particular activity does not mean that the permit holder will be immune from liability in a delictual claim for damages.

With regard to criminal offenses, the liability of directors or employees of corporate bodies is of significant importance. Under Section 332(5) of the Criminal Procedure Act, when an offense has been committed, whether by performance of any act or by the failure to perform any act, for which any corporate body is or was liable to prosecution, any person who was at the time of the commission of the offense, a director or employee of the corporate body shall be deemed in their personal capacity to be guilty of the said offense unless it is proven that such person did not take part in the commission of the offense and could not have prevented it.

The foregoing Section of the Criminal Procedure Act has far-reaching implications. Under South African company law principles, a director may well be a party to the reckless or fraudulent conduct of a company's business even in the absence of positive steps taken in carrying out the company's business.

III. New Developments In A Developing Economy

If one steps back and observes the extent of environmental legislation and the number of public bodies charged with the administration of environmental laws, one might conclude that a legal minefield exists in South Africa for any would-be polluter. However, the availability of human resources to monitor and control polluting activities has been severely limited largely due to financial constraints in the budgets of the various regulatory authorities. The number of prosecutions for illegal activities, which may contravene more than one of the available environmental protection statutes, has traditionally been relatively minimal. Recent statements made and steps taken by, for example, the Minister of Water Affairs and Forestry, indicate the South African Government's intention to take a more stringent approach to prosecuting environmental offenders.

South Africa is not a country of unlimited natural resources. In the interests of preserving those resources for a developing economy, more attention will be paid in future to the concept of sustainable development and the implementation of South Africa's environmental laws. Sustainable development has been acknowledged in the Reconstruction and Development Program.

As stated above, with the advent of democracy, environmental matters are now engaged on a political level. In post-April 1994 South Africa, a number of legislative and policy reform efforts have been initiated in order to address various inadequacies in the environmental legislation and its administration. These inadequacies have their origin in a superseded racist political order, namely, the apartheid order, which exercised political powers in the interests of a minority of South Africans.

In 1995, the formulation of a new environmental policy for South Africa was commissioned by the Department of Environmental Affairs and Tourism. In order to ensure widespread consultation and the development of national environmental policy, a national conference was called in August 1995, titled "Connep" (Consultative Conference on National Environmental Policy), where representatives from different stakeholder groups formulated the process to be followed. In April 1996, as a first step in the Connep process, the Department of Environmental Affairs and Tourism published a Discussion Document which has several sections covering a wide range of environmental, institutional and governance issues. An objective of the Connep process is to produce a White Paper on environmental policy and possibly subsequent legislation to replace the present Environment Conservation Act.

In 1995, the Minister of Water Affairs and Forestry initiated a process for the revision of South Africa's 1956 Water Act and other water laws. The Minister of Water Affairs and Forestry appointed a Water Law Review Panel in mid-1995 which drafted a set of principles on which a new South African water law could be based. The Water Law Review Panel reported to the Minister and the process of drafting principles was taken further by a Water Law Steering Committee, comprised of three members of the Water Law Review Panel and four members of the Department of Water Affairs and Forestry. The Water Law Steering Committee finalized a further set of Draft Principles in April 1996, which have been published for public comment. The process of revising the Water Act continues with a number of research initiatives and public consultation processes currently taking place in South Africa.

In 1992, the Department of Environmental Affairs and Tourism initiated the National Holistic Policy for Integration of Pollution Control ("IPC") project. The ambit of the IPC project was extended in 1995 to address the need to create integrated regulatory structures to effectively control waste management. A tangible result of the IPC and Waste Management project is the preparation of a White Paper on Integrated Pollution Control and Integrated Waste Management. The IPC and Waste Management project has recently been subsumed into the Connep process discussed above.

Perhaps the most significant development in the context of the environment under South Africa's new democracy is the entrenchment of a right to an environment that is not detrimental to a person's health and well-being as a fundamental right under Section 29 of the Interim Constitution's Bill of Rights. Although the Constitutional Court has recently held that the fundamental rights embodied in the Bill of Rights under the Interim Constitution are not enforceable as between private citizens, it appears that the New Constitution as adopted by the Constitutional Assembly on May 8, 1996 will change this. The environmental rights clause under Section 24 of the New Constitution's Bill of Rights provides that everyone has the right (i) to an environment that is not harmful to their health or well-being and (ii) to have the environment protected, for the benefit of present and future generations, through reasonable legislative and other measures that (a) prevent pollution and ecological degradation, (b) promote conservation and (c) secure ecologically sustainable development and use of natural resources while promoting justifiable economic and social development.

IV.   Conclusion

Future development of the environmental laws in South Africa will undoubtedly take place in a legislative environment that endorses the need for integration and coordination at the various tiers of government and their regulatory authorities. This should remedy the currently fractured and disparate state of the laws regulating environmental matters and their administration. The South African Government has undertaken to ensure that all South

Africans, present and future, have the right to a decent quality of life through the sustainable use of resources. The pace of change in environmental law and its administration should ensure that environmental standards in South Africa compare favorably with international standards.

Johannesburg, South Africa
June 1996

CHAPTER 14

RESOLVING COMMERCIAL DISPUTES IN SOUTH AFRICA

By David W. Butler

I. Introduction

This chapter deals with the resolution of commercial disputes with a South African connection, from the perspective of a foreign lawyer advising a client who has business dealings with South African parties. In the context of international commercial disputes, arbitration is an attractive option, because of a distrust felt by two parties from different countries regarding the other's legal system and courts. This distrust becomes more acute when the one party is a state or state-controlled corporation. A foreign arbitral award is also often easier to enforce than a foreign judgment. This is also the case in South Africa. Furthermore the right to appear in South African courts is limited to those lawyers who have been formally admitted to practise there. As a result, a foreign disputant wishing to litigate in South Africa will invariably have to brief local lawyers. This restriction does not apply to arbitration.

For these reasons, greater emphasis is placed in this contribution on arbitration rather than on litigation. The high costs and long delays associated with both litigation and the more formal type of arbitration are causing the business sector in South Africa to give increasing attention to the techniques of alternative dispute resolution for resolving their disputes. These techniques are consensual and voluntary, and, outside the labour field, are free from statutory regulation. Therefore, mediation, as the most important of the ADR techniques, is only briefly considered in the final section of this contribution. Nevertheless, particularly parties entering into a long-term commercial relationship would be well advised to make some contractual provision for mediation or conciliation procedures as a precondition to using litigation or arbitration to resolve a commercial dispute.

II. Litigation
    A.   Structure And Jurisdiction Of The Courts

The superior courts consist of the Constitutional Court, which is the court of final instance over all matters relating to the interpretation, protection and enforcement of the Constitution, including a violation of any fundamental right entrenched by the Bill of Rights and the constitutionality of any Act of Parliament (see s. 98(2) of the Constitution of the Republic of South Africa, Act 200 of 1993) and the Supreme Court, which consists of an Appellate Division and the various provincial and local divisions. Magistrates' courts, established by the Inferior Courts Act 32 of 1944, now have civil jurisdiction in claims up to R100 000, but are not really suited for dealing with complex commercial claims, even if their value falls within the jurisdiction of the magistrates' courts. The remainder of this section is devoted to the civil jurisdiction of a provincial or local division of the Supreme Court, as the court most likely to hear a dispute regarding a substantial claim of a commercial nature in the first instance. Only a brief summary of a complex subject is attempted.

A provincial or local division of the Supreme Court has inherent jurisdiction under the common law and the jurisdiction conferred on it by statute. Such division has jurisdiction over all persons residing in its area of jurisdiction (Supreme Court Act 59 of 1959

s. 19(1)(a)). A domestic corporation is resident at the place where its registered office is located or where it has its principal place of business, i.e. the seat of its central management and control. In the case of an external company, with a registered office in South Africa as required by s 322 of the Companies Act 61 of 1973, the company will be resident at its registered office (see Malan et al. 1995 *TSAR* 115-6).

A court will also have jurisdiction in causes arising within its jurisdiction, (a) if the defendant is an *incola* of South Africa (i.e. resident there), or (b) in the case of a peregrine defendant (ie a defendant residing outside South Africa) there has either been an attachment to establish jurisdiction or a submission to jurisdiction. A contractual claim will be a cause arising, if the contract was entered into there or was to have been performed there, in whole or in part, or if the breach on which the plaintiff relies was committed there. A claim in tort arises in the area where the tort was committed. It must be noted that submission to jurisdiction by a peregrine defendant (in the sense used above) can only provide a substitute for attachment where the cause of action is one arising within the court's jurisdiction. Where the cause of action is not one arising within the jurisdiction, attachment of person or property is essential to give the court jurisdiction over a foreign resident. (See further Malan et al. 1995 *TSAR* 117-122; Erasmus A1-20 - A1-31.)

Where a South African court otherwise has jurisdiction, but the parties have chosen a foreign court to hear their dispute by incorporating an appropriate clause in their contract, that clause is not absolutely binding and the South African court retains a discretion to hear the matter itself and not to refer it to the foreign court (see Butler v. Banimar Shipping Co SA 1978 (4) SA 753 (SE) 761G-H; Yorigami Maritime Construction Co Ltd v. Nissho-Iwai Co Ltd 1977 (4) SA 682 (C) 694A-B). Conversely, there is some support for the view that a South African court may decline to exercise jurisdiction which it otherwise has over a defendant by virtue of the forum conveniens doctrine, if the defendant is able to show compelling reasons why the matter should rather be tried by a competent foreign court (see Estate Agents Board v. Lek 1979 (3) SA 1048 (A) 1067E; Forsyth 155-8).

The jurisdiction of South African courts over foreign states is regulated by the Foreign States Immunities Act 87 of 1981. The courts only have jurisdiction where provided by the Act (s. 2(1)), for example in relation to a commercial transaction (s 4). A foreign state entity which is distinct from the organs of government shall only be immune in respect of acts performed in the exercise of sovereign authority and in circumstances where the foreign state would have been immune (s.15(1)). Property of the foreign state which is being used for commercial purposes is not immune from attachment (s. 14(3)).

B.   Legal Practitioners

South Africa, following the practice in England, still has a dual bar system, with lawyers being admitted to practise either as attorneys or as advocates. Advocates are classified either as junior or senior advocates. The right to represent clients in court is presently regulated by the Right of Appearance in Courts Act 62 of 1995. An advocate is entitled to appear on behalf of any person in any court in South Africa (s. 2). Particularly in civil (as opposed to criminal) matters, an advocate will only appear if briefed by an attorney, and a senior advocate will usually be briefed together with a junior. An attorney has the right to appear on behalf of any person in any court except the Supreme Court or the

Constitutional Court (s. 3(1)). Attorneys may therefore appear on behalf of clients in the magistrates' courts. An attorney complying with certain conditions can now however acquire the right to appear on a client's behalf in the Supreme Court (ss. 3(2) and 4). Such attorneys may also appear in the Constitutional Court s. 3(3)). It is envisaged that because of the nature of a busy attorney's practice, attorneys specialising in commercial work will still continue to brief advocates, as trial specialists, in complex matters.

C. Basic Litigation Procedures

South African civil procedure is English in origin and contains the features of the English version of the adversarial model. The parties' lawyers play a dominant role in the proceedings and decide what evidence to present. South African law of evidence is also based on that of England and is characterised by exclusionary rules. The judge plays a largely passive role. There are no juries. The discussion below relates to the proceedings in the Supreme Court.

The two basic procedures in civil matters are (a) application proceedings and (b) an action. Evidence in application proceedings is on affidavit. Thus, although application proceedings are quicker than an action, they are usually not appropriate where a material question of fact is in dispute, which will have to be resolved by oral evidence.

The action procedure commences by means of a summons with the issues in dispute being defined by way of an exchange of pleadings. In practice, pleadings are often drafted to promote trial by ambush, by disclosing as little as possible about the parties' cases. Only after the close of pleadings is a party usually entitled to call on the other party to make discovery of all relevant documents in that party's possession or under his control. The party calling for discovery is entitled to inspect the documents discovered, except those for which privilege is claimed. In complex commercial disputes, this unrestricted right to discovery can result in unnecessary expense and in the proceedings being submerged in a mass of insufficiently relevant documents. There is no procedure for the pre-trial oral examination of the opposing party's witnesses. A party wishing to call an expert witness must give notice to the other side and provide a summary of the expert's evidence, although in practice these summaries tend to be very brief. Except in the Commercial Court, discussed below, there is no provision for the exchange of lists of witnesses or witness statements by witnesses of fact before the trial, which again promotes trial by ambush. At the trial great reliance is placed on the cross-examination of witnesses by the opposing party's counsel to test the reliability of their evidence. A judge may not call a witness, including an expert, without the consent of the parties. S. 19 *bis* of the Supreme Court Act 59 of 1959 allows the court, with the consent of the parties, to refer matters of a technical nature to a referee for investigation and report to the court, which then decides to what extent it will accept the report. This provision is little used in practice.

Where an important witness is outside the country and unwilling or unable to come to the court, the court may, on application, permit the appointment of a commissioner to receive the evidence abroad. The evidence will then be received by the commissioner in the presence of the parties and their counsel, with the witness being examined and cross-examined in the usual way. To reduce expense, the court may be prepared to allow the evidence on commission to be obtained by means of interrogatories. Specific questions from the parties, approved by the court, are then put to the witness by the commissioner in the absence of the parties and their counsel. (See the Uniform Rules of Court rule 38(3) and (5).) To ensure the attendance of the witness, the party seeking the appointment of a commissioner may apply to the court for the issue of a letter of request for appropriate assistance, addressed to the government of the country in which the witness resides and in which the commission will sit.

In claims for payment of money on a so-called liquid document, the plaintiff can use an expedited form of procedure known as provisional sentence proceedings. The court also has a discretionary power to issue a declaratory order, on the application of an interested person, where no consequential relief is sought (see the Supreme Court Act 59 of 1959 s. 19(1)(a)(iii).)

Some of the difficulties inherent in present trial procedures referred to above can be countered by having the matter tried by the Commercial Court, established within the Witwatersrand Local Division (WLD) of the Supreme Court during 1993 and regulated by a Practice Direction, authorising certain departures from the usual rules. Commercial cases are allocated to judges with particular commercial experience. Only matters in which the WLD has jurisdiction can be referred to the Commercial Court. Both parties must apply jointly for the action to be designated as a commercial matter, after the close of pleadings. To qualify, the action must be a substantial matter of a broadly commercial nature, including a matter relating to international trade. If the Judge President decides to designate it as a commercial matter, he allocates it to a specific judge who will from then on be actively involved in the pre-trial procedures, including the hearing of the application for directions which will regulate the further conduct of the case. The most important innovation in the Commercial Court is that written statements of witnesses of fact will normally be exchanged well before the trial. While the statements must contain the complete oral evidence which the party intends to lead from the witness at the trial, the statements are not in themselves evidence. Furthermore, the witness, if called, will give evidence in chief at the trial in the usual way unless the judge otherwise directs.

The Commercial Court provides for a degree of case management by the trial judge and moves away from trial by ambush by normally requiring an exchange of all witnesses' statements. However, because the Commercial Court operates by a Practice Direction, and not by its own Rules of Court, it only has jurisdiction by consent, which must be obtained at the close of pleadings. This is a fundamental weakness, as a party with a weak case and wishing to delay the outcome is unlikely to consent. (See generally regarding the Commercial Court Erasmus D2-8 - D2-15.)

Regarding class actions, s. 7(4)(b)(iv) of the Constitution of the Republic of South Africa Act 200 of 1993 makes specific provision for the use of a class action to remedy an infringement or threatened infringement of a fundamental right entrenched in the bill of rights in Chapter 3 of the interim constitution. For the rest, class actions are not well developed in South African law and are presently being investigated by the South African Law Commission. A class action is presently not available for those seeking compensation or damages, caused for example to consumers by the marketing of a defective medication. (See further Erasmus A2-31 - A2-33.)

D. Urgent Interlocutory Remedies

After some initial uncertainty, it is now clear that South African courts will be prepared to grant the equivalent of the English Anton Piller order for the preservation of evidence. To obtain the order in camera and without notice to the respondent, it will be necessary for the applicant to establish prima facie that (a) the applicant has a cause of action against the respondent which the applicant intends to pursue; (b) the respondent has in his possession specified documents or things constituting evidence of great importance in substantiating the applicant's case but to which the applicant has no real or personal right; and (c) there is a real and well-founded fear that the evidence may be hidden or destroyed before the case comes to trial or to the stage of discovery. (See Shoba v. Officer Commanding, Temporary Police Camp, Wagendrift Dam 1995 (4) SA 1 (A) 15G-I, where the court also held at 17E that there was no reason to restrict the remedy to intellectual property cases.)

South African law also recognises an anti-dissipation interdict derived from the civil law, which performs the same function as the Mareva injunction of English law. The applicant must establish prima facie that he has a well-grounded fear of irreparable loss because (a) the respondent has no bona fide defence against the applicant's apparently valid claim; (b) the respondent has assets in South Africa; and (c) the respondent intends defeating the applicant's claim by secreting or disposing of those assets or by removing them beyond the jurisdiction of the court. The applicant can apply to have the application heard in camera and, in an appropriate case, may also obtain an ancillary order compelling the respondent to disclose his assets in South Africa. (See Knox D'Arcy Ltd v. Jamieson 1994 (3) SA 700 (W) 705A-710F.)

E. Costs

In South African law, the successful party is usually entitled to be awarded costs, in other words costs follow the event. The purpose of an award of costs is to indemnify the successful litigant for the expense occasioned by his having been unjustly forced by his opponent to institute or defend legal proceedings. Because the amount recoverable is subject to taxation (i.e. assessment) by the taxing master of the court, and because "party and party" as opposed to "attorney and client" costs are usually awarded, the successful party can only hope to recover a substantial portion of his costs and not a full indemnity. Legal practitioners in South Africa are presently not permitted to take cases on a contingency fee basis. A party who believes he will ultimately be successful and receive a costs award may for this reason be reluctant to settle if the effect will be to deprive him of recovering those costs. The question of costs is therefore likely to be an important factor in settlement negotiations at any stage prior to judgment, once substantial costs have been incurred.

Although the court has a wide discretion to award costs, this discretion must be exercised judicially, failing which the award may be set aside on appeal. The court should therefore only depart from the rule that costs follow the event if special circumstances are present. A plaintiff who has achieved "substantial success" by recovering more than the defendant offered, even if this amount is much less than the plaintiff claimed, is usually still entitled to costs, particularly if he has proved a substantial right. However, where the claim is exorbitant and this has resulted in unnecessary costs being incurred, the successful party will usually be deprived of at least a portion of his costs. The successful party may also be deprived of a portion of his costs or be ordered to pay wasted costs where he has taken unnecessary steps or followed the wrong procedure. Misconduct by a party or his lawyers in connection with the litigation may constitute special circumstances justifying a special award of costs.

Costs are normally awarded as between party and party. These do not include all the costs which a party incurred but only those which appear to the taxing master to have been *necessary* for the attainment of justice. Additional expenses incurred by the successful party cannot be recovered from the party ordered to pay costs, in the absence of an order for "attorney and client" costs, which will only be granted in exceptional circumstances. Normally, some form of serious misconduct by a party in connection with the litigation will be required to justify such an order against him.

The law of costs is a complex subject which has generated much case law. The purpose of the brief discussion above is merely to warn foreign parties of the basic implications of costs awards if contemplating litigation in South Africa. (See further e. g. Cilliers The Law of Costs; Cilliers "Costs" in LAWSA vol. 3 441-541.)

F. Judgments In A Foreign Currency

South African courts are prepared to give judgment in a foreign currency, also on a claim for damages, whether arising from breach of contract or a tort, where the loss has been felt in a foreign currency. The damages are then assessed as at the date of the breach or tort, following the usual rules, but in the foreign currency. It is possible for the defendant to satisfy a judgment given in a foreign currency by paying the rand equivalent of the foreign currency as at the date of payment. (See e. g. Elgin Brown and Hamer (Pty) Ltd v Dampskibsselskabet Torm Ltd 1988 (4) SA 671 (N) 674F-J; Standard Chartered Bank of Canada v. Nedperm Bank Ltd 1994 (4) SA 747 (A) 775A 777C-D.) The ability of a South African debtor to pay in a foreign currency and the ability of a foreign judgment creditor to take a payment in rands out of the country is presently subject to exchange control regulations.

G. Recovery Of Interest

Although, as stated above, South African courts are prepared to give judgment in a foreign currency, they have given insufficient attention to the rate at which interest should be paid on such judgments. For several years South Africa has experienced relatively high inflation and interest rates when compared to major Western countries. Logically, when giving judgment in a foreign currency, a court should award interest at a rate appropriate to the foreign currency, where it is empowered to do so. Otherwise, where rates applicable to the foreign currency are lower than those usually applicable in South Africa to judgment debts, the result will be to over-compensate the plaintiff. When enforcing foreign judgments in a foreign currency under their common-law powers, South African courts have been prepared to award interest at the rate and from the date specified in the foreign judgment (see Barclays Bank of Swaziland Ltd v. Mnyeketi 1992 (3) SA 425 (W); Gabelsberger v Babl 1994 (2) SA 677 (T) 680B-D). However, in the Elgin Brown and Standard Chartered cases referred to in para 2.5 above, interest was awarded on damages in a foreign currency at the usual rate applicable to South African judgment debts in terms of the Prescribed Rate of Interest Act 55 of 1975. It should also be noted that under South African law, in the absence of a contractual provision to the contrary, interest only runs on a claim for damages once the amount of the damages has been fixed by the court. This rule operates to protect the defendant, who will therefore benefit from procedural delays prior to judgment. (See further Butler (1995) 6 Stell LR 291 315-20.)

Lawyers acting for foreign parties contracting with South African businesses should therefore try to ensure that the contract contains appropriate provisions to avoid the problems referred to in this paragraph.

H. Enforcement Of Foreign Judgments

The judgment of a foreign court is presently not directly enforceable in South Africa but constitutes a cause of action for enforcement proceedings in South African courts, providing that the conditions set out below are complied with (see Jones v. Krok 1995 (1) SA 677 (A) 685B-E). (Provided the foreign judgment is for a fixed sum of money, it will be possible to enforce it by expedited provisional sentence proceedings as opposed to an ordinary action: see Jones v. Krok above at 685I-686B.) The first condition is that the foreign court which gave the judgment must have had "international competence" to do so under South African law. Therefore, in the case of judgments sounding in money, the defendant must have been resident or domiciled in the foreign country or must have submitted to the jurisdiction of the foreign court. Jurisdiction established by the attachment of property or because the cause of action arose in the foreign country will not suffice for this purpose. Secondly, the judgment must be final and conclusive in its effect and not have become superannuated. A judgment is final once it cannot be altered by the court which delivered it, even if it is subject to appeal to a higher court. However, where the judgment is shown to be subject to appeal or that an appeal is pending, the South African court asked to enforce the judgment enjoys a discretion to stay the enforcement proceedings pending the final determination of the appeal in the foreign jurisdiction (see further Jones v. Krok above at 692B-G). Thirdly, the recognition and enforcement of the judgment must not be contrary to public policy. (See further the discussion of public policy in the context of punitive damages below.) Fourthly, the judgment must not have been obtained by fraudulent means. Fifthly, the judgment must not involve the enforcement of a penal or revenue law of the foreign state. Finally, the enforcement of the judgment must not be precluded by the Protection of Businesses Act 99 of 1978, discussed below. Apart from this, the South African court will not go into the merits of the case adjudicated upon by the foreign court or review or set aside its findings of fact or law.

In terms of s. 1 of the Protection of Businesses Act 99 of 1978, no judgment or arbitral award made outside South Africa shall be enforced inside South Africa without the consent of the Minister of Trade and Industry, if the judgment or award arose from an act or transaction "connected with the mining, production, importation, exportation, refinement, possession, use or sale of or ownership to any matter or material, of whatever nature, whether within, outside, into or from [South Africa]". The provision applies notwithstanding any other law or legal rule to the contrary. It was apparently originally enacted to protect

South African businesses "from the far-reaching tentacles of American anti-trust legislation". "Matter or material" has been interpreted as referring to raw materials or substances from which physical things are made. A transaction involving the charter or possession of a ship (as a manufactured item) has therefore been held to fall outside the section (see Tradex Ocean Transportation SA v. MV Silvergate (or Astyanax) 1994 (4) SA 119 (D) 121A).

The Act was subsequently amended by the insertion of additional provisions to restrict the enforcement of judgments from the United States in product-liability cases, particularly against South African asbestos producers. A foreign judgment arising from a transaction referred to above and directing the payment of multiple or punitive damages cannot be enforced in South Africa even with the Minister's consent (s. 1A). However, where punitive damages, whether contractual or in tort, are awarded to an American party against a South African party by reason of the breach of a joint venture agreement for the production of a product in the United States according to a process developed in South Africa, this is a right in contract or in tort sounding in money and does not therefore arise from a transaction within the ambit of the Act, rendering ss. 1 and 1A inapplicable (Jones v. Krok 1996 (1) SA 504 (T) at 509I-510G). A South African party, who has paid out punitive damages in response to a foreign judgment, may be able to recover the payment, especially from assets of the foreign recipient situated in South Africa. If the recipient is a corporation, local assets of a corporation in the same group may possibly be used for this purpose (s. 1B). Furthermore, no judgment or arbitration award arising from a transaction of the type described above can be enforced, with or without the Minister's consent if the judgment or award is connected with any liability arising from any bodily injury to any person resulting from the consumption or use of or exposure to any natural resource of South Africa, unless the same liability would have arisen under South African law (s. 1D). Once again, this provision prevents the recovery of multiple or punitive damages, but compensatory damages would be recoverable with the Minister's consent, under s. 1. Although the wording of these sections is unnecessarily wide, they may be regarded as a statutory expression of public policy aimed at preventing the enforcement of certain judgments or awards providing for punitive or multiple damages against South African businesses. In the two reported cases to date, the provisions have been restrictively interpreted by the courts.

It remains to consider the enforcement of judgments for punitive damages falling outside the ambit of the Protection of Businesses Act. It was held in Jones v. Krok (1996 (1) SA 504 (T) 515H) that the mere fact that an award of damages is made on a basis not recognised in South Africa does not necessarily make the award contrary to public policy. Although the principle behind the award of punitive damages is not necessarily unconscionable (at 516E), the court held that the award of double the amount claimed as punitive damages because of the defendant's reprehensible conduct was so excessive and exorbitant as to render it contrary to public policy in South Africa (at 517G-H). (Leave to take the judgment on appeal to the Appellate Division has since been granted (see Jones v. Krok 1996 (2) SA 71 (T).)

The Enforcement of Foreign Civil Judgments Act 32 of 1988 appears to create a statutory exception to the cumbersome enforcement procedure described above, by providing for the enforcement of certain judgments on their mere registration by the appropriate magistrate's court in South Africa (ss. 3 and 4). However, the Act only applies to judgments given in a foreign country designated for this purpose by the Minister of Justice (s. 2(1)). As yet, no foreign countries have been so designated.

(In addition to the cases referred to above see generally on the enforcement of foreign judgments Forsyth 332-82 and Edwards "Conflict of Laws" in LAWSA vol. 2 384-94.)

III. Arbitration
A. Sources Of South African Arbitration Law

Although Roman-Dutch arbitration law continued to apply in the Cape after the second British occupation in 1806, it was not particularly well developed. As a result, legislation based on English arbitration legislation was adopted at the turn of the century, and the present Arbitration Act 42 of 1965 which replaced the colonial legislation is based mainly on English models. However, English common law on arbitration was not adopted along with the legislation. The purpose of the arbitration legislation was not to repeal the Roman-Dutch law, but it was intended to facilitate the reference of a dispute to arbitration and the conduct of those proceedings and to provide a better and more efficient means of enforcing arbitral awards. As a result, there are important differences between English and South African arbitration law. Some of the most important of these differences are referred to below. When adopted in 1965, the current South African Arbitration Act was in advance of those in many other jurisdictions, but it is now showing its age. Shortly after the country's transition to majority rule, the South African Law Commission, with the approval of the current Minister of Justice, began work on a project to consider the reform of the country's arbitration legislation, including the question as to what response South Africa should make to the UNCITRAL Model Law on International Commercial Arbitration.

The present Arbitration Act makes no distinction between domestic and international arbitrations and therefore applies to both. The statute commences by dealing with arbitrability: matrimonial matters and matters relating to status may not be resolved by arbitration (s. 2). Although "status" is not defined, it has been suggested that it relates to matters of status which parties are not capable of determining for themselves by agreement. The statute also deals with the effect of the arbitration agreement (ss. 3-8), the appointment of arbitrators and umpires (ss. 9-13), arbitration proceedings (ss. 14-22), the award (ss. 23-33) and miscellaneous matters (ss. 34-43). South Africa acceded to the New York Convention on the Recognition and Enforcement of Arbitral Awards of 1958 during 1976 without making the reciprocity or commercial reservations. The Recognition and Enforcement of Foreign Arbitral Awards Act 40 of 1977 was subsequently enacted to give effect to South Africa's treaty obligations. South Africa has not yet ratified the Convention on the Settlement of Investment Disputes (the ICSID or Washington Convention of 1965).

B. Overview Of South African Arbitration Practice

Arbitration has been widely used for many years in South Africa for the resolution of disputes in the construction industry, but it is also used, albeit less frequently, for the resolution of other types of commercial disputes. More recently, arbitration has been extensively used for resolving labour disputes. Arbitrations in the construction industry, particularly if the disputes are complex and involve large amounts, tend to be relatively formal, especially if the parties are represented by lawyers. Arbitrations in labour disputes are however usually characterised by greater informality and the use of expedited procedures.

Arbitration is also increasingly used for the resolution of international commercial disputes with a South African connection. When drafting the arbitration clause in an international commercial contract, it appears that South African lawyers will usually recommend that the arbitration should take place under the auspices of the International Chamber of Commerce (ICC) and subject to its rules. South African lawyers are however becoming aware that the ICC Rules are not necessarily the most expeditious or cost-effective method of resolving a dispute through arbitration. They should therefore be open to suggestions for the use of possible alternatives like the rules of the London Court of International Arbitration. Because of the similarity between the International Arbitration Rules of the American Arbitration Association (AAA) and the UNCITRAL Rules of 1976 (allowing for the fact that the latter are intended for an ad hoc arbitration), and the relatively modest administrative charges of the AAA, a South African lawyer can have no objection in principle against recommending their rules instead of the ICC Rules.

The best established arbitration association in South Africa is the Association of Arbitrators (Southern Africa) which was established in 1979. It is based in Johannesburg, with branches in some of the other main centres. The Association has formal agreements with a number of arbitration associations in other countries and informal links with several more, including the AAA. It has recently published a Directory of Fellows with profiles of Fellows from whose ranks the Association's nominations of arbitrators are made. Although the majority of its members are from the construction industry, more than 25% of its Fellows are lawyers. The Association has published Rules for the Conduct of Arbitration Proceedings, and their use is commonly prescribed by arbitration clauses used in the construction industry.

The Independent Mediation Service of Southern Africa (IMSSA) is a non-profit organisation established in 1983 which specialises in mediations and arbitrations in labour disputes. As a result of a recent initiative by members of the Johannesburg bar, the Arbitration Foundation of Southern Africa (AFSA) is in the process of being established. It will be based in Sandton, just north of Johannesburg and aims to promote the use of arbitration and mediation for the settlement of commercial disputes and will also provide the necessary physical facilities there.

C. Arbitration Procedure

In this section, the main features of arbitration proceedings under South African law are briefly discussed.

1. The Arbitration Act

S 1 of the Arbitration Act 42 of 1965 defines an arbitration agreement as a written agreement providing for the reference to arbitration of an existing or future dispute relating to a matter specified in the agreement, whether an arbitrator is named therein or not. The

Act does not require the agreement to be signed by the parties, nor does it expressly envisage an exchange of documents in the alternative (compare article II(2) of the New York Convention). An oral arbitration agreement is still valid under South African law, but is regulated by the common law as opposed to the Arbitration Act. The death of party or the sequestration of the estate of a party to an arbitration agreement covered by the Act will not have the effect of terminating the agreement, in the absence of a contractual provision to that effect (see ss. 4 and 5). Court assistance to enforce an arbitration agreement is discussed below.

2. Composition And Appointment Of The Arbitral Tribunal

Unless the arbitration agreement provides otherwise, a reference to arbitration under South African law is to a single arbitrator (Arbitration Act 42 of 1965 s. 9). Where the arbitration agreement provides for a reference to three arbitrators, one of whom is to be appointed by the other two, it is necessary to specify that the third arbitrator will function as an arbitrator, and not as an umpire, otherwise it will be assumed that the intention was that the third arbitrator should function as an umpire (Arbitration Act s. 11(1)(b)). (An umpire fulfills the same function as one in English law, namely to resolve a deadlock on a point where the arbitrators cannot agree. In this event, the umpire, unlike a third arbitrator, is vested with exclusive jurisdiction to decide the point.) Where each party is entitled to appoint an arbitrator, a party appointee must act impartially and is not the agent of the party who appointed him. (In this respect the requirements of South African law are basically the same as the AAA International Arbitration Rules.)

If the parties are unable to agree on the appointment of the arbitrators or a body to perform that function, it is possible to approach the court to appoint an arbitrator (Arbitration Act s. 12). Unless the arbitration agreement provides otherwise, the appointment of an arbitrator cannot be terminated except with the consent of all the parties. The court may however, on application, remove an arbitrator from office on good cause shown (s. 13).

An arbitrator, when accepting appointment, should ensure, when his appointment is subject to South African law, that the basis of his remuneration is fixed by an agreement between him and the parties to the reference, otherwise the arbitrator runs the risk that a party who is dissatisfied with his award can apply to the taxing master of the court to tax (assess) his fees, even if the fees have already been paid (s. 34(1)). This could result in his fees being considerably reduced.

3. Representation Of Parties

A party to arbitration proceedings in South Africa is entitled to be represented by the person of his choice (compare the Arbitration Act 42 of 1965 s 15(1)). The representative need not be a South African lawyer, and could be a person with technical expertise in the subject-matter of the dispute or a foreign lawyer, subject to any applicable requirements regarding work permits.

4. Arbitration Procedure

The arbitrator in South Africa is master of his procedure, subject to the arbitration agreement, the provisions of the Arbitration Act and the rules of natural justice (see Anshell v. Horwitz 1916 WLD 65 at 67; Butler & Finsen 97). Regarding the statutory powers of the arbitral tribunal prior to and during the hearing, the Arbitration Act 42 of 1965 confers a number of specific powers on the tribunal which are therefore available except to the extent that they are modified or excluded in the arbitration agreement. (There is no general statutory power to conduct the arbitration in such manner as the tribunal deems appropriate, comparable to article 19(2) of the UNCITRAL Model Law.) Certain of these specified statutory powers may only be exercised on the application of a party: namely the power to order discovery of documents, the power to require the parties to deliver pleadings or statements of claim and defence, the power to require a party to allow the inspection of goods or property involved in the reference which is in his possession or under his control and the power to appoint a commissioner to take evidence on commission (s. 14(1)(a)). Thus, in the absence of a contrary provision in the arbitration agreement, the arbitrator has the power to restrict excessive discovery of documents which will merely cause unnecessary delay and expense. The arbitrator should also endeavour to ensure that the statements of claim and defence are accompanied by copies of all relevant documents, as this will then obviate the need for full discovery as in the Supreme Court. Other statutory powers may be exercised on the tribunal's own initiative, for example the power to decide the date and place of any hearing, the power to administer oaths to or take affirmations from witnesses, the power to examine witnesses and the power to inspect any goods or property involved in the reference (s. 14(1)(b)). If a party has received reasonable notice of the hearing and fails to attend, the arbitrator may proceed with the hearing in that party's absence (s. 15(2)). However, one statutory power, namely the power to receive evidence on affidavit, may only be exercised with the consent of the parties or by order of court (s. 14(1)(b)(vi)). Although s. 14 does not deal specifically with the point, it would appear that unless the arbitration agreement provides otherwise, the arbitrator is not obliged to apply the formal rules of evidence, as long as the procedure which he follows complies with the rules of natural justice (see Butler & Finsen 220-1).

S. 20 of the Arbitration Act also provides for the arbitrator before making his award, on application, to refer a question of law to the court or to an advocate for opinion (a "consultative case"). The opinion of the court or advocate is binding on the arbitrator and the parties and is not subject to appeal. The arbitrator has a limited discretion to refuse the application, unless convinced that the application is not bona fide (see e. g. Government of the Republic of South Africa v. Midkon (Pty) Ltd 1984 (3) SA 552 (T)). Although the provision differs materially from the repealed section 21 of the English Arbitration Act 1950, which unlike s. 20, also permitted the arbitrator to formulate his award as a stated case for consideration by the court, thereby in effect creating a right of appeal on a question of law, s. 20 is still open to abuse by a party wishing to delay the reference. It is as yet uncertain whether the provision can be validly excluded in the parties' arbitration agreement. (See further on s. 20 Butler & Finsen 206-11.)

The arbitrator's statutory powers have certain gaps. He has no power to subpoena witnesses and a party needing to subpoena a witness must do so through the magistrates' court with jurisdiction in the area where the arbitration is held (Arbitration Act s. 16). Although the arbitrator may examine a witness called by the parties, he has no power to call a witness (including an expert) on his own initiative, unless this power is conferred on him in the arbitration agreement. Likewise, the arbitrator will only have the power to order interim measures for the protection of goods and security for costs if the arbitration agreement so provides.

5. The Award

The arbitral tribunal's award must be in writing and signed by the arbitrators. The refusal by a minority to sign will not invalidate the award (Arbitration Act 42 of 1965 s. 24). Particularly because of the delays involved in international arbitration, the arbitration agreement should provide for the award to be made within a stipulated or reasonable time from the conclusion of the hearing, thereby effectively neutralising the statutory time-limits for making an award (in s. 23 of the Arbitration Act). Where South African law applies to the arbitration procedure, an arbitral tribunal of more than one arbitrator should also note s. 14(3) and (4) of the Arbitration Act regarding the method of arriving at decisions. Basically, where there is no unanimity, the majority must agree on the amount to be awarded and may not award the least amount or an average amount. Where the required level of agreement cannot be achieved on an award or on a procedural matter, the Act envisages that the matter should be referred to an umpire to break the deadlock unless the arbitration otherwise provides (see ss. 14(4) and 18). The parties should therefore consider giving the presiding arbitrator the power to decide the matter to avoid the delay and expense of a reference to an umpire, where no majority award or ruling is possible.

As to its contents, the award should be certain, final, possible, lawful and within the arbitral tribunal's powers in terms of the reference. Unless the arbitration agreement provides otherwise, South African law does not require the arbitral tribunal to give reasons for its award. Unless the arbitration agreement provides otherwise, the tribunal is empowered to make an interim award (s. 26).

The Arbitration Act does not give an arbitrator power to award interest. It merely provides that an award for the payment of a sum of money shall, unless the award provides otherwise, carry interest as from the date of the award at the same rate as that prescribed for judgment debts (see s. 29).

The arbitral tribunal has a limited statutory power to correct a clerical mistake or patent error in its award arising from an accidental slip or omission (s. 30)). The provision clearly does not extend to a situation where the arbitrator after delivering the award changes his mind on one of the findings.

6. Costs

The parties to an arbitration under South African law may only validly agree that each party shall pay his own costs or any part thereof, once the dispute to be referred to arbitration has arisen (Arbitration Act 42 of 1965 s. 35(6)). Unless the arbitration agreement provides otherwise, the award of costs in connection with the reference and the award is in the discretion of the arbitral tribunal (s. 35(1)). The costs of the award comprise the arbitrator's fees and disbursements, the costs of the venue and other administrative charges. The costs of the reference are the costs properly incurred by the party in whose favour costs are awarded in preparing and presenting his case, excluding the costs of the award. There is however no difference between the two concepts in relation to the way in which the arbitrator must exercise his discretion.

Although s. 35(1) of the Arbitration Act gives the arbitrator the discretion to award costs, it is not an unqualified discretion, and the arbitrator must exercise his discretion judicially and in accordance with recognised principles. If the arbitrator exercises his discretion improperly, the court will interfere and set aside or remit the award of costs (see para 3.4.3 below for these remedies). The courts will regard the arbitrator as having exercised his discretion improperly, if the arbitrator fails to consider all the relevant facts or fails to act in accordance with the settled practice and principles upon which costs are generally awarded by the courts (see especially Kathrada v. Arbitration Tribunal 1975 (2) SA 673 (A) 678E 680H-681A). The basic principle is that the a party who is substantially successful is entitled to be awarded costs in the absence of special circumstances. Costs will normally be awarded as between party and party and, where the party was represented by lawyers, on the supreme court scale. The award of attorney and client costs, in the absence of an agreement, will only be justified if there are special circumstances. Before there are special circumstances present, which justify a departure from the usual rule, there must be reprehensible conduct in relation to the arbitration proceedings on the part of the party against whom the special order is made, as opposed to unsatisfactory conduct before the commencement of the reference (see Joubert T/A Wilcon v. Beacham 1996 (1) SA 500 (C) 502I). A party ordered to pay costs is entitled to have those costs taxed (i.e. assessed) in order to determine the precise amount which he has to pay. Subject to the arbitration agreement, taxation can be performed either by the arbitrator or by the taxing master of the Supreme Court (s. 35(1) and (3)).

A defendant wishing to protect himself against the possibility of an adverse costs order where a reasonable offer of settlement made "without prejudice" has been rejected by the claimant, in the event of the award being less than the amount tendered in settlement, can do so by making the offer "without prejudice save as to costs". In these circumstances the existence and amount of the settlement will be disclosed to the arbitrator only after he has made his award on the merits but prior to his making an award on costs.

(For a more detailed discussion of costs in arbitration proceedings see Butler & Finsen 276-85; Loots 1053-1056, 1067-1075.)

D. The Role Of The Courts In Relation To Arbitration

In this section, the principal powers of a South African court concerning arbitration proceedings are discussed. A "court" for purposes of the Arbitration Act is defined in s. 1 as a provincial or local division of the Supreme Court having jurisdiction. (For an overview of the court's statutory and common-law powers in arbitration proceedings, see Butler & Finsen 61-2.)

1. Enforcing The Arbitration Agreement

In terms of article II of the New York Convention, the court of a contracting state, when confronted with a case concerning a dispute subject to an arbitration agreement (as defined in article II(1) and (2)), is required to refer the parties to arbitration, should one of them so request, unless the court finds that the arbitration agreement is "null and void, inoperative or incapable of being performed". Although South Africa acceded to the New York Convention without reservation, the legislation to give effect to the accession (namely the Recognition and Enforcement of Foreign Arbitral Awards Act 40 of 1977) contains no equivalent to this provision, with the result that the court's ordinary discretionary power concerning the enforcement of the arbitration agreement continues to apply. (An assumption to this effect in Polysius (Pty) Ltd v. Transvaal Alloys (Pty) Ltd 1983 (2) SA 630 (W) 646G-H, 647B was not referred to in the judgment on appeal, namely Transvaal Alloys (Pty) Ltd v. Polisius (Pty) Ltd 1983 (2) SA 653 (T).) Under s 6(2) of the Arbitration Act, the court has a discretion to refuse to stay court proceedings to allow the dispute to be referred to arbitration, if the party resisting arbitration is able to show a sufficient reason. The courts regard that party as bearing a heavy onus which is not easily discharged. Nevertheless, in one case involving an international arbitration agreement, the court declined to stay court proceedings so that the dispute could be referred to arbitration under Japanese law in Japan, because the witnesses would mainly come from Cape Town, and more importantly, because of the danger of a multiplicity of proceedings leading to conflicting decisions on the same issues (see Yorigami Maritime Construction Co. Ltd v. Nissho-Iwai Co. Ltd 1977 (4) SA 682 (C) 692H-694D). The position under South African law regarding the enforcement of an arbitration agreement therefore differs substantially from that under §§ 3 and 4 of the Federal Arbitration Act 1925. South African arbitration law also makes no provision for the consolidation of separate arbitration proceedings between different parties pursuant to separate arbitration agreements without the consent of all the parties involved.

South African law is also experiencing difficulty in recognising fully the doctrine of the severability of the arbitration clause from the contract containing that clause. The arbitration clause in a contract which was voidable because of misrepresentation has been recognised, at least by implication, as severable from the main contract (see the obiter dictum in Van Heerden v. Sentrale Kunsmis Korporasie (Edms) Bpk 1973 (1) SA 17 (A) 30B-H). However, in Wayland v. Everite Group Ltd (1993 (3) SA 946 (W) 951H-I), the court emphatically rejected the doctrine of severability where the main contract was alleged to be void, holding a declaration by the parties that the clause should be severable from the main agreement as having no effect. This decision is contrary to the trend in most other jurisdictions, particularly those who have implemented legislation based on article 16(1) of the UNCITRAL Model Law.

2. Enforcing An Arbitral Award

There are three procedures for enforcing an arbitration award under South African law. First, an award made outside South Africa may be enforced under the Recognition and Enforcement of Foreign Arbitral Awards Act 40 of 1977 (see s. 1 "foreign arbitral award"), which, as stated above, was enacted to give effect to South Africa's accession to the New

York Convention of 1958. The Act even confers jurisdiction on a South African court to enforce a foreign arbitral award between two foreigners (peregrini) subject only to an attachment of property or person to ensure that jurisdiction is effective (see Laconian Maritime Enterprises Ltd v. Agromar Lineas Ltd 1984 (3) SA 233 (D) 239F). The grounds upon which the enforcement of a foreign arbitral award may be refused under s. 4(1) of this Act are basically the same as those contained in article V of the New York Convention, although there are some minor differences between the wording of the two provisions. A South African court hearing an application for enforcement may postpone the hearing of the application if satisfied that an application for the setting aside or suspension of the award is pending before a court of the country in which or under the law of which the award was made (s. 4(2), which corresponds to article VI of the Convention).

Secondly, an award made inside or outside South Africa can be enforced as a contractual obligation under South Africa's common law (see Benidai Trading Co. Ltd v. Gouws & Gouws (Pty) Ltd 1977 (3) SA 1020 (T) 1038H, which concerned an award made in London).

In both cases, the enforcement of a foreign arbitral award will be subject to the provisions of ss. 1 and 1D of the Protection of Businesses Act 99 of 1978 (discussed above), where applicable. Even where this Act does not apply, enforcement of a foreign arbitral award providing for punitive or multiple damages, as opposed to compensatory damages, may possibly be refused as being contrary to public policy where the court regards the amount awarded as exorbitant (compare Jones v. Krok (1996 (1) SA 504 (T) 517G-H).

Thirdly, an award made inside South Africa may be enforced by an application to court under s. 31 of the Arbitration Act 42 of 1965, upon the applicant satisfying the court that the award was validly made (see above) by an arbitrator duly appointed under a valid arbitration agreement. Where the award is valid but tainted by a procedural irregularity, a party resisting enforcement should normally bring an application for setting aside or remittal, discussed below (see MM Fernandes (Pty) Ltd v. Mahomed 1986 (4) SA 383 (W) 389B-C)). If the court however regards the award as being so tainted by a procedural irregularity committed during the hearing as to render the award void, the court may decide to dismiss the application for enforcement (see Wilton v Gatonby 1994 (4) SA 160 (W) 168B-C).

3. Remedies For Attacking An Arbitral Award

The rule of English law, prior to its repeal in 1979, whereby a court could set aside an award by reason of an error of fact or law on the face of that award has never been part of South African law (see Dickenson & Brown v Fisher's Executors 1915 AD 166 at 177-81). There is also no equivalent to the limited right of appeal to the courts on a question of law introduced by s. 1(2) of the English Arbitration Act of 1979. An arbitrator is generally expected to arrive at his award by applying the relevant rules of law to the matters in dispute. Clauses authorising the arbitrator to have regard to fairness and reasonableness in making the award do however occasionally occur in practice (see e.g. Amalgamated Clothing & Textile Workers Union of South Africa v. Veldspun (Pty) Ltd 1994 (4) SA 162 (A) 167H), but their effect has not yet been considered in a reported judgment.

The Arbitration Act 42 of 1965 provides two separate remedies for attacking an award, namely setting aside and remittal. The purpose of the latter is to refer the award back to the same arbitral tribunal which made the award to enable it to remedy some defect. An application to court for the setting aside (s. 33(2)) or remittal (s. 32(2)) of an award should generally be brought within six weeks after the publication of the award to the parties, unless that period is extended by the court on good cause shown (s. 38). There are four statutory grounds on which an award may be set aside and these grounds have been held by the courts to be exhaustive. They are (a) misconduct by a member of the arbitral tribunal; (b) a gross procedural irregularity; (c) where the tribunal has exceeded its powers; and (d) where the award has been improperly obtained. To establish misconduct it is necessary to show mala fide, wrongful or other improper conduct on the part of the arbitrator in relation to his duties as arbitrator (see Dickenson & Brown v. Fisher's Executors above at 176; Bester v. Easigas (Pty) Ltd 1993 (1) SA 30 (C) 38F). The courts have generally rejected the notion that "misconduct" should be widely interpreted to include the "legal" or "technical" misconduct of English law. Where an arbitrator, without moral turpitude, has made a serious procedural error leading to a party being unfairly treated, the award should be attacked under ground (b) above. A bona fide mistake by the arbitrator in reaching his conclusion on the merits of the dispute, whether on the law or the facts, is not a basis for setting aside an award as misconduct or on some other ground (see Dickenson & Brown v. Fisher's Executors above at 176; Hyperchemicals International (Pty) Ltd v. Maybaker Agrichem International (Pty) Ltd 1992 (1) SA 89 (W) 100B-C)).

As an alternative to setting aside, the aggrieved party can apply to court to have the award remitted back to the same arbitrator on "good cause shown". Grounds recognised by the South African courts as "good cause" for remittal are (a) the grounds for setting aside an award (in appropriate circumstances); (b) where fresh evidence has been discovered after the publication of the award and (c) an admitted mistake by the arbitrator not amounting to "second thoughts" (see Butler & Finsen 287-9).

4. General Powers Of The Courts

Apart from the powers of the court referred to above, the most important statutory powers of the court are the general powers of the court contained in s. 21 of the Arbitration Act 42 of 1965. These powers include the power to order security for costs; the power to order the interim preservation of property; and the power to grant an interim interdict or similar relief.

IV. Mediation

Some standard-form contracts in South Africa, for example those used in construction projects involving civil engineers, have contained provisions for mediation or conciliation procedures for many years, but their function has not always been properly understood. Some persons have tended to regard mediation as a type of informal arbitration. However, there was of course no intention that the procedures would be subject to the Arbitration Act 42 of 1965 or to the courts' powers under that Act.

In their widest sense, mediation or conciliation procedures may be understood as a voluntary process whereby a mutually acceptable third party helps to bring the parties to a dispute to an agreed solution. There are two basic types of mediation procedure, depending on whether or not the third party is expected to recommend a solution if he fails in his attempts to bring the parties to a negotiated settlement. The terminology used to distinguish the two types is not consistent. Where the third party is expected to recommend a solution (by giving a non-binding opinion), he is referred to as a conciliator in industrial disputes but is usually termed a mediator in the construction industry. Conversely, a third party who is not required to recommend a solution if his attempts to guide the parties to a negotiated settlement fail, is termed a mediator in industrial disputes but a conciliator in the construction industry.

As the process is entirely voluntary, having its origin in an agreement between the parties, the lack of consistency in terminology is not important, as long as the disputants are agreed on the function of the third party and the extent of his powers, which should therefore be spelt out with sufficient clarity in the agreement. The proceedings before the mediator are confidential and, in so far as they are concerned with attempts to settle the dispute, will also be regarded as being "without prejudice". As a result, no reference may be made to the contents of such proceedings in subsequent arbitration or court proceedings if the negotiations are unsuccessful. As the mediation or conciliation is an attempt to settle the dispute without resorting to arbitration or litigation, and possibly on the basis of commercial interests as opposed to legal rights, there is no intention to designate a losing party. Therefore, the mediator's fees and expenses are usually shared equally between the parties, and for the rest, each party will bear his own costs, in the absence of an agreement to the contrary.

An agreement resulting from settlement negotiations involving a mediator or from the subsequent acceptance of the mediator's opinion by both disputants will be enforceable by means of court proceedings on the same basis as any other agreement.

(See further Butler & Finsen 10-16; Loots 1011-1014.)

Stellenbosch, South Africa
June 1996

Bibliography:

Brooks, P. E. J., "Jurisdiction" in LAWSA (Joubert W A (ed)) vol 11 (1981) Butterworths Durban

Butler, David W., "The recovery of interest in arbitration proceedings: an agenda for lawmakers" (1995) 6 Stellenbosch Law Review 291-323

Butler, David W. & Finsen, Eyvind N., Arbitration in South Africa: Law and Practice 1993 Juta Cape Town

Cilliers, A. C., The Law of Costs (2 ed) 1984 Butterworths Durban

Cilliers, A. C., "Costs" in LAWSA (Joubert W A (ed)) vol 3 (1985) Butterworths Durban

Edwards, A. B., "Conflict of Laws" in LAWSA (Joubert W A (ed)) vol 2 (1st reissue 1993) Butterworths, Durban

Erasmus, H. J., Superior Court Practice 1994 Juta Cape Town

Forsyth, C. .F, Private International Law (2 ed) 1990 Juta Cape Town

Loots, Philip C., Construction Law and Related Issues 1995 Juta Cape Town

Malan, F. R., Neels, J. L., O'Brien, P. H. & Boshoff, A., "Transnational litigation in South Arican law" 1995 Tydskrif vir Suid-Afrikaanse Reg 106-26, 282-99, 460-70

Pretorius, Paul (ed) Dispute Resolution 1993 Juta Cape Town

CHAPTER 15

SOUTHERN AFRICAN REGIONAL LEGAL FRAMEWORK

By Robin B. Camp

Many foreign investors use South Africa as a base for expanding into other parts of southern Africa. This chapter briefly highlights some of the more important legal rules relevant to doing business in the other countries in southern Africa that form important markets for foreign investors expanding beyond South Africa.

To the northwest of South Africa lies Namibia, a sparsely populated country enjoying a democratic government and a strong press. Namibia is cattle-farming and mining country, tending from semi-desert in the east to the Namib desert along the Atlantic Coast, which has a cold current offshore, like Patagonia and the Atacama. The capital is Windhoek in the center of the country; a charming town founded by German Missionaries and settlers in the last century.

To the north of South Africa lies Botswana, a semi-desert bushveld country with a population of 1.4 million, although the size is equivalent to France and Belgium combined. Because of the diamond boom and a conservative government, Botswana enjoys a relatively high measure of prosperity and stability. Botswana's industries are mining, cattle-farming (the cultural pivot of the Batswana people) and tourism. The game parks in the north of Botswana are probably without parallel. Botswana, with its 80,000 elephants, has a situation where the tuskers alone, never mind the buffalo, hippo, lion, zebra, etc., press down many many times heavier on the face of the country than do the humans! Botswana has an embryonic stock exchange and a surprisingly sophisticated infrastructure for such a young, sparsely populated and remote country.

To the northeast of South Africa lies Zimbabwe, a beautiful country with a friendly and efficient people. The Victoria Falls on the Zambezi River are one of the wonders of the world, and a visitor will probably share the one and a half mile long Falls with no more than a handful of other tourists and not a neon sign in sight. Indeed, the walk along the lip of the falls is one through spray and in sight of the usually shy bush buck and rare bushveld avifauna. Zimbabwe is a thriving country, but one somewhat hampered by a history of socialist attempts and over-population.

To the further northeast of South Africa is Mozambique. Once again a very beautiful country, tending towards the Indian Ocean tropical shoreline, but one ravaged by years of civil war following decolonization by Portugal. Its infrastructure is more or less destroyed and its legal system in tatters. For this reason, Mozambique's legal system is not addressed in this chapter.

The same can be said for Angola, similarly an ex-Portuguese colony, which is to be found to the north of Namibia. Angola is a country wealthy in natural resources, but at present moribund as a result of the civil war which raged there for fifteen years, and is perhaps still not quite over. Angola's legal system also is not addressed in this chapter.

To the west of Angola again and to the north of Zimbabwe lies Zambia. Like Zimbabwe, once a British colony, and extremely wealthy in natural resources, Zambia was cruelly struck by the drop in copper prices of two decades ago and by misgovernment for a lengthy period. It is attempting to re-establish itself.

Fully encompassed geographically by South Africa is the tiny mountain country of Lesotho. Beautiful, particularly when the snows lie thick in winter, Lesotho's economy was based on exporting manpower to the Witwatersrand gold mines. The call for this labor is diminishing and the country is suffering economically.

Similar in size to Lesotho is the Kingdom of Swaziland, which lies between South Africa and Mozambique and is also landlocked. This is a country with a wonderful climate. Its people are friendly. It is struggling to come to grips with democracy and its economy, which is based on agriculture such as sugar and timber, is still embryonic.

These then are countries which fall naturally into the southern African region. Several factors tie these countries in with South Africa. Namibia was taken by South African forces in World War I and, thereafter, for a period of several decades, administered by South Africa. Many Afrikaaners had lived there from the earliest times, with family ties back in South Africa. Mozambique provided ports through which Zimbabwe, Zambia and northern South Africa communicated. Botswana, in colonial times, was administered from South Africa. Close examination will reveal that the borders, often colonial remnants, divided tribes arbitrarily. Thus, for instance, linking people in South Africa to their cousins in Botswana, and folk in Botswana to their cousins in Zimbabwe on the one side and South West Africa on the other side.

South Africa's influence diminishes as one moves northwards. Zaire, to the north of Angola, was Belgian in colonial times. The dream of a Cape-to-Cairo railway nurtured by Cecil John Rhodes ended no further north than Zambia. Tropical forests and extremely difficult terrain impeded further communication from south to north.

I. **Namibia**
    A. **Type Of Government**

Namibia is a multi-party democracy.

B. **Legal System**

When South Africa was given the mandate over this former German Colony by the League of Nations, the common law as applied in the Cape Province (Roman Dutch Law) was introduced as the common law of Namibia. English law has also had a bearing, mainly on commercial law.

The Constitution of Namibia preserved all laws in force immediately before the date of independence until repealed or declared unconstitutional by a competent court. Consequently, many laws passed by the South African legislature prior to independence still apply and there are areas of statute law in which no or minimal differences exist between the two countries.

C. **Forms Of Business Organizations**

Various forms of enterprise are available to the businessman, both under common and statute law. Under statute law, companies and close corporations are available. Under common law, agency, licensing and distribution arrangements, partnerships and trusts are available.

D. Formation Of A Business

It is necessary for enterprises in specific areas to obtain licenses or other permits. Examples are road carrier permits for transportation of persons or goods, prospecting licenses for mining concerns, import and export permits, liquor licenses for businesses selling liquor and registration of certain industries. Formalities and procedures in obtaining licenses or permits vary significantly. Work and residence permits also must be obtained before entering Namibia.

E. Customs And Excise

On independence, Namibia elected to remain part of the South African Customs Union, whose members are Lesotho, Namibia, South Africa and Swaziland ("SACU"), and as such is bound by the applicable regulations as determined by the member states.

The Export Processing Zones Act came into operation on April 18, 1995. The first and only zone so far is in Walvis Bay. The idea behind the Act is to encourage export, manufacture and production in such areas. This entails, among other things, tax holidays, duty and general sales tax exemptions and employees' salary subsidies.

F. Foreign Investment

The Namibian Constitution expressly encourages foreign investment. Realizing the importance of foreign investments to the country, the Namibian government passed the Foreign Investments Act in 1990. The Act establishes an Investment Centre as part of the Ministry of Trade and Industry to assist in the administration of the Act.

G. Intellectual Property

Rights to intellectual property are protected under Namibian law, largely by statute, but also at common law. The statutes applicable are basically identical to those of South Africa, which in turn are based on internationally accepted principles.

H. Labor

The Labour Act is applicable to all employees in the private sector and stipulates basic conditions of employment, prohibits discrimination on various grounds in relation to a person's employment or occupation and authorizes affirmative action.

Like most other African countries, Namibia experiences high unemployment, essentially of unskilled labor, and has shortages of skilled labor. Expertise is often obtained from outside the country.

I. Taxation

Namibia's tax legislation is similar to that of neighboring countries, notably South Africa.

The principal statute is the Income Tax Act. Income tax is presently levied at 35% in respect of companies. This is also the highest rate of tax for individuals, who are taxed on a sliding scale.

General sales tax is levied on the consideration payable in respect of the sale of goods or services. The rate applicable to goods is presently 8% and that for services is 11%.

Importers and manufacturers of goods are obliged to pay additional sales duty at a rate which ranges from 5% to 15% covering the range of goods from necessities to luxuries. This rate is calculated on the value of the goods at the time of import or sale of goods respectively.

Transfer duty is payable by the purchaser of immovable property, be it improved or unimproved, ranging from 1% to 8%, at the upper percentage for land valued at in excess of N$250,000.

Stamp duty is levied on various legal documents at specified rates pursuant to the Stamp Duties Act.

There is no estate duty or donation tax in Namibia. Capital gains are not taxable and, although municipalities and similar local authorities levy rates and taxes based on the valuation of immovable property in order to cover for municipal expenses, these are moderate.

Namibia has double-taxation treaties with the United Kingdom, the Republic of South Africa and Germany and other such treaties are being negotiated.

1. Natural Resources Legislation

Mineral resources, such as diamonds, gold, uranium, copper, tin, lead and zinc, as well as marble, are abundant and have formed the basis of Namibia's commercial economy. Based to some extent on German colonial mining legislation, mineral rights are owned by the State and not by private persons or bodies, but are passed on to them for prospecting exploration and mining in the form of licenses, grants or concessions. The applicable statute is the Minerals (Prospecting and Mining) Act which came into operation on April 1, 1994.

J. Currency System; Securities Markets

Namibia's economy is still largely influenced by that of South Africa due to the historic ties between the two countries. Until September 1993, when Namibia introduced its own currency, the Namibian Dollar, the South African Rand was also the currency of Namibia. The Rand remained legal tender for a transitional period of two years. After independence, Namibia remained part of the South African Rand monetary area, and, despite declared Government policy to wean itself economically from South Africa, it seems that Namibia will retain the Rand as its currency for the foreseeable future.

The Stock Exchange Control Amendment Act introduced a stock exchange in Namibia which opened in September 1992 and has twenty listings to date.

II. Botswana

A. Type Of Government

Botswana is a multi-party democracy.

B. Legal System

Botswana inherited the Roman-Dutch Law extant in the Cape Colony in 1881 and the Botswana legal system is, in large part, similar to that of South Africa.

C. Forms Of Business Organizations

Each of the following forms of business organizations is recognized in Botswana:
- private or public limited liability company;
- external company (branch of foreign company);
- company limited by guarantee;
- partnership;
- common law trust;
- sole proprietorship; and
- societies being associations of persons.

D. Formation Of A Business

Societies, trusts and companies must be registered with the appropriate authorities in Gaborone. There is no requirement for registration of a trust, although the practice is to register a trust with the Registrar of Deeds. A business generally has to register with the Commissioner of Income Tax. Trading licenses are required for wholesale, retail and agency activities.

E. Taxation

Tax is levied on income which is actually derived or deemed to be derived from Botswana sources. The corporate tax rate is 15% and companies are liable for an additional company tax of 10%. The effective tax rate of manufacturing companies is 15%. There is a 15% withholding tax on all dividends. The aggregate of the tax so withheld is available for and capable of set off/credit against the 10% additional company tax. A listed company in which at least 25% of the paid up capital was held by the general public in a tax year, and the wholly owned subsidiary thereof, is, for tax purposes, entitled to a deduction from chargeable income of 12.5% of its chargeable income.

There is capital gains tax at the income tax rate of the particular taxpayer in respect of:
- immovable property as to 100% of the gain, which is calculated by deducting from the sale price the cost of acquisition and the cost of any improvements and escalator factor applied to such costs; and

- any other property as to 50% of the gain, which is calculated by deducting from the sale price the cost of acquisition and the cost of any improvements or capital maintenance.

Capital gains tax is not payable on the sale of shares of a company listed on the Botswana Share Market.

For individual taxpayers, the top marginal tax rate is 30%.

Botswana has double taxation agreements with South Africa, the United Kingdom and Sweden.

F. **Foreign Investment**

Botswana welcomes foreign investment. A direct investor (an investor which invests more than 10% of the issued share capital in a company and has a right to appoint directors and control management) may invest with Bank of Botswana ("BOB") approval. That approval is readily given where the investment is in:
- a new company, upon proof that the funds are received from foreign sources; or
- an existing company, upon satisfaction that fair value is being paid for the shares.

A portfolio investor (an investor which invests in less than 10% of the entire issued share capital of a company and has no right to appoint a director to and has no say in management) may invest in up to 5% of the entire issued share capital of a company without BOB approval, and up to 10% with BOB approval. The aggregate foreign portfolio investment in a company may not exceed 49% of the free stock of the company (that is, stock which does not give rise to control of the company).

Once an investment has been approved by BOB:
- dividends are freely remittable out of Botswana, subject to audited financial statements being lodged with an authorized dealer (i.e., the commercial bank concerned) and payment of withholding tax; and
- capital gains on a subsequent sale are freely remittable out of Botswana, subject, in the case of an unlisted company, to payment of capital gains tax.

Non-residents may make loans to Botswana entities. The loan and the terms thereof require BOB approval and interest payable on the loan may then be remitted, subject to payment of a 15% withholding tax, and the capital may be repaid and remitted after two years.

In addition to current account allowances for travel, royalties, franchise and management fees, companies and businesses may remit up to P1 million for direct investment abroad without BOB approval.

Persons in Botswana are permitted to hold foreign currency accounts in U.S. dollars, British pounds, German marks or South African Rand.

Temporary resident individuals are allowed to remit out of Botswana 65% of actual earnings each year.

G. Regulatory Environment

The Trading Act regulates wholesale, retail representative and agency businesses. The Trading Act requires licenses for each of these types of businesses. The insurance and pension and provident industry is regulated by the Insurance Act and Pension and Provident Fund Act and regulations. There is no regulation of competition or of mergers, acquisitions and takeovers.

The Botswana Share Market trades in the shares of fourteen public companies. The Botswana Stock Exchange Act governs dealings on the Botswana Stock Exchange.

H. Intellectual Property

Intellectual property protection is provided for by statute.

I. Registries

Botswana has registries for business names, designs, patents and trademarks. As far as registration of designs, patents and trademarks is concerned, Botswana does not issue original licenses, but registers designs, patents and trademarks already registered in South Africa and the United Kingdom.

J. Tariffs

Botswana is a member of SACU, imposing the same import tariffs as South Africa, subject to the Uruguay Round of the General Agreement on Tariffs and Trade ("GATT"). A trade agreement with Zimbabwe exists pursuant to which certain goods are exempted from import and export duty.

K. Incentives

Financial assistance to manufacturing operations exists by way of the financial assistance policy ("FAP"), which was previously effectively limited to manufacturing, medium and small-scale mining and agriculture other than cattle and most rain fed crops. The Government intends extending the FAP to the service sector, including tourism.

Under the FAP, the following grants are available to an investor in a new enterprise:
- a five year "step down" tax holiday (involving reimbursement of company tax paid) of 100% in each of the first two years of operation and 75%, 50% and 25% in the third, fourth and fifth years, respectively;
- a step down reimbursement of unskilled labor costs of 80% in the first two years of operation and 60%, 40% and 20% in the third, fourth and fifth years, respectively; and
- a training grant reimbursement of 50% of approved training costs in the first five years of operation.

Alternatively, the following grants are available on a case-by-case basis:
- a capital grant equal to the lesser of a fixed percentage of the capital

investment (the minimum being 40% of capital investment in urban areas and the maximum being 85% of capital investment in certain rural areas) and P1,000 per citizen job created where the investor is a non-citizen;
- a step down sales augmentation grant equal to up to 8% of sales revenue in each of the first two years of operation and 6%, 4% and 2% in years three, four and five, respectively; and
- the above-mentioned reimbursements of unskilled labor costs and training costs.

Grants under the FAP are exempted from income tax.

L. Membership In International And Regional Organizations

Botswana is a member of the Southern African Development Community ("SADC"), the World Bank, the International Monetary Fund (the "IMF"), the Organization of African Unity (the "OAU"), the United Nations, the British Commonwealth and the Lome Convention and is a signatory to GATT.

III. Zimbabwe

A. Type Of Government

Zimbabwe is a multi-party democracy.

B. Forms Of Business Organizations

The following forms of business organizations are recognized in Zimbabwe:
- public limited liability companies (whether or not listed on the Zimbabwe Stock Exchange);
- private limited liability companies;
- foreign companies (i.e., subsidiaries or branches of foreign companies);
- private business corporations (which are almost identical to South African close corporations);
- partnerships;
- trusts; and
- sole proprietorships.

C. Formation Of A Business

Companies and private business corporations are registered and regulated by the Companies Act. Listed public companies are, in addition, regulated by the rules of the Zimbabwe Stock Exchange. There is a central registry of companies in Harare.

Generally, shop and trading licenses are required for most businesses. These are largely dealt with by local authorities. Registration of businesses is required for various purposes, including with the National Social Security Authority, Accident Prevention and

Compensation Scheme. There are compulsory pension and other benefits schemes and various employment councils.

D. Taxation

The corporate tax rate is 37.5%. However, profits earned from new projects by manufacturing companies operating in designated growth areas are taxed at 20% in the year in which operations commence and for the four years thereafter. Foreign incorporated companies pay, in addition to income tax, profit tax at the rate of 15% per dollar on 50% of the taxable income they derive from Zimbabwean sources. There is a 30% capital gains tax on the sale of shares and immovable property.

Dividends paid by a Zimbabwean company to another Zimbabwean company are not taxable, although foreign dividends earned by Zimbabwean companies are taxable at 20%. Dividends distributed by Zimbabwean companies to individuals are subject to a deduction of 20%. This does not apply to dividends paid to a holding company. The same applies to interest paid to non-residents.

Export Processing Zone concessions are available to companies operating in such zones. There is a 100% drought levy for the year 1995-1996 raised on tax paid for the year 1994-1995.

Individuals earning less than Z$9000 are not liable for income tax. Child credits are Z$880.00 per annum per child for a maximum of four children.

Double taxation agreements are in place with South Africa, Bulgaria, Canada, Germany, Mauritius, the Netherlands, Norway, Poland, Sweden and the United Kingdom. Further double taxation agreements are soon to be signed with France and Malaysia.

E. Foreign Investment

Foreign investment in Zimbabwe is encouraged. A government agency, "The Zimbabwe Investment Centre," deals with new in Zimbabwe projects and investments. Staff at the Centre are most helpful. Local participation in any investment projects is encouraged.

F. Exchange Control

Exchange controls have been substantially liberalized. Dividend remittances are allowed at 100% of current after-tax profits. Capital is blocked, although it may be remitted through 30-year government bonds, denominated in Zimbabwe dollars. Pursuant to the terms of these bonds, capital is repaid in ten equal annual installments at the end of years eleven through thirty. Interest on the bonds, which is tax free, is 4% per annum and is payable semi-annually.

G. Regulatory Environment

Zimbabwe does not have a Monopolies Commission, although public demand for it is growing. The Zimbabwe Stock Exchange has regulations governing dealings in securities listed on it.

H. Intellectual Property

Intellectual property protection is provided by statute.

I. Registries

Zimbabwe had public registries for trademarks, designs and patents. Zimbabwe is a signatory of the Berne and Paris Conventions.

J. Tariffs

Import controls exist in Zimbabwe. There are a limited number of goods on a negative list, which include clothing, armaments and nuclear materials. Zimbabwe is a member of GATT.

K. Membership In International And Regional Organizations

Zimbabwe is a member of the United Nations, the British Commonwealth, the Non-aligned Movement, the Association of Southern African States, SADC, the World Bank, the IMF, the OAU and the Preferential Trade Area (the "PTA") and is a signatory to GATT.

IV. Zambia

A. Type Of Government

Zambia is a multi-party democracy with a written constitution containing a bill of rights.

B. Forms Of Business Organizations

Each of the following forms of business organizations is recognized in Zambia:
- private or public limited liability company;
- company limited by guarantee;
- unlimited company;
- foreign company branch;
- partnership; and
- sole proprietorship.

C. Formation Of A Business

Companies and foreign companies must be registered with the Registrar of Companies in Lusaka. Partnerships and sole proprietorships trading under a name other than their own must register their business name. Various registrations are required for tax purposes, national provident fund and workmens' compensation. Business licenses are required for certain activities.

D. Taxation

Tax is levied on income from actual and deemed Zambian sources. The corporate and marginal personal tax rate is 35%. However, income from farming and the export of non-traditional exports is taxed at 15%. Additional taxes include:
- value added tax ("VAT"), at a rate of 20%;
- a withholding tax, at a rate of 10% on dividends paid to residents and non-residents, reducible to 5% or 0% under certain taxation agreements; and
- property transfer tax (in lieu of capital gains tax), at a rate of 2.5% on the sale of real property or shares not listed on the Lusaka Stock Exchange.

Zambia has double taxation agreements with most major industrialized and African countries.

E. Foreign Investment

Zambia welcomes foreign investment and virtually all businesses (other than certain types of retail trade, road haulage and building minerals) are open to foreign investors. There are no exchange controls and foreign currencies can be bought and sold at market-determined exchange rates.

Investors proposing to establish businesses in Zambia in the field of manufacturing, mining and processing of gemstones, agriculture, transport, communications, construction, tourism and the provision of services are required to apply for an investment certificate. General incentives available to the holders of such certificates include, for rural enterprises, a reduction by one seventh of income tax otherwise payable for the first five years, various capital allowances, exemption from tax for five years on dividends from farming and residence/work permits for qualifying investors. Special incentives which may be available include exemption from customs duty on the import of machinery and equipment.

F. Regulatory Environment

A number of pieces of legislation have recently been introduced (not all of which are yet operational) to regulate the securities industry, banking and financial services, environmental protection and competition. The Lusaka Stock Exchange has recently published its listing requirements.

G. Intellectual Property

Intellectual property protection is provided by statute for copyrights, patents, trademarks and registered designs.

H. Registries

There are public registries for lands and deeds, mining titles, companies, business names and intellectual property rights.

I. Tariffs

Import tariffs and direct controls such as import permits exist. Customs duties generally range between 20% and 40% plus VAT, although lower duties are payable on goods coming from fellow members of the PTA. Import permits are issued by commercial banks.

J. Membership In International And Regional Organizations

Zambia is a member of the Common Market for East and Southern Africa, the PTA, the World Bank, the IMF, the OAU, the United Nations and the British Commonwealth and is a signatory to GATT.

V. Lesotho

A. Business Entities

The following forms of business entities are recognized in Lesotho:
- private or public limited liability companies;
- external companies, which are branches of foreign corporate bodies;
- partnerships, which include consortia and joint ventures; and
- sole proprietorships.

Private and public limited liability companies and external companies must be registered in accordance with the Companies Act, 1967. Partnerships must be registered in accordance with the Partnerships Proclamation, 1957.

1. Companies

The private limited company is the most common form of business entity used in Lesotho. The following requirements apply to private limited companies:
- the minimum authorized and issued share capital must be M1,000;
- there must be a minimum of two shareholders (and a maximum of 50), with a minimum of one director;
- at least 51% of the shareholding in the company must be held by Lesotho citizens to the extent that certain trading licenses are required by the company; otherwise there is no restriction on who may hold shares;
- the Public Officer must be a resident in Lesotho, unless there is a special dispensation; and

- the financial accounts of the company must be audited by an auditor registered to practice in Lesotho.

The company registration process should not take longer than one month at a cost of approximately M2,000, which includes all fees paid to the Registrar of Companies and initial secretarial work, but which does not cover licensing and related procedures.

2. External Companies

A foreign company may register as an external company in Lesotho and must do so within six months of opening a place of business. The registration will require, among other things, the nomination of a person within Lesotho upon whom notices and processes can be served and the address of the principal place of business of the company in Lesotho.

3. Partnerships

Partnership agreements must be reduced to writing and attested to before a notary public. These agreements are then registered in the Deeds Registry in Maseru under the Partnerships Proclamation, 1957 (the "Proclamation"). A partnership agreement must likewise be cancelled in writing. Partnerships are restricted to twenty persons. The Proclamation essentially codifies the common law as regards partnerships.

B. Taxation

The Income Tax Act, 1993, as amended, together with the regulations promulgated thereunder, governs taxation. Tax rates are as follows:
- a manufacturing company is taxed at a rate of 15% and all other companies, including external branches, at a rate of 40%;
- an external company is subject to tax at a rate of 40% on repatriated income, in addition to income tax on its chargeable income.
- residents are subject to a progressive tax, the first M20,000 in income being taxed at the rate of 35%, the second M20,000 in income at a rate of 35% and all income over M40,000 at a rate of 40%.

Withholding tax is required to be deducted at source at the standard tax rate on dividends, interest, royalties, natural resource payments or management charges for a management or administrative service and at a rate of 10% on the gross amount of any payment under a Lesotho-source services contract paid to a non-resident. Capital gains tax does apply in Lesotho.

C. Exchange Control; Customs Union

Lesotho is part of the Rand Common Monetary Area. Exchange controls apply, as provided in the Exchange Control Order and Exchange Control Regulations of the Central

Bank of Lesotho, which functions in conjunction with the South African Reserve Bank. The commercial banks in Lesotho are appointed as authorized foreign exchange dealers up to certain limits.

Lesotho is a member of the PTA and SADC.

D. Trading Licenses

The issuance of licenses is governed by the Trading Enterprises Order, 1987 and the Trading Enterprises Regulations, 1989. There is a 1993 Order but no regulations have as of yet been promulgated thereunder. Certain licenses are restricted to local citizens or companies controlled by local citizens.

VI. Swaziland

A. Type Of Government

Swaziland is a constitutional monarchy with a Parliament and Senate partly elected (through an intricate process) and partly appointed by the monarch.

B. Forms Of Business Organization

Each of the following forms of business entities is recognized in Swaziland:
- private or public limited liability company;
- external company (i.e., a branch of a foreign company);
- partnership;
- trading trust; and
- sole proprietorship.

C. Formation Of A Business

Companies, trusts and external companies must be registered with the authorities in Mbabane. A business generally has to register for various tax purposes, workmens' compensation, graded tax and the Swaziland National Provident Fund. Business licenses are required for certain activities.

D. Taxation

Tax is levied on income from actual and deemed Swaziland sources. The corporate tax rate is 37.5%. In addition there is a withholding tax of 10% of dividend payments to non-residents and a sales tax of 10%. There is no capital gains tax or tax on dividends from companies and distributions paid to residents.

Swaziland has double taxation agreements with various countries in Africa, including South Africa.

E. Foreign Investment

Swaziland welcomes foreign investment and most business activities are open to foreign investors. Exchange control still exists. However, South Africa, Lesotho, Namibia and Swaziland have no exchange control restrictions in effect between them by virtue of their membership in the Common Monetary Union.

The following are the main incentives available to investors in Swaziland:
- substantial investors can apply to the Ministry of Commerce for an income tax holiday which is usually granted for a five-year period;
- machinery imported into the country for the purposes of setting up a business is exempt from sales tax; and
- non-Swazi citizens are able to purchase immovable property and investors who purchase property in the Matsdapha Industrial Area are exempt from applying for and obtaining the consent of the Land Speculation Control Board.

Revenue and original capital investment can be repatriated, subject to the consent of the Central Bank of Swaziland first having been obtained. Such revenue and capital can be repatriated in the currency in which the original investment was made in Swaziland.

F. Regulatory Environment

The Swaziland Stock Exchange has regulations governing dealings in securities listed on it which are in line with those of the Johannesburg Stock Exchange.

The Swazi legal system is totally independent and follows the principles of Roman Dutch law.

G. Intellectual Property

Intellectual property protection is provided for by statute.

H. Registries

There are public registries for trademarks and patents. Swaziland is a signatory to the Berne and Paris Conventions.

I. Tariffs

Import tariffs and direct controls such as import permits exist but are subject to the provisions of GATT. There is a free and virtually unimpeded exchange of goods between member states of SACU. In addition Swaziland is partly to many preferential trade agreements in Africa and Europe and with the United States. There are a number of export incentives available to genuine exporters.

Gaborone, Botswana
June 1996

ABOUT THE AUTHORS

LEORA BLUMBERG is the Deputy Chairperson of the South African Board of Tariffs and Trade, where she is focusing upon the restructure of South Africa's anti-dumping legislation and practice. Ms. Blumberg's address and telephone numbers are:
>Board on Tariffs and Trade
>Private Bag X753
>Pretoria 0001, South Africa
>Telephone: 011-27-12-310-9851
>Telecopy: 011-27-12-320-2085

Prior to her appointment to the Board of Tariffs and Trade, Ms. Blumberg was a partner at the Webber Wentzel Bowens law firm in Johannesburg, South Africa. Ms. Blumberg specialized in the practice of international trade, investment and competition law. Ms. Blumberg has also practices at law firms in Luxembourg, Singapore and in the United States and has lectured on international law at the University of Witwatersrand in South Africa.

PIERRE E.J. BROOKS, Chairman of the Competition Board in Pretoria, South Africa, is Emeritus Professor of Law at the University of South Africa ("UNISA") and a Member of the Securities Regulation Panel. Dr. Brooks was previously Head of the Department of Mercantile Law at UNISA, Vice-Dean of the Faculty of Law at UNISA and Director of the Institute of Foreign and Comparative Law at UNISA. Dr. Brooks' professional fields of interest include company law, competition law, transnational business law, private international law and EEC law. He is an Advocate of the Supreme Court of South Africa. Dr. Brooks is a graduate of UNISA and of University of Exeter, England.

DAVID W. BUTLER is a professor of mercantile law at the University of Stellenbosch in South Africa. His address and telephone numbers are:
>University of Stellenbosch
>Faculty of Law
>Stellenbosch 7600, South Africa
>Telephone: 011-27-21-808-3486
>Telecopy: 011-27-21-886-6235
>E-Mail: DWB@MATIES.SUN.AC.ZA.

Professor Butler is also an attorney of the Supreme Court of South Africa. Professor Butler has also taught international commercial arbitration at the University of Florida College of Law.

ROBIN B. CAMP is a partner at the Armstrongs law firm in Gaborone, Botswana. His address and telephone numbers are:
>Armstrongs
>Box 1368
>Fifth Floor
>Barclays House, Khama, Crescent
>Gaborone, Botswana
>Telephone: 267-353-481
>Telecopy: 267-352-757

Mr. Camp received his Bachelor of Commerce and Bachelor of Laws from the University of Stellenbosch in South Africa in 1973 and 1976, respectively. Mr. Camp is admitted to practice in Johannesburg, South Africa, and also at the High Court of Lesotho and the High Court of Botswana. Mr. Camp is a fellow of the South African Association of Arbitrators and a member of the Kalahari Conservation Society.

DELOITTE & TOUCHE, SOUTH AFRICA is the South African affiliate of Deloitte Touche Tohmatsu International. Deloitte & Touche's services in South Africa include, but are not limited to, accounting and auditing, management consulting, tax and corporate finance services. The business address of Deloitte & Touche's Johannesburg office is:
> Deloitte & Touche
> Private Bag X6
> Gallo Manor
> Sandton 2052, South Africa

Inquiries to Deloitte & Touche should be directed to Michael H. Rippon. His telephone number is 011-27-11-806-5000 and his telecopy number is 011-27-11-806-5003.

MICHAEL J.R. EVANS is a director of Mallinicks Inc., a Cape Town law firm. His address and telephone numbers are:
> Mallinicks Inc.
> 6th Floor 2 Long Street
> Cape Town 8001, South Africa
> Telephone: 011-27-21-419-4411
> Telecopy: 011-27-21-217-7207
> Internet: Malnick@1access.za.

Mr. Evans received his B.A., his Honors degree (Comparative African Government and Law), his L.L.B. and his Postgraduate Diploma in Tax Law from the University of Cape Town. Mr. Evans specializes in corporate law and has advised a number of foreign companies which have established themselves in South Africa in the post-sanction era.

LEE FALKOW is a professional assistant (that is, an associate) at the Werksmans law firm in Johannesburg, South Africa. Her address and telephone number are:
> Werksmans Chambers
> 22 Girton Road
> Parktown 2193, South Africa
> Telephone: 27-11-488-0000
> Telecopy: 27-11-484-3100

Ms. Falkow obtained her law degree from the University of the Witwatersrand. Ms. Falkow specializes in the practice of international trade and commercial law. Ms. Falkow has written various papers on international trade, competition law, intellectual property, agency and distributorships.

LENORE GLANZ, a law librarian at the Library of International Relations and at the ITT Chicago-Kent College of Law Library, works primarily with reference and international documents. She specializes in responding to inquiries about and retrieving documents issued by non-governmental organizations such as the UN, EU, GATT, FAO, WTO and World Bank, as well as the central banks or statistical arms of foreign countries. Ms. Glanz's writings have appeared in PTA Today, Special Libraries, the Sixteenth Century Journal and World Events, the newsletter of the Chicago Council on Foreign Relations. Ms. Glanz is a member of the American Association of Law Libraries and several other library or historical associations.

Ms. Glanz is a graduate of Loyola University, Chicago with a Ph.D. in legal history, and of the University of Illinois, Urbana, where she earned a B.A. (magna cum laude), M.A. and M.S.L.S.

JOHN JANKS is a partner at the Werksmans law firm in Johannesburg, South Africa. His address and telephone numbers are:
>Werksmans Chambers
>22 Girton Road
>Parktown 2193, South Africa
>Telephone: 27-11-488-0000
>Telecopy: 27-11-484-3100

In addition to his law degree, Mr. Janks has higher diplomas in tax and in company law, and is currently in post-graduate study in constitutional law. Mr. Janks specializes in the practice of general commercial law, including the negotiation and drafting of contracts, and tax and estate matters. Mr. Janks also has an interest in constitutional law and environmental law. Finally, Mr. Janks has written various papers on leases, trusts, privacy (especially in respect of computer and electronic messaging), VAT in relation to property transfers, joint venture and supply agreements, constitutional law and environmental law.

KEVIN JOSELOWITZ is a director of the Edward Nathan Friedland Inc. law firm in Johannesburg, South Africa. His address and telephone numbers are:
>Edward Nathan & Friedland Inc.
>P.O. Box 3370
>23rd Floor Sanlamsentrum
>206-214 Jeppe Street
>Johannesburg 2000, South Africa
>Telephone: 27-11-337-2100
>Telecopy: 27-11-333-6942

Mr. Joselowitz received his B.A. and L.L.B., both with distinction, from the University of the Witwatersrand. Mr. Joselowitz specializes in the practice of corporate law, particularly in mergers and acquisitions.

MICHAEL M. KATZ is the Senior Partner and a Director of Edward Nathan & Friedland Inc., a law firm in Johannesburg, South Africa. His address and telephone numbers are:
>Edward Nathan & Friedland Inc.
>P.O. Box 3370
>23rd Floor Sanlamsentrum
>206-214 Jeppe Street

Johannesburg 2000, South Africa
Telephone: 27-11-337-2100
Telecopy: 27-11-333-6942

Mr. Katz received his B. Com. L.L.B. from the University of Witwatersrand and his L.L.M. from Harvard Law School. Mr. Katz is a member of the Standing Advisory Committee on Company Law, the Chairman of the Tax Advisory Committee to the Minister of Finance, a member of the Securities Regulation Panel and the Chairman of the Commission of Inquiry to Investigate the Taxation System of South Africa. Mr. Katz is also an Honorary Professor of Company Law at the University of Witwatersrand. In addition, Mr. Katz is a former member of the State President's Economic Advisory Council.

PETER S.G. LEON is a partner in the Webber Wentzel Bowens law firm in Johannesburg, South Africa and heads its Financial Services Unit. His address and telephone numbers are:

Webber Wentzel Bowens
60 Main Street
Johannesburg 2107, South Africa
Telephone: 011-27-11-240-5000
Telecopy: 011-27-11-240-5111

Mr. Leon specializes in the practice of securities law and securities regulation, competition law, international banking and general corporate law. Mr. Leon is also the Leader of the Democratic Party in the Gauteng Legislature.

PUKE MASERUMULE is a partner in the Tshabalala Maserumule law firm in Johannesburg, South Africa. His address and telephone numbers are:

Tshabalala Maserumule
Suite 1003
Kelhof Building
112 Pritchard Street
Johannesburg 2001, South Africa
Telephone: 011-27-11-337-8501
Telecopy: 011-27-11-337-6914

In addition to his law degree, Mr. Maserumule has a post graduate diploma in labor law and specializes in the practice of labor law.

TIEGO MOSENEKE is a senior partner at the Moseneke & Partners law firm, the largest black-owned corporate law firm in Johannesburg, South Africa. His address and telephone numbers are:

Moseneke & Partners
First Floor
Surrey House
35 Rissik Street
Johannesburg 2001, South Africa
Telephone: 011-27-11-492-1610
Telecopy: 011-27-11-838-1556

Mr. Moseneke's practice includes the representation of multinational foreign investors in South Africa. He is the co-author of the Report on Privatization in South Africa.

NICOLA F. NEWTON-KING is the legal counsel to the Johannesburg Stock Exchange. Her address and telephone numbers are:
Johannesburg Stock Exchange
17 Diagonal Street
Johannesburg 2001, South Africa
Telephone: 011-27-11-377-2200
Telecopy: 011-27-11-834-7402

When Ms. Newton-King wrote her article for the Guide, she was a partner at the Webber Wentzel Bowens law firm in Johannesburg, South Africa. Ms. Newton-King's practice at Webber Wentzel Bowens specialized in securities law and securities regulation, derivatives and banking, law and general corporate law.

DAVID F. SHEPPARD is a partner in the Pretoria, South Africa office of the Adams & Adams law firm. His address and telephone numbers are:
Adams & Adams
1140 Prospect Street
Pretoria 0001, South Africa
Telephone: 011-27-12-481-1500
Telecopy: 011-27-12-342-7730

Mr. Sheppard specializes in the practice of patent litigation, particularly in the chemical field. Mr. Sheppard has a degree in chemistry from the University of London and is a British chartered patent agent and a South African patent agent and attorney. Mr. Sheppard is also the South African reporter for the European Intellectual Property Review and is the author of numerous papers on South African intellectual property law.

ROBYN STEIN is a director at the Bowman Gilfillan Hayman Godfrey Inc. law firm in Johannesburg, South Africa. Ms. Stein's address and telephone numbers are:
Bowman Gilfillan Hayman Godfrey Inc.
9th Floor
Twin Towers West
Sandton City
Sandton 2146, South Africa
Telephone: 011-27-11-881-9800
Telecopy: 011-27-11-883-4505

ABOUT THE EDITORS

VAUGHN C. WILLIAMS is a partner in the Skadden, Arps, Slate, Meagher & Flom law firm in New York, New York. His address and telephone numbers are:
Skadden Arps Slate Meagher & Flom
919 Third Avenue
New York, New York 10022
Telephone: 212-735-3470
Telecopy: 212-735-2000

Mr. Williams specializes in litigation, including corporate and securities litigation, merger and acquisition litigation, class action litigation and general commercial litigation. Mr. Williams received his J.D. from Stanford Law School, where he was President of the Stanford Law Review.

The Skadden Arps firm has 21 offices worldwide, including 12 offices in Asia, Australia, Canada and Western and Central Europe. Its international practice includes international corporate transactions, international energy project finance, international project finance, international trade, privatization, and international litigation and arbitration.

WILLIAM M. HANNAY, Vice-Chair of the ABA Section of International Law, has been a member of the Section's Council for the past four years and served as Deputy to the General Division Vice-Chair (1994-95). He previously chaired the International Criminal Law Committee. Mr. Hannay served as Annual Meeting chair for the meetings in 1990 and 1995 in Chicago and has also served as a member of the A.B.A.'s ad hoc Committee on an International Criminal Tribunal.

Mr. Hannay is a partner in the Chicago-based law firm of Schiff Hardin & Waite, concentrating his practice in the area of U.S. and international antitrust and trade regulation. His address and telephone numbers are:
Schiff Hardin & Waite
7200 Sears Tower
Chicago, Illinois 60606-6473
Telephone: 312-876-1000
Telecopy: 312-258-5600

Mr. Hannay is an Adjunct Professor at IIT/Chicago-Kent College of Law in Chicago and recently led the American Bar Association's ILEX Briefing Trip to South Africa in November 1995. Among his publications, he is the author/editor of Butterworth Legal Publishers' International Trade: Avoiding Criminal Risks. He is a graduate of Yale College and Georgetown University Law Center.

MICHAEL R. LITTENBERG is an attorney at the Schulte Roth & Zabel law firm in New York, New York. His address and telephone numbers are:
Schulte Roth & Zabel
900 Third Avenue
New York, New York 10022
Telephone: 212-758-0404
Telecopy: 212-593-5955

Mr. Littenberg specializes in cross-border transactions, including mergers and acquisitions, joint ventures and securities offerings. He represents U.S. companies in connection with their activities in Africa and African companies in connection with international capital raising and strategic transactions with foreign participants. Mr. Littenberg also has been active in cross-border transactions involving North America, South America, Europe, Asia and Australia.

Mr. Littenberg has published and spoken extensively on Africa. He also is the South Africa country editor for Bowne's International Securities Handbook. Mr. Littenberg is a member of the African Law Committee of the International Law Section of the American Bar Association, the Africa coordinator for the Section's International Securities Transactions Committee and a member of the African International and Comparative Law Society. Mr. Littenberg also is a member of the South Africa-America Organization.

Mr. Littenberg obtained his B.S. in Business Administration (with a concentration in International Business) from Indiana University. He obtained his J.D., magna cum laude, from Tulane University School of Law, where he was an editor of the Tulane Law Review.

LAUREN ROBINSON, an associate at Schiff Hardin & Waite in Chicago, Illinois, primarily practices general corporate and real estate law, with a focus on affordable housing development, including the representation of not-for-profit corporations seeking the purchase of multi-unit residential property under federal statutes funding such acquisitions and the syndication of low income housing tax credits. Her address and telephone numbers are:

> Schiff Hardin & Waite
> 7200 Sears Tower
> Chicago, Illinois 60606-6473
> Telephone: 312-876-1000
> Telecopy: 312-258-5600

Ms. Robinson is the co-author of "Landlord's Duties and Liabilities," a chapter in the Illinois Institute for Continuing Legal Education's 1996 Handbook on commercial landlord-tenant practice in Illinois. She has also written and lectured on rural land reform in South Africa. Ms. Robinson is a graduate of New York University School of Law, New York University Graduate School of Public Service and Vassar College (Honors Thesis).

APPENDIX A

RESOURCES ABOUT SOUTH AFRICAN LAW IN THE UNITED STATES

By Lenore Glanz

All of the following publications are available in business and law libraries in the United States. For items that are difficult to find, one should visit a public or private library which has computer search facilities and refer to a librarian who can conduct a computer search (such as OCLC or RLIN databases). Materials may also be obtained from Juta & Co., Ltd., one of the leading publishers of materials regarding South African law and business.[1]

I. **On-Line Resources**

- The Law Library Of Congress (U.S.) has a site listing the laws of all nations, including those for the Republic of South Africa: http://law.house.gov/83.htm
- Legal and business information regarding South Africa may be accessed via LEXIS and WESTLAW as follows:
- LEXIS: access the Mideast/Africa Library (MIDEAFR) via NEXIS.
- WESTLAW: access the International Business Database on DIALOG.

II. **Publications**
    A. **Commercial Law**

- Commercial Laws Of The World: South Africa. Ormond Beach, FLA: Foreign Tax Law Publishers: current (looseleaf).
  (A full text translation of the laws, statutes, and regulations regarding commerce.)
- De Kock's Industrial Laws Of South Africa. By C. Thompson & P. Benjamin. Cape Town: Juta: current. (looseleaf)
  (Will soon take the title: South African Labour Law.)
- Digest Of Commercial Laws Of The World. Ed. by Lester Nelson. Dobbs Ferry, NY: Oceana: current. 3 vols. (looseleaf)
- Foreign Law: current sources of codes and basic legislation in jurisdictions of the world. By Thomas H. Reynolds and Arturo A. Flores. Littleton, CO: Rothman: current.

---

[1] Juta & Co., Ltd, Legal and Business Publications. Head Office, Mercury Crescent Hillstar Industrial Township, Wetton 7764, P.O. BOX 14373, Kenwyn 7790, CapeTown, South Africa. TEL: (021) 797-5101; FAX: (021) 762-7424. Juta is represented in the United States and Canada by Wm. H. Gaunt & Sons, Inc., Gaunt Building, 3011 Gulf Drive, Holmes Beach, FLA 34217-2199. TEL: (800) 942-8683 and (813) 778-5211; FAX: (813) 778-5255.

(The chapter on South Africa identifies recent treatises on various areas of the laws as well as the applicable statutes on company law, corporations, environmental protection, foreign investments, etc.)

- Fundamentals Of The South African Financial System. Ed. by L. J. Fouries et al. Halfway House: Southern Book Publishers: 1992.
- Guide To The Close Corporations Act & Regulations. By W. Geach & T. Schoeman. Cape Town: Juta: current. (looseleaf)
- Guide To The Companies Act And Regulations. By T. Schoeman & W. Geach. Cape Town: Juta: current. (looseleaf)
- Juta's Business Law, ed. by Peter Dawe & Coenrad Visser. Cape Town: Juta: 1993.
(A quarterly journal containing articles on legal matters relevant to the business community.)
- Practical Guide To Document Authentication: legalization of notarized and certified documents. By John P. Sinnott. Dobbs Ferry, NY: Oceana: current. (looseleaf)
(Includes legalization procedures for each country.)
- South African Mercantile Law. Ed. by C. Visser et al. Cape Town: Juta: current. (Published three times per year)
(This journal succeeds Modern Business Law.)

B. **Environmental Law**

- International Environment Reporter. Washington, DC: BNA: current.
(The information on South Africa includes environmental agency addresses and phone numbers.)
- International Execution Against Judgement Debtors. General Editor: Dennis Campbell. London: Sweet & Maxwell; Deerfield, IL: Clark Boardman Callaghan: current. (looseleaf)

C. **Foreign Exchange**

- Exchange Arrangements and Exchange Restrictions. Annual Report. Washington, DC: International Monetary Fund: current.
(Each annual report has a chapter on South Africa.)

D. **Foreign Investment**

- Investing, Licensing & Trading Conditions Abroad: Africa/Middle East. London & New York: The Economist Intelligence Unit (EIU): current.
(The reports on South Africa are published quarterly and may be obtained by contacting the EIU at The Economist Building, 111 West 57th Street, New York 10019. TEL: (212) 554-0600; FAX: (212) 586-1181.)
- McGregor's Quick Reference To The JSE. By Robin McGregor. Cape Town: Juta: semiannual.

(This book provides listed companies' annual reports, addresses, transfer registers, subsidiaries, etc.)
- McGregor's Who Owns Whom: the investor's handbook. By Robin McGregor. Cape Town: Juta: 1993. (13th ed.)
(This is a comprehensive listing with indices of approximately 25,000 companies.)
- Portfolio of Black Businessmen in Southern Africa. Johannesburg: WR Publications: 1994.
- South Africa Yearbook. Ed. by South African Communication Service. Pretoria: CTP Book Printers on Behalf of the Government Printer: current. (Originally known as the South Africa Official Yearbook.)
- Trade Policy Review: The Republic of South Africa. Geneva: GATT: 1993.
- U.S. - South Africa Economic Yearbook. Washington, D.C.: U.S. - South Africa Business Council: current.
- Stock Exchanges of the World: Selected Rules and Regulations. Robert C. Rosen, General Editor. Dobbs Ferry, NY: Oceana: current. (looseleaf) (Includes the rules and regulations of the Johannesburg Stock Exchange.)

E. **General Business**

- African Business Handbook: a practical guide to business resources for U.S./Africa trade and investment. Washington: 21st Century Africa, Inc: (biannual; new issue will appear in Autumn 1996). TEL: (202) 659-6473; FAX: (202) 659-6475.
- Business Blue-Book of South Africa. Edited by Lorna White. Cape Town: The Business Press Division of the Communications Group: current.

F. **Intellectual Property**

- Copyright Laws and Treaties of the World. Paris: UNESCO; Washington, DC: BNA: current. 3 vols. (looseleaf)
- Protection of Corporate Names: a country-by-country survey by the U.S. Trademark Association. New York: Clark Boardman Callaghan, current. (looseleaf)
- Trademarks Throughout the World. Ed. by Alan J. Jacobs. New York: Trade Activities (Clark Boardman Callaghan): current.
(Includes a digest of South African trademark law.)

G. **Labor Law**

- Guide to South African Labour Law. By A. Rycroft & B. Jordaan. Cape Town: Juta: 1992. (2d ed.)

- Industrial Relations Handbook. By A. Pons et al. Cape Town: Juta: current. (looseleaf)
- Industrial Relations in South Africa. By Sonia Bendix. Cape Town: Juta: 1992. (2d ed.)
- International Encyclopedia for Labour Law and Industrial Relations. Editor-in-chief: R. Blanpain. Deventer, Netherlands: Kluwer, current. (looseleaf)
- Rieckert's Basic Employment Law. By John Grogan. Cape Town: Juta: 1993. (2d ed.)
- Worker Participation-South African Options and Experience. Ed. by M. Anstey. Cape Town: Juta: 1990.
- World Trademark Law and Practice. By John P. Sinnott. London: Sweet & Maxwell; New York: M. Bender: current. (looseleaf)
(Includes a chapter on South Africa.)

H. **Tax Law**

- International Tax Summaries. By the Coopers & Lybrand International Tax Network. New York: Wiley: current.
(This annual publication presents an overview of the tax system of 123 countries, including South Africa.)
- Tax Laws of the World: South Africa. Ormond Beach, FLA: Foreign Tax Law Publishers: current. (looseleaf).

Chicago, Illinois
June 1996

APPENDIX B

SELECTED BUSINESS, TRADE AND LEGAL ASSOCIATIONS AND GOVERNMENT AGENCIES

I. **Accountants**

- The Association for the Advancement of Black Accountants. P.O. Box 1470, Durban 4000 South Africa. TEL: (12) 27-31-305-1804; FAX: (12) 27-31-305-1823.
- The Institute of Commercial and Financial Accountants of SA. P.O. Box 61010, Marshalltown 2107 South Africa. TEL: (12) 27-11-838-7070; FAX: (12) 27-11-838-7075.
- The South African Institute of Chartered Accountants. P.O. Box 59876, Kengray 2100 South Africa. TEL: (12) 27-11-622-6655; FAX: (12) 27-11-622-3321.

II. **Advertising/Marketing**

- Advertising Standards Authority of SA. P.O. Box 41555, Craighall 2024 South Africa. TEL: (12) 27-11-880-4440/1; FAX: (12) 27-11-880-5547.
- Association of Advertising Agencies Ltd. P.O. Box 2302, Parklands 2121 South Africa. TEL: (12) 27-11-880-3908; FAX: (12) 27-11-447-1174.
- Association of Marketing. P.O. Box 98859, Sloane Park 2152 South Africa. TEL: (12) 27-11-706-1633; FAX: (12) 27-11-706-4151.
- Direct Selling Association. Private Bag 34, Auckland Park 2006 South Africa. TEL: (12) 27-11-726-5300; FAX: (12) 27-11-726-8421.
- Print Media Association. P.O. Box 47180, Parklands 2121 South Africa. TEL: (12) 27-11-447-1264; FAX: (12) 27-11-447-1289.
- SA Advertising Research Foundation. P.O. Box 98874, Sloane Park 2152 South Africa. TEL: (12) 27-11-463-5340; FAX: (12) 27-11-463-5010.
- SA Marketing Research Association. P.O. Box 91879, Auckland Park 2006 South Africa. TEL: (12) 27-11-482-1419; FAX: (12) 27-11-726-3639.

III. **Bar Associations**

- Association of Law Societies of the Republic of South Africa. P.O. Box 36626, Menlo Park 0102 South Africa. TEL: (12) 27-12-342-3339; FAX: (12) 27-12-342-3305.
- Association of Legal Advisors of South Africa. P.O. Box 95194, Grant Park 2051 South Africa. TEL: (011) 483-3071.
- Black Lawyers Association. P.O. Box 5217, Johannesburg 2000 South Africa. TEL: (12) 27-11-337-1535/6; FAX: (12) 27-11-337-1539.
- General Council of the Bar of South Africa. P.O. Box 2260, Johannesburg 2260, Johannesburg 2000 South Africa. TEL: (011) 293-976; FAX (011) 298-970.

- National Democratic Lawyers Association. P.O. Box 3934, Johannesburg 2000 South Africa. TEL: (12) 27-11-331-9726/7; FAX: (12) 27-11-331-9728.
- Society of Advocates of South Africa. Momentum Centre, East Tower, 343 Pretorius Str., Pretoria 0002 South Africa. TEL: (12) 27-12-322-1511; FAX: (12) 27-12-322-1535.

IV. Business And Trade Information

- Bureau of Market Research (UNISA). P.O. Box 392, Pretoria 0001 South Africa. TEL: (12) 27-12-429-3070; FAX: (12) 27-12-429-3221.
- Central Statistical Service. Private Bag X44, Pretoria 0001 South Africa. TEL: (12) 27-12-310-8911; FAX: (12) 27-12-310-8500.

V. Embassies

- Consulate General of the Republic of South Africa. 333 E. 38th Street, 9th Floor, New York, NY 10016. TEL: (212) 213-4880; FAX: (212) 213-0102. *Also,* 200 S. Michigan Avenue, 6th Floor, Chicago, IL 60604. TEL: (312) 939-7929; FAX: (312) 939-2588.
- Embassy of the Republic of South Africa. 3051 Massachusetts Avenue, N.W., Washington, D.C. 20008. TEL: (202) 232-4400; TELEX: 248364; FAX: (202) 265-1607.
- Embassy of the USA. Thibault House, 7th Floor, 877 Pretorius Street, Pretoria, South Africa. TEL: (12) 342-1048; TELEX: 322143; FAX: (12) 342-2244.
(The Foreign Agricultural Service, which promotes agricultural trade and investment, and the Economic Section, which distributes information about overall economic conditions in South Africa and U.S. government agency programs involving South Africa, are located at the Embassy in Pretoria.)

VI. Foreign Exchange

- The South African Reserve Bank: Exchange Control Division. P.O. Box 3125, Pretoria 0001 South Africa. TEL: (12) 27-12-313-3911; FAX: (12) 27-12-313-3771.

VII. Franchising

- The Franchise Association of Southern Africa. P.O. Box 31708, Braamfontein 2017 South Africa. TEL: (12) 27-11-403-3468; FAX: (12) 27-11-403-1279.

VIII. Government

- Ministry of Environmental Affairs of South Africa. Private Bag X482, Pretoria 0001. TEL: (011) 27-12-326-1110/1/2; FAX: (011) 27-12-323-2275.
- Ministry of Finance of South Africa. Private Bag X115, Pretoria 0001.
  TEL: (011) 27-12-323-1891; FAX: (011) 27-12-323-3262.
- Ministry of Labour of South Africa. Private Bag X499, Pretoria 0001. TEL: (011) 27-12-322-6523; FAX: (011) 27-12-320-1942.
- Ministry of Trade and Industry. Private Bag X84, Pretoria 0001. TEL: (011) 27-12-310-9791; FAX: (011) 27-12-322-2701.
- United States Department of State: South Africa Desk. Washington, D.C. 20520. TEL: (202) 647-8433; FAX: (202) 647-5007.

IX. Import and Export

- Board of Tariffs and Trade. Private Bag X753, Pretoria 0001 South Africa. TEL: (12) 27-12-322-8244; FAX: (12) 27-12-322-0149.
- Commissioner for Customs and Excise Department of Finance. Private Bag X47, Pretoria 0001 South Africa. TEL: (12) 27-12-314-9911; FAX: (12) 27-12-325-7992.
- Department of Trade and Industry Directorate: Import and Export Control. Private Bag X192, Pretoria 0001 South Africa. TEL: (12) 27-12-310-9791; FAX: (12) 27-12-322-0298.

X. Intellectual Property

- Department of Trade and Industry. Office of the Registrar; Patents, Trade Marks, Designs & Copyright. Private Bag X400, Pretoria 0001 South Africa. TEL: (12) 27-12-310-9791; FAX: (12) 27-12-323-4257.
- South African Institute of Intellectual Property Law. P.O. Box 1014, Pretoria 0001 South Africa. TEL: (12) 27-12-320-8500; FAX: (12) 27-12-320-1850.

XI. Investing/Debt And Equity Markets

- The Bond Market Association (BMA). P.Xo. Box 144, Newtown 2113 South Africa. TEL: (12) 27-11-836-2921; FAX: (12) 27-11-834-2211.
- Industrial Development and Investment Centre (IDIC). Directorate of Department of Trade and Industry. Private Bag X753, Pretoria 0001 South Africa. TEL: 012-310-9791; FAX: 012-322-0149.
- The Johannesburg Stock Exchange (JSE). P.O. Box 1174, Johannesburg 2000 South Africa. TEL: (12) 27-11-377-2200; FAX: (12) 27-11-834-7402.

- The South African Futures Exchange (SAFEX). P.O. Box 4406, Johannesburg 2000 South Africa. TEL: (12) 27-11-728-5960; FAX: (12) 27-11-728-5970.
- The South African Reserve Bank. P.O. Box 427, Pretoria 0001 South Africa. TEL: (12) 27-12-313-3911; FAX: (12) 27-12-313-3197/3929.

XII. The Reconstruction And Development Program (RDP)

(The RDP is the government's five-year plan to address the extensive social and economic needs of South Africans, to increase living standards, and to create economic opportunity for all South Africans. The plan embodies providing education, training and health care; developing housing; building roads and other basic infrastructure; and creating jobs. The RDP coordinates economic activity and investment between the government, the private sector and providers of foreign aid. Total expenditures are projected to reach between $10-20 billion.)

- Africa Growth Network. P.O. Box 260205, Excom 2023 South Africa. TEL: (12) 27-11-350-6111; FAX: (12) 27-11-350-5317.
- Association of Black Securities and Investment Professionals. 3rd Floor, 2 Sturdee Avenue, Rosebank 2196 South Africa. TEL: (12) 27-11-280-2219; FAX: (12) 27-11-447-5369.
- Black Entrepreneurship and Enterprise Development. P.O. Box 30804, Braamfontein 2017 South Africa. TEL: (12) 27-11-339-3237; FAX: (12) 27-11-403-7359.
- Black Management Forum. P.O. Box 62070, Marshalltown 2107 South Africa. TEL: (12) 27-11-333-8532/3; FAX: (12) 27-11-333-7806.
- Development Action Group (DAG). 101 Lower Main Road, Observatory 7925 South Africa. TEL: (12) 27-21-448-7886/7/8; FAX: (12) 27-21-47-1987.
- Development Bank of Southern Africa. P.O. Box 1231, Halfway House 1685 South Africa. TEL: (12) 27-11-313-3911; FAX: (12) 27-11-313-3086.
- Foundation for African Business and Consumer Services (FABCOS). P.O. Box 8785, Johannesburg 2000 South Africa. TEL: (12) 27-11-832-1911; FAX (12) 27-11-836-5920.
- Independent Development Trust. P.O. Box 16114, Vlaeberg 8018 South Africa. TEL: (12) 27-21-238-030; FAX: (12) 27-21-234-512.
- National African Federation of Chambers of Commerce (NAFCOC). P.O. Box 61213, Soshanguve 0152 South Africa. TEL: (12) 27-1214-3204/6; FAX: (12) 27-1214-2024.
- National Business Initiative for Growth, Development & Democracy. P.O. Box 294, Auckland Park 2006 South Africa. TEL: (12) 27-11-482-5100; FAX: (12) 27-11-482-5507.

- National Economic Development and Labour Council (NEDLAC). P.O. Box 443, Auckland Park 2006 South Africa. TEL: (12) 27-11-482-2511; FAX: (12) 27-11-482-4650.
- National Industries Chamber. P.O. Box 845, Kempton Park 1620 South Africa. TEL: (12) 27-11-394-2228; FAX: (12) 27-11-970-2543.
- Reconstruction and Development Programme (RDP). Private Bag X1000, Pretoria 0001 South Africa. TEL: (12) 27-12-328-4708; FAX: (12) 27-12-323-9512.
- Secretariat of the Economic Community of Southern Africa. Private Bag X321, Pretoria 0001 South Africa. TEL: (12) 27-12-341-4313; FAX: (12) 27-12-341-0506.
- South African Import & Export Association. P.O. Box 9736, Johannesburg 2000 South Africa. TEL: (12) 27-11-839-1385/2750; FAX: (12) 27-11-839-1386.

XIII. Regional Administrations For Economic Affairs

- Eastern Cape. Private Bag X0054, Bisho South Africa. TEL: (12) 27-401-992468; FAX: (12) 27-401-91883.
- Free State. P.O. Box 264, Bloemfontein 9300 South Africa. TEL: (12) 27-51-407-1128; FAX: (12) 27-51-448-8361.
- Gauteng. P.O. Box 62302, Marshalltown 2107 South Africa. TEL: (12) 27-11-240-1531/2; FAX: (12) 27-11-836-8558.
- Kwazulu-Natal. Private Bag 54323, Durban 4000 South Africa. TEL: (12) 27-31-360-6570; FAX: (12) 27-31-360-6568.
- Mpumalanga. Private Bag X11215, Nelspruit 1200 South Africa. TEL: (12) 27-1311-554004; FAX: (12) 27-1311-554006.
- North West. Private Bag X2008, Mmabatho 2735 South Africa. TEL: (12) 27-1408-41690; FAX: (12) 27-1408-841696.
- Northern Cape. Private Bag X5016, Kimberley 8300 South Africa. TEL: (12) 27-531-814136; FAX: (12) 27-531-829464.
- Northern Province. P.O. Box 3490, Pietersburg 0700 South Africa. TEL: (12) 27-1522-97-4414; FAX: (12) 27-1522-97-4415.
- Western Cape. P.O. Box 979, Cape Town 8000 South Africa. TEL: (12) 27-21-483-4301; FAX: (12) 27-21-483-3886.

XIV. Trade Organizations

- Cape Chamber of Industries. P.O. Box 11536, Cape Town 8000 South Africa. TEL: (12) 27-21-215180; FAX: (12) 27-21-419-5982.
- Cape Town Chamber of Commerce. P.O. Box 204, Cape Town 8000 South Africa. TEL: (12) 27-21-23-2323; FAX: (12) 27-21-24-1878.
- Durban Regional Chamber of Business. P.O. Box 15063, Durban 4000 South Africa. TEL: (12) 27-31-301-3692; FAX: (12) 27-31-304-5255.

- Free State Chamber of Business. P.O. Box 87, Bloemfontein 9300 South Africa. TEL: (12) 27-51-447-3368/9; FAX: (12) 27-51-447-5064.
- Foundation for African Business and Consumer Services (FABCOS). P.O. Box 8785, Johannesburg 2000 South Africa. TEL: (12) 27-11-832-1911; FAX (12) 27-11-836-5920.
- Industrial Development Corporation of South Africa, Ltd. P.O. Box 784055, Sandton 2146 South Africa. TEL: (11) 883-1600; TELEX: 427174; FAX: (11) 883-1655.
- International Trade Bureau. CC Box 99003, Carlton Centre 2001 South Africa. TEL: (12) 27-11-331-3418/9; FAX: (12) 27-11-331-3442.
- Johannesburg Chamber of Commerce and Industry (JCCI). Private Bag 34, Auckland Park 2006 South Africa. TEL: (12) 27-11-726-5300; FAX: (12) 27-11-482-2000.
- National African Federation of Chambers of Commerce (NAFCOC). Private Bag X81, Soshanguve 0152 South Africa. TEL: (12) 27-1214-3204/6; FAX: (12) 27-1214-2024.
- Sandton Chamber of Commerce. P.O. Box 650846, Benmore 2010 South Africa. TEL: (12) 27-11-884-8907; FAX: (12) 27-11-884-8905.
- South African Chamber of Business (SACOB). P.O. Box 91267, Auckland Park 2006 South Africa. TEL: (11) 27 11 482-2524; FAX: (11) 27 11 726-1344.
- South African Foreign Trade Organization (SAFTO). P.O. Box 782706, Sandton 2146 South Africa. TEL: (11) 883-3737; TELEX: 424111; FAX: (11) 883-6569.
- U.S.-South Africa Business Council: National Foreign Trade Council. 1625 K Street, NW, Washington, DC 20006. TEL: (202) 887-0278; FAX: (202)452-8160.
- Vaal Triangle Chamber of Business. P.O. Box 4000, Vanderbijlpark 1900 South Africa. TEL: (12) 27-16-810165; FAX: (12) 27-16-33-8801.

APPENDIX C

SOUTH AFRICA FACT SHEET

I. **Location**

South Africa is 455,318 square miles and located on the southernmost tip of the African continent. On its southern border, South Africa is bounded by the Atlantic Ocean to the west and the Indian Ocean to the east. Namibia, Botswana, Zimbabwe, and Mozambique bound the country along its northern border. The countries of Swaziland and Lesotho are located within South Africa.

II. **Standard Time**

Seven hours ahead of Eastern Standard Time, four hours ahead of Greenwich Mean Time and one hour ahead of Central European time.

III. **Population**

The country's population is 43 million of which 32 million are Black, 5.5 million are White, 4.2 million are Coloured (descendants of the indigenous Khoikhoi and people of mixed ancestry of the Khoikhoi, Whites, and slaves from Madagascar) and one million people are of Asian or Indian descent. The population is skewed toward youth. Sixty percent of the Black population, or 45% of the entire country's entire population, is under the age of 25.

IV. **Capital**

Pretoria is the seat of government.

V. **Provinces**

The country is divided into nine provinces as follows:
- Eastern Cape
- Free State
- Gauteng (also known as "PWV", *i.e.*, Pretoria, Witwatersrand, Vaal Triangle)
- KwaZulu-Natal
- Mpumalanga ("Land of the Rising Sun") (formerly Eastern Transvaal)
- North West
- Northern Cape
- Northern Province
- Western Cape

As part of the transition from apartheid, the country is in the process of changing the names of the provinces as a means of ridding itself of the vestiges of apartheid.

VI. Urbanization

Sixty percent of the population lives in urban locales. The Black population is divided evenly between urban and rural locations. By 2010, it is predicted that the trend toward urbanization will continue and 75% of Blacks will be urbanized.

VII. Economy

South Africa has evolved from an agricultural-based economy to a mining-based economy and currently, to a manufacturing-based economy. In 1993, its GDP reached $112 billion, of which exports comprised $25 billion.

Johannesburg is the economic capital of South Africa as economic activity in the city accounts for approximately 40% of the country's GDP. Black South Africans often refer to it as I'goli ("City of Gold") -- a reference to the country's mining wealth. The country is in the process of "unbundling" the concentration of the country's wealth, the majority of which is controlled by a handful of conglomerates.

South Africa produces 50% of the electrical output of Africa, 45% of the continent's mining output and 40% of the continent's GDP. It is also Africa's largest agricultural exporter. Seventy-five percent of the exports and 68% of the imports of southern Africa are transported through South Africa's seven ports.

The manufacturing sector comprises 23% of GDP producing chemicals, basic metals, paper, machinery, and automobile parts. Roughly 1.4 million people work in manufacturing trades which are concentrated in Gauteng.

Despite its decreased dominance in the South African economy, mining remains central to the economy nonetheless as the country is the world's leading supplier of gold, chromium, manganese, and platinum. Mining accounts for approximately 60% of exports and 10% of GDP. The sector employs over 600,000 people.

The agricultural sector accounts for 5% of GDP and is a leading employer of Black labor. Despite this sector's decrease of total GDP, it remains a significant component of the economy evidenced by the fact that South Africa is one of the few net exporters of agricultural products in Africa. The sector's principal crops are tobacco, potatoes, wheat, sugar, fruit, and maize. The country also exports wool which is the second largest agricultural export commodity after maize. Seven percent of the country's exports are agricultural-based. South Africa also exports wood products and produces sufficient wood, paper and pulp products for virtually its entire need.

The remaining leading sectors of the economy are finance, communications, transportation and energy. Unemployment nationally is 40% and is 45% among Black South Africans.

VIII. Currency

The currency is the South African rand. The exchange rate of a rand against the U.S. dollar at June 3, 1996 was as follows: U.S. $1.00 = R4.36.

IX. **Language**

South Africa has 11 official languages as follows: Afrikaans, English, Ndebele, Sepedi, Sestho, Setswana, Swazi, Tshivenda, Xhosa, Xitsonga, and Zulu.

X. **The Transition from Apartheid**

In February 1990, Nelson Mandela was released from prison after 27 years of incarceration. Thereafter, the government began repealing the statutes comprising the legal framework of apartheid. In December 1991, delegates from all of South Africa's political parties except extreme right wing parties attended the Convention for a Democratic South Africa (CODESA) to form a transitional, multi-racial government and to draft an Interim Constitution. The convention culminated with the Parliament adoption of a transitional Constitution under which the country was governed until the country held democratic elections by Parliament in November 1993. The people of South Africa elected Nelson Mandela, the world-renowned anti-apartheid leader, president in the country's first democratic national election on April 27, 1994. The first post-apartheid government was named the Government of National Unity and operated by consensus pursuant to the interim Constitution. Pursuant to the interim Constitution, Parliament comprised 26 parties -- each of whom received a constitutionally-defined minimum of the national vote. The Cabinet was comprised of representatives of the three largest parties - the ANC, the National Party, and the Inkatha Freedom Party. The interim constitution was enacted as the governing document of the country for five years until democratically-elected representatives could draft a permanent document. On May 8, 1996, Parliament adopted a final permanent Constitution. The final Constitution will replace the interim document over three years. The final South African Constitution, similar to those of the leading democracies of the world, enshrines majority rule and a bill of rights guaranteeing individual liberties. In particular, South Africa's bill of rights prohibits discrimination based on "race, gender, sex, pregnancy, marital status, ethnic or social origin, colour, sexual orientation, age, disability, religion, conscience, belief, culture, language, and birth." The Constitutional Court, the highest court of South Africa, has final jurisdiction regarding the interpretation of the Constitution.